The Traumatic Colonel

America and the Long 19th Century

GENERAL EDITORS
David Kazanjian, Elizabeth McHenry, and Priscilla Wald

The Traumatic Colonel

*The Founding Fathers, Slavery,
and the Phantasmatic Aaron Burr*

Michael J. Drexler and Ed White

NEW YORK UNIVERSITY PRESS
New York and London

NEW YORK UNIVERSITY PRESS
New York and London
www.nyupress.org

For Library of Congress Cataloging-in-Publication data, please contact
the Library of Congress.

ISBN: 978-1-4798-7167-4 (cl.)
ISBN: 978-1-4798-4253-7 (pap.)

References to Internet Websites (URLs) were accurate at the time of
writing. NEither the author nor New York University Press is responsible
for URLs that may have expired or changed since the manuscript was
prepared.

New York University Press books are printed on acid-free paper, and
their binding materials are chosen for strength and durability. We
strive to use environmentally responsible suppliers and materials to the
greatest extent possible in publishing our books.

Manufactured in the United States of America
c 10 9 8 7 6 5 4 3 2 1
p 10 9 8 7 6 5 4 3 2 1

Also available as an ebook

THE
AMERICAN
LITERATURES
INITIATIVE

A book in the American Literatures Initiative (ALI), a collaborative
publishing project of NYU Press, Fordham University Press, Rutgers
University Press, Temple University Press, and the University of Virginia
Press. The Initiative is supported by The Andrew W. Mellon Foundation.
For more information, please visit www.americanliteratures.org.

To Amisha
To Kimberley

There is no subject so interesting and important to the real lovers of their country, as that of slavery, because there is none which involves the happiness, prosperity and glory of our country in so great a degree—none attended with so many difficulties in remedying. It is admitted by all parties, slave-holders or not, that slavery is the greatest curse our country is afflicted with—it is a foul stain upon our national escutcheon—A canker which is corroding the moral and political vitals of our country. There is but one voice on this subject, and that is the voice of condemnation, as an enormous, and an alarming evil.

—Daniel Raymond, *The Missouri Question*

It has been made a question among the learned, whether most good or evil has resulted to mankind, from the discovery of America. That the munificent gift of a new world, should have given rise to such a question, is of itself a melancholy proof of human depravity.

Although there may be no serious difficulty in deciding this question, yet, when we consider what oceans of blood have been shed—how many human beings have been butchered—how many nations of brave, high-minded men have been exterminated; and when we add to this the mass of human suffering which has been already caused by negro slavery, the philanthropist is almost ready to drop the tear of regret, and exclaim, alas, that America was ever discovered!

—Daniel Raymond, *Thoughts on Political Economy*

Contents

Acknowledgments

Portions of this project were presented at the Bucknell University English Department and Faculty Colloquium, the University of Florida English Department's Americanists' Colloquium, the Aaron Burr Association, Indiana University's Center for Eighteenth-Century Studies, the Research Center for Urban Cultural History at the University of Massachusetts at Boston, the University of Texas at Austin, Emory University, the University of Glasgow, Rutgers University, the University of Wisconsin–Madison, American University in Beirut, and Tulane University. From colleagues too numerous to attempt to list here—they include faculty, graduate students, and undergraduates—we received generous and thoughtful suggestions and insights, essential to the growth of this project, and all through a time of widespread institutional austerity. We thank student assistants Emily Anderson, Deanna Koretsky, and Stephanie Scherer for their hard work. We owe our thanks, as well, to University of Florida students in ENG 3011 and AML 6017 and Bucknell University students in ENG 306. A version of chapter 2 appeared as "Secret Witness, or the Fantasy Structure of US Republicanism," in *Early American Literature* 44.2 (2009): 333–63. We thank the anonymous reviewers, David Shields, departing from the journal's editorship, and Sandra Gustafson, entering, for their help. A portion of chapter 4 appeared as "The Constitution of Toussaint: Another Origin of African American Literature," in *A Companion to African American Literature*, ed. Gene Jarrett, 59–74 (New York: Wiley-Blackwell, 2010). We are grateful to Gene for his suggestions and encouragement. We are grateful, too, at NYU Press, to the series editors, Priscilla Wald, David Kazanjian, and Elizabeth McHenry, as well as to Eric Zinner and Alicia Nadkarni.

The Traumatic Colonel began with a conversation in October of 2005. Since then, we have worked in fits and starts, time permitting, with hours on the phone, hundreds of emails, conversations with friends, and above all the tremendous patience and support of loved ones. We acknowledge a few personal ties, those who understand that there are a lot of facets to this, a lot of interested parties: Jim Lavine, Kevin Daly, Daniel Juan Gil, Ed Cahill, Duncan Faherty, and Molly Rothenberg. Ed is especially grateful to Amisha Sharma, who appreciated this very complicated case—a lotta ins, lotta outs, lotta what-have-yous. He cannot adequately thank her for making this come together. Michael wishes to thank his children, Hannah, Mariah, and Caleb for a few quiet hours, and most especially Kimberley—getting there is half the fun; being there is all of it.

Burrology—Extracts

In the case of Mr. Jefferson, there is nothing wonderful; but Mr. Burr's good fortune surpasses all ordinary rules, and exceeds that of Bonaparte. All the old patriots, all the splendid talents, the long experience, both of federalists and antifederalists, must be subjected to the humiliation of seeing this dexterous gentleman rise, like a balloon, filled with inflammable air, over their heads. And this is not the worst. What a discouragement to all virtuous exertion, and what an encouragement to party intrigue, and corruption!
—John Adams to Elbridge Gerry, 1800

Few men, if any, in the United States have done more to produce the late change in the representation of the people, than colonel BURR. His Eagle eye penetrated thro' every scheme, of the adverse party, and he has combated with success the *"evil genius of America."* While some were distracting their brains, with jarring elements and component parts, the capacious soul of Burr, conceived the harmony of the *great whole*. While others were collecting their materials, he erected his fabric. A man whose active genius is every where & whose goodness of heart and purity of morals have never been impeached, is an admirable *second* and may be a suitable *successor* to the sagacious *Jefferson*.
—Morgan J. Rhees, Esq.,
Inauguration Day Oration, 1801

What is the language the people of America express in this vote? Why certainly that in their opinion Mr. Jefferson is equal to Colonel Burr, and Colonel Burr equal to Mr. Jefferson!
—*Washington Federalist*, 1801

It is in the camp of the Enemy that we must look for a Deliverer. In the choice of Mr. Burr, there is yet a remedy for the evils I have enumerated. . . . It is often difficult to trace with precision, the proportion of each, in that compound of motives, by which the conduct of statesmen is usually governed. To borrow a familiar illustration—we can see, as in a changeable silk, that there is a variety of colors; but it is difficult to say where one ends or the other begins. —Epaminondas, *New-York Gazette*, 1801

It is time to tear away the veil that hides this monster, and lay open a scene of misery, at which every heart must shudder. Fellow Citizens, read a tale of truth, which must harrow up your sensibility, and excite your keenest resentment. It is, indeed, a tale of truth! And, but for wounding, too deeply, the already lacerated feelings of a parental heart, *it* could be authenticated by all the formalities of an oath.
—*Aaron Burr!*, handbill, 1801

Something "is rotten in Denmark"; that under an exterior, which, though not altogether pleasing, is calculated to make false impressions on unsuspicious minds, SOMETHING EXCEEDINGLY UNPROPITIOUS TO THE FREEDOM OF THE UNION, IS AT THIS MOMENT CONTEMPLATED BY THE VICE-PRESIDENT.
—James Cheetham, *Narrative of the Suppression*, 1802

It cannot escape notice, that in the toasts given by the Anti-Constitutionalists on the anniversary of independence, the VICE-PRESIDENT is either omitted, or mentioned with pointed disrespect. In one he is called the "Burr of democracy."
—*New-York Gazette and General Advertiser*, July 20, 1802

The lovers of *secret history*, and those who listen with pleasure to the tales of party intrigues, or smile at the arts of authorship, may find some amusement in the perusal of this pamphlet.

As a considerable portion of it is occupied in detailing the contents of the *suppressed* history, it is unnecessary for us to be particular in our account of it; since, in the next article, the reader will perceive that this same history has, after all, come forth into open day.

The author of this narrative makes some very severe strictures on the character and conduct of Mr. BURR, and it appears to be the main design of his performance to hold him up to the contempt and detestation of the world. . . .

That such accusations should be made by one of the same political party against so distinguished a character as the accused, may, at first sight, be thought unaccountable; and the mystery will disappear to those only who are acquainted with all the subdivisions of party and the springs which influence their political movements.

—*American Review, and Literary Journal,* 1802

The character faithfully drawn of Mr. Burr in the following pages is so complex, so stript of precise and indelible marks; so mutable, capricious, versatile, unsteady and unfixt, one to which no determinate name can be given, and on which no reliance can be placed, that serious questions may arise from it.

—James Cheetham, *A View of the Political Conduct of Aaron Burr, Esq.,* 1802

To a genius of singular perspicacity, Mr. *Burr* joins the most bland and conciliating manners. With a versatility of powers, of which, perhaps, *America* furnishes no other example, he is capable of yielding an undivided attention to a single object of pursuit.

—John Davis, *Travels of Four Years and a Half,* 1803

Perhaps no man's language was ever so apparently explicit, and, at the same time, so covert and indefinite.

—William Plumer, *Memorandum,* 1804

I trust . . . that the world will do me the justice to believe that I have not censured him on light grounds nor from unworthy inducements. I certainly have had strong reasons for what I have said, though it is possible that in some particulars I may have been influenced by misconstruction or misinformation.

—Alexander Hamilton, statement before the duel, 1804

O thou agent of our sorrows! who by the people's voice wast raised
so near the highest honors thy nation could bestow, couldst thou not
forgive? . . . Where is that honor now thou heldest so dear? Gone; for
ever gone. . . . . Honor, at best, is but a noisy breath.—Methinks if ever
re-applied to thy sinking name, it will be emptier than a puff of air.
                   —Hezekiah N. Woodruff, sermon at Scipio, NY, 1804

Doctor! Doctor! help, help!—the people want your *bolusses*, your
panacea's and your remedies—The Multitude want your skill—they
are sorely afflicted, with an itching for Col. Burr—and you have
a sovereign remedy that will cure half a million a minute—I will
vouch for your pills being genuine, and that one box will cure all the
infected—Your skill is more famous than the man, who advertises
that secrecy and honor may be depended on, on moderate *terms!*—
And as this famous empiric is famous for curing the ——, I think
you may fairly be put in competition with him as the curer of the
Burr-itch.   —P.Q., *American Citizen*, 1804

On Monday evening last, the day preceding the commencement
of the election, Mr. Burr had assembled at this house, by special
invitation, a considerable number of *gentlemen of colour*—upwards
of twenty. These gentlemen were headed by a celebrated perfumer in
Broadway. They were invited by Mr. Burr to a ball and supper, *in his
own house*, and the federal candidate, the *rejected* Vice-President,
did himself the honor of superintending their *elegant amusements*.
This, as the reader will perceive, was to the court the favour of the
people of colour in aid of his election.
                              —*American Citizen*, 1804

THE MODERN CAIN.

The last account we have seen of the murderer BURR, is a paragraph
in a New York paper, stating on the authority of a letter from Mr.
Burr himself, that he is now in Spanish America. Who would suffer
the goadings of this man's conscience for the high rank in this
democratick administration which he has occupied?
                       —*Repertory*, September 21, 1804

To analise his face with physiognomical scrutiny, you may discover many unimportant traits; but upon the first blush, or a superficial view, they are obscured like the spots in the sun, by a radiance that dazzles and fascinates the sight. —*Port Folio*, 1805

They would often meet together at sun-down in the woods and caves, and hold *kintikoys*, where they drank largely of the Burr decoction; stripped themselves star[k] naked, and sung, and fiddled, and capered, and danced, and played the fool all night long. They would mark themselves too in the day time, and dress themselves up like mountebanks, jugglers, and rope dancers. Then they would run along upon the tops of the fences, tumble in the dirt, act pantomimes and make speeches, with many other diverting tricks, to the amusement of the bye-standers. At such times too they had a remarkable fondness for filth, and would lie down in the drains and ditches, and smear and daub themselves all, and throw nasty matter at the travelers. —*American Citizen*, 1805

Thus Mr. Burr, for aye intriguing,
With this side, and with that side leaguing,
Has late contriv'd a scheme quite handy,
To make himself, for life, a grandee.
—Thomas Fessenden, "Democracy Unveiled," 1805

There is a chain of connection through the continent—of which Burr has been and still is the master link.
—*Aurora*, October, 13, 1806

This is indeed a deep, dark, and widespread conspiracy, embracing the young and the old, the Democrat and the Federalist, the native and the foreigner, the patriot of '76 and the exotic of yesterday, the opulent and the needy, the "ins" and "outs"; and I fear it will receive strong support in New Orleans from a quarter little suspected.
—General James Wilkinson
to President Thomas Jefferson, November 1806

Col. Osmun and Lyman Harding Esq. were bound in the sum
of 2500 dols. as sureties of Burr. It is a singular fact that the late
Vice President of the United States, is now advertised in all the
public places in this Territory, as well as in the Newspapers, as a
runaway.   —*Trenton Federalist*, 1807

The debate on the bill to prohibit the importation of slaves was
resumed, but seemed to have lost all its interest.
                          —memoirs of John Quincy Adams, January 26, 1807

Mr. Burr and his conspiracy have begun to occupy our attention.
          —John Quincy Adams to John Adams, January 27, 1807

I never, indeed thought him an honest, frank-dealing man, but
considered him as a crooked gun, or other perverted machine,
whose aim or stroke you could never be sure of.
                      —Thomas Jefferson to William Branch Giles, 1807

A gentleman, the other day, remarked to another, as a singular
fact, that the initials of the name of A. Burr, were those of
the two greatest conquerors that had ever spread ruin and
devastation over the face of the earth, to wit, Alexander and
Buonaparte. It is by no means singular, retorted his facetious
friend; they will stand for the vilest traitor that ever disgraced
humanity, Benedict Arnold, but in fact they will stand for ANY
BODY.   —*Miller's Weekly* (Pendleton, SC), 1807

Colonel Burr (*quantum mutates ab illo!*) passed by my door the day
before yesterday, under a strong guard. So I am told, for I did not
see him, and nobody hereabouts is acquainted with his person. . . .
To guard against inquiry as much as possible he was accoutered in
a shabby suit of homespun, with an old white hat flapped over his
face, the dress in which he was apprehended. . . . His very manner
of traveling, although under arrest, was characteristic of the man,
enveloped in mystery.
                          —John Randolph to Joseph H. Nicholson, 1807

I am anxious to see the Progress of Burr's Tryal; not from any Love or hatred I bear to the Man, for I cannot say that I feel either. He is, as you say a Nondescript in natural History. But I think something must come out on the Tryal, which will strengthen or weaken our Confidence in the General Union. I hope something will appear to determine clearly, whether any foreign Power has or has not been tampering with our Union. If it should appear that he is guilty of Treason and in Concert with any foreign Power, you and your twelve thousand Copetitioners might petition as earnestly as you did for Fries, if I was President, and the Gallows should not lose its prey. An ignorant Idiot of a German, is a very different Being from a Vice President of the United States. The one knew not what Treason was; the other knows all about it. The one was instigated by Virginians and Pensilvanians who deserved to be hanged much more than he did. The other could be instigated only by his own ambition, avarice or Revenge. But I hope his Innocence will be made to appear, and that he will be fairly acquitted.

—Benjamin Rush to John Adams, 1807

A stranger presents himself. It is Aaron Burr. Introduced to their civilities by the high rank which he had lately held in his country, he soon finds his way to their hearts, by the dignity and elegance of his demeanor, the light and beauty of his conversation, and the seductive and fascinating power of his address. . . . Such was the state of Eden, when the serpent entered its bowers!

—William Wirt, for the prosecution
against Aaron Burr, 1807

If I were to name this, I would call it the Will o' wisp treason. For though it is said to be here and there and everywhere, *yet it is nowhere.* It only exists in the newspapers and in the mouths of the enemies of the gentleman for whom I appear; who get it put in the newspapers.

—Luther Martin, in defense of Aaron Burr, 1807

The rebellion had been crushed, it was said, in the womb of speculation; the armies of Colonel Burr were defeated before they were raised.

—Edward Livingston, *A Faithful Picture,* 1808

And there was the fascinating colonel Burr. A man born to be
great—brave as Cæsar, polished as Chesterfield, eloquent as Cicero.
Lifted by the strong arm of his country, he rose fast, and bade fair
soon to fill the place where Washington had sat. But alas! lacking
religion, he could not wait the spontaneous fall of the rich honors
ripening over his head, but in an evil hour stretched forth his hand
to the forbidden fruit, and by that fatal act was cast out from the
Eden of our republic, and amerced of greatness for ever.

> —Mason Weems, *Life of George Washington*,
> 6th ed., 1808

Of Burr I will say nothing, because I know nothing with certainty.

> —John Adams to James Lloyd, 1815

For more than thirty years Colonel Burr has been assailed and
abused in public journals, at home and abroad. Some of them
have misrepresented him from ignorance of the facts; others
from party purposes or malicious feelings. It is sometimes
amusing to read some of these misrepresentations. It is not Mr.
Wirt alone who has gained fame by indulging the imagination
on the wonderful sorceries of Colonel Burr. Others have given
him the eye of the basilisk, from whose glance it was impossible
to recede, and that when once fixed on an object the destruction
of it was certain. They have represented his voice as sweeter than
that of the Sirens, and that he used this charm as successfully
as the fabled enchantresses. Even his gait had something of
necromancy about it, and reminded these lovers of the wonderful
of the stealthy step of Tarquin approaching the couch of the
chaste Lucretia. In their legends, he was more successful in his
intrigues than Apollo, for no Diana could interfere between him
and the object of his pursuit. These exaggerations and fictions
often reached his ear, but did not disturb him. He took no
pains to make explanations or excuses. When asked in a proper
manner for his opinions, he always gave a direct and prompt
answer to the inquirer, but never permitted any one to put a
supercilious interrogatory to him.

> —Samuel Lorenzo Knapp, *The Life of Aaron Burr*, 1835

Remembering what has been said of the power of Burr's personal influence, his art to tempt men, his might to subdue them, and the fascination that enabled him, though cold at heart, to win the love of woman, we gaze at this production of his pen as into his own inscrutable eyes, seeking for the mystery of his nature. How singular that a character, imperfect, ruined, blasted, as this man's was, excites a stronger interest than if it had reached the highest earthly perfection of which its original elements would admit! It is by the diabolical part of Burr's character, that he produces his effect on the imagination.
—Nathaniel Hawthorne, "A Book of Autographs," 1844

Sprang from the best Puritan blood of New England, identified with the only genuine Pilgrim aristocracy—that of the clergy—and, with this prestige, ushered into active life at the close of the French and opening of the American War, with that band of select heroes and statesmen now idolized as the purest constellation in the firmament of history; he, who called Jonathan Edwards grand-father, in whose fraternity fell the gallant Montgomery, who had been domesticated with Washington, and Vice President of the United States,—who had extended manorial hospitality to a king,—hunted as a felon, sleeping on a garret floor in Paris, and skulking back to his native land in disguise—offers one of those rare instances of extreme and violent contradictions which win historians to antithetical rhetoric, and yield the novelist hints "stranger than fiction."
—review of James Parton's *Life and Times of Aaron Burr,* in the *Southern Literary Messenger,* May 1858

He was one of those persons who systematically managed and played upon himself and others, as a skillful musician on an instrument.
—Harriet Beecher Stowe, *The Minister's Wooing,* 1859

His eyes were of a dark hazel, so dark, no sign of a pupil could be seen, and the expression of them, when he chose, was wonderful— they could be likened only to those of a snake, for their fascination was irresistible.
—Charles Burdett, *Margaret Moncrieffe: The First Love of Aaron Burr: A Romance of the Revolution,* 1860

What Burr meant to do I know no more than you, dear reader. It is none of our business just now.

> —Edward Everett Hale,
> "The Man without a Country," 1863

My material is enormous, and I now fear that the task of compression will be painful. Burr alone is good for a volume.

> —Henry Adams to Henry Cabot Lodge, July 1880

If I find [John] Randolph easy, I don't know but what I will volunteer for Burr. Randolph is the type of a political charlatan who had something in him. Burr is the type of a political charlatan pure and simple, a very Jim Crow of melodramatic wind-bags.

> —Henry Adams to John T. Morse, Jr., April 1881

The idea implied a bargain and an intrigue on terms such as in the Middle Ages the Devil was believed to impose upon the ambitious and reckless. Pickering and Griswold could win their game only by bartering their souls; they must invoke the Mephistopheles of politics, Aaron Burr.

> —Henry Adams, *History of the*
> *Jefferson Administration*, 1889

I regard any concession to popular illusion as a blemish; but just as I abandoned so large a space to Burr—a mere Jeremy Diddler—because the public felt an undue interest in him, so I think it best to give the public a full dose of General Jackson.

> —Henry Adams to Charles Scribner, May 1890

"What a head!" was the phrenologist's first whisper. . . . "His head is indeed a study—a strange, contradictory head."

> —James Parton, *The Life and Times of Aaron Burr*, 1892

Aaron Burr, whose homicidal (?) and treasonable (?) deeds have been thrown into the shade by more splendid achievements of the kind in our day, was certainly in advance of the men of his time in his ideas on the capacity and education of women.

> —Grace Greenwood in *The Aaron Burr Memorial*, 1903

Some time ago, I received a letter, presumably from an admirer of Alexander Hamilton, in which I was informed that if I did not cease publishing books reflecting upon General Hamilton, his friends would publish some secret memoirs which would reflect more seriously upon the character of Colonel Burr than anything which had yet been published.

—Charles Felton Pidgin
in *The Aaron Burr Memorial*, 1903

Burr was a typical man, the beginning of a new species, destined to become *a*, if not *the* dominant one in the future of civilized people.

—Thaddeus Burr Wakeman
in *The Aaron Burr Memorial*, 1903

The Aaron Burr Legion, which has just had a gathering in Newark, the birthplace of Aaron Burr and the old home of his family, was organized to clear the fame of this notable personage, who is one of the *betes noirs* of American history, from the alleged scandals which blackened his career, and brought it to an ignominious close. The motive of such reconstructive ambition must always be deemed worthy of laudation, and it is a satisfying set-off against the spirit of iconoclasm, which also cuts up such interesting and ingenious capers in historical research. We can even pat that brilliant German on the back who undertakes to set Judas Iscariot on a high pedestal.   —*Newark News*, 1903

Since a child, forty-five years ago, I have been interested in Colonel Burr's character, and in spite of all the prejudiced flings by writers, I have held and maintained that he was not a traitor to our Government, but one of its patriots. I read Parton's "Life of Burr" when a boy, and before I enlisted in the Confederate Army. It is the only book in Burr's favor that I have ever read. When will the memorial volume be issued? I wish to get one. I am a Mississippian and know very well the vicinity in which he resided when arrested.

—W. W. Mangum in *The Aaron Burr Memorial*, 1903

The Aaron Burr Legion is devoted to the rehabilitation of Aaron
Burr. It probably wants to vote him in the primaries with the dead
dogs and four-year-old negroes.

                                    —*Memphis Commercial Appeal*, 1903

New Jersey has an "Aaron Burr Legion" whose object is to "clear the
name of Colonel Burr" and to erect a monument to him at Newark,
where he was born. That is, they talk about the monument after
the "clearing" has been done. Funny what fads folks will foster just
because they have nothing else to do. The Legion should have for a
motto: "The devil isn't as black as he's painted."

                                    —*Brooklyn Standard Union*, 1903

As the transports began to arrive and the eleven hundred
disembarked, Captain Howard, commandant of Fort Westward, came
up from the landing with the most notable of the guests. It was upon
the reckless, dashing Arnold that all eyes were turned. Jacataqua's
Abenakis stood in the same stolid silence, still a group apart, but
the maiden herself, for once yielding to the wild pulses of her heart,
stepped between the sturdy squires to a point of vantage whence she
might gaze upon the warrior whom all men seemed to honor.

   One swift glance she gave the hero, then her black eyes met a pair
as dark and flashing as her own, met and were held. She turned to
the man at her side.

   "That, that Anglese! Who?"

   "Thet? Thet's young Burr, the one Cushing said got off a sick bed
to come."

   Startled, she stepped back among her people.

                      —William Carlos Williams, *In the American Grain*, 1925

But where are the facts?

   His enterprise in Mexico.

   Not yet. That one thorn on which they did impale him was a later
growth. It did not come until the end of years of vicious enmity by
Hamilton and might well be called a deed of desperation.

   It proved the soundness of their logic.

   They hounded him to it to prove their logic.

                      —William Carlos Williams, *In the American Grain*, 1925

He might have talked in another language, in which there was nothing but evocation. When he was seen so plainly, all his movements and his looks seemed part of a devotion that was curiously patient and had the illusion of wisdom all about it. Lights shone in his eyes like travelers' fires seen far out on the river. Always he talked, his talking was his appearance, as if there were no eyes, nose, or mouth to remember; in his face there was every subtlety and eloquence, and no features, no kindness, for there was no awareness whatever of the present. Looking up from the floor at his speaking face, Joel knew all at once some secret of temptation and an anguish that would reach out after it like a closing hand. He would allow Burr to take him with him wherever it was that he was meant to go.

—Eudora Welty, "First Love," 1943

Burr's letter's like, "You dissed me!" And then, Hamilton writes back like, "Dude lighten up." . . . The thing I love about writing about history and, especially historical reenactments is that . . . no one ever says what it's about, they never say the thing, which is like: They're morons. These are two of the smartest guys in the history of the country being total idiots. . . . Yeah, [the reenactment] was totally accurate, like Burr was a black woman.

—Sarah Vowell, interviewed on *The Daily Show with Jon Stewart* on July 14, 2004

You can call me Aaron Burr from the way I'm droppin' Hamiltons.

—Andy Samberg and Chris Parnell, "Lazy Sunday," 2005

Cheney's shooting of his friend is a lot easier to explain than Burr's shooting of Hamilton: the Vice President was drinking while "hunting" semi-domesticated birds, and got so excited when he heard a quail fluttering for its life that he whirled and fired with complete disregard for the human beings standing around him. . . . Quite un-Burr-like, you see.

—*Unitary Moobat* (blog), November 18, 2007

Biden thinks Cheney is the most dangerous vice president we've ever had? What about Burr?

—Ramesh Ponnuru, 2008

Until I was reading this snotty novel called "Burr," by Gore
Vidal, and read how he mocked our Founding Fathers. And as
a reasonable, decent, fair-minded person who happened to be a
Democrat, I thought, "You know what? What he's writing about,
this mocking of people that I revere, and the country that I love, and
that I would lay my life down to defend—just like every one of you
in this room would, and as many of you in this room have when you
wore the uniform of this great country—I knew that that was not
representative of my country."

> —Michelle Bachman, Michigan speech, 2010

"Fortunately his name is not Alexander Hamilton, George
Washington or Thomas Jefferson," he said. "That's helped my
budget."

> —Brian D. Hardison, quoted in
> "Making a Case to Remember Burr," 2012

The Traumatic Colonel

Introduction

> Ancient historians compiled prodigies, to gratify the credulous curiosity of their readers; but since prodigies have ceased, while the same avidity for the marvelous exists, modern historians have transferred the miraculous to their personages.
>
> —Charles Brockden Brown, "Historical Characters Are False
> Representations of Nature"

In November 1807, six years into retirement from the presidency, John Adams spelled out for his regular correspondent Benjamin Rush his thoughts about the tremendous and mysterious popularity of George Washington. He ventured to outline ten qualities that explained Washington's "immense elevation above his fellows": his "handsome face"; his height; his "elegant form"; his grace of movement; his "large, imposing fortune"; his Virginian roots ("equivalent to five talents," he added parenthetically); "favorable anecdotes" about his earlier years as a colonel; "the gift of silence"; his "great self-command"; and finally the silence of his admirers about his flaws, particularly his bad temper.[1] "Here you will see," he concluded, "I have made out ten talents without saying a word about reading, thinking, or writing. . . . You see I use the word talents in a larger sense than usual, comprehending every advantage. Genius, experience, learning, fortune, birth, health are all talents" (107).

This was far from the first time Adams had tried to explain Washington's status, a topic that had arisen regularly since Adams and Rush began their correspondence in early 1805. At one point he stressed the hypocrisy of those "who trumpeted Washington in the highest strains" but who "spoke of him at others in the strongest terms of contempt" (January 25, 1806, 49).[2] Later he emphasized a public complicity in certain fictions of Washington's life, such that his professed "attachment to private life, fondness for agricultural employments, and rural amusements were easily believed; and we all agreed to believe him and make the world believe him" (September 1807, 101). At another point he stressed the class-motivated theatrics "played off in the funerals of Washington, Hamilton, and Ames," which are "all calculated like drums and trumpets and fifes in an army to drown the unpopularity of speculations, banks, paper money, and mushroom fortunes" (July 25, 1808, 123–24). Washington's acting abilities deserved mention too, for "we may say of him, if he was not the greatest President, he was the best actor of presidency we have ever had," even achieving "a strain of Shakespearean and Garrickal excellence in dramatical exhibitions" (June 21, 1811, 197). So too the clever financial maneuverings beneath Washington's alleged "sacrifices," such that "he raised the value of his property and that of his family a thousand per cent, at an expense to the public of more than his whole fortune" (August 14, 1811, 201). As late as 1812, Adams was stressing Washington's special status as a "great character," *"a Character of Convention,"* explaining, "There was a time when northern, middle, and southern statesmen and northern, middle, and southern officers of the army expressly agreed to blow the trumpet of panegyric in concert, to cover and dissemble all faults and errors, to represent every defeat as a victory and every retreat as an advancement, to make that Character popular and fashionable with all parties in all places and with all persons, as a center of union, as the central stone in the geometrical arch" (March 19, 1812, 230, emphasis in original). A similar process was under way in France with Napoleon, and "something hereafter may produce similar conventions to cry up a Burr, a Hamilton, an Arnold, or a Caesar, Julius or Borgia. And on such foundations have been erected Mahomet, Genghis Khan, Tamerlane, Kublai Khan, Alexander, and all the other great conquerors this world has produced" (ibid.).

This range of observations should illustrate the uncertainty and inconsistency of Adams's speculations, which were by no means confined to Washington. Indeed, the topic of reputation and mystique seems to have been prompted by comments exchanged in 1805, about the Spanish American adventurer Francisco de Miranda. Adams had written Rush of "a concurrence, if not a combination, of events" that struck him (December 4, 1805, 47). "Col. Burr at Washington, General Dayton at Washington, General Miranda at Washington, General Hull returning from his government, General Wilkinson commanding in Louisiana, &c., &c." (ibid.). Rush answered that Miranda had in fact recently paid a visit and had reminded him, "in his anecdotes of the great characters that have moved the European world for the last twenty or thirty years, of *The Adventures of a Guinea*, but with this difference—he has passed through not the purses but the heads and hearts of all the persons whom he described" (January 6, 1806, 48). "I never had the good fortune to meet General Miranda nor the pleasure to see him," answered Adams:

> I have heard much of his abilities and the politeness of his manners. But who is he? What is he? Whence does he come? And whither does he go? What are his motives, views, and objects? Secrecy, mystery, and intrigue have a mighty effect on the world. You and I have seen it in Franklin, Washington, Burr, Hamilton, and Jefferson, and many others. The judgment of mankind in general is like that of Father Bouhours, who says, "For myself, I regard secret persons, like the great rivers, whose bottoms we cannot see, and which make no noise; or like those vast forests, whose silence fills the soul, with I know not what religious horror. I have for them the same admiration as men had for the oracles, which never suffered themselves to be understood, till after the event of things; or for the providence of God, whose conduct is impenetrable to the human mind" (January 25, 1806, 49).

A few months later, Adams returned to these observations with this outburst: "Secrecy! Cunning! Silence! *voila les grands sciences de temps modernes.* Washington! Franklin! Jefferson! Eternal silence! impenetrable secrecy! deep cunning! These are the talents and virtues which are triumphant in these days," he concluded, quickly adding, "When I group Washington with Franklin and Jefferson, I mean only in the article of silence" (July 23, 1806, 64).

How are we to read these exchanges? Let us start by considering two likely responses of contemporary readers. On the one hand, we might enjoy a certain gratifying titillation at hearing perhaps unknown, gossipy details about the Founding Fathers. This pleasure results not only from a familiarity with the Founders but also from a certain defamiliarization, as these mythical figures are made somewhat new. At the same time, however, many readers—above all, scholars—may feel a certain distaste at the continued fetishization of the elites of the past. After all, hasn't much scholarship of the past century tried to move us away from such historiography, toward social or structural histories? Isn't the history of the early republic to be found in histories from below, in the lives of women, workers, farmers, slaves, and Native Americans, rather than in the same old arcana of a few white, male elites? Isn't a return to Adams's musings about Washington and others somehow reactionary, a sign of that irritating phenomenon known as "Founders Chic"? Shouldn't this Founders Chic be resisted?[3]

We would note, first, that this combination of responses—of guilty pleasure and critical disgust, of fascination and of knowing better—perfectly characterizes the musings of Adams himself. In the letters with Rush, he simultaneously indulges in and resists the aura of the Founders. His persistent enumeration of humanizing details and secret histories, shared with Rush in order to puncture the mystique of the already mythically enhanced elites, simultaneously exposes *and* perpetuates their perplexing prominence. Indeed, we would argue that *this* particular affective combination is exactly what defines Founders Chic. Like Adams, those who succumb to Founders Chic imagine that *others* naively, blindly, uncritically admire and worship the Founders—whether they are the fools voting for Jefferson or the modern purchasers of a best-selling biography. But it is this complex of fascination, this desire to decipher and interpret an inexplicably compelling cultural formation, that defines the phenomenon, and to cure ourselves we must begin by acknowledging that the logic of debunking will not get us very far. As Roland Barthes realized upon completion of *Mythologies*, myth debunking had become a myth in itself, a classroom exercise that any student could execute with facility, but without any ultimate threat to myth itself.[4] In short, the critique of myth is often essential to its enjoyment. Nor can we say that debunking is a later phenomenon. In the case of Founders Chic, the seemingly contrary tendency toward humanizing details, context, and "secret" histories was present from the start, an integral part of the *formation* of the Founders Fantasy. Thus, when contemporary hagiographies startle their readers by telling them, first, the shocking details of a Jefferson or a Franklin and, second, that lo and behold these details *actually appeared in the newspapers of the time!!*, they fundamentally obscure the problem. This favorite rhetorical move makes one marvel at the Founders all the more, for they seem to have become larger than life *despite* knowledge of their sexual histories, their racial politics, or their political maneuvers. Actually the reverse is the case: the Founders emerged as significant symbolic figures *because of* these biographical, semic details.[5] We see precisely this relationship in the Adams-Rush correspondence, in which the secret histories and private details of the Founders, dished to deflate their mystique, rather amplify it instead. This phenomenon is more pertinent than ever today, when ostensibly humanizing and demythologizing biographical details preserve and renew the Founders' mythological status.[6]

If we want to cure ourselves of Founders Chic, then, we cannot have recourse to the details that fill the letters of Adams and Rush: they are part of the problem we need to address. Instead, we must focus on the *formal* insights indirectly articulated in these letters. Two related observations seem particularly important. The first is that the Founders are constituted by a carefully structured emptiness. Adams and Rush touch on this point again and again when they speak of the secrecy, silence, mystery, and intrigue that characterize such figures, when the Founders are compared to deep rivers and silent forests, or when Washington is described as a stone that fills a gap in a geometrical arch.[7] These gaps are then restlessly filled by semic details. Adams's list of Washington's ten talents is exemplary of this manic overlay. And the observation that those who lauded Washington "in the highest strains" also held him in the "strongest terms of contempt" confirms that this *content* need not be consistent in fact or affect. Thus, vitriol, scandal, and rumor may as easily fill that empty space as heroic feats, gestures, and words. The point is that biographical details are subordinate to this *fundamental structuring* of the Founder figure.

Second, and consequently, we see Adams refer, again and again, to the Founders as fictional constructs. We see this in the references to the portrayal of Washington as "the best actor of presidency we have ever had" but even more so in the description of "*a Character of Convention*," a phrase we should read in the most literal sense. Rush goes a step further in the comparison with the guinea, the object passed through numerous hands in the 1767 novel *Chrysal; or, The Adventures of a Guinea*. The point is clear: the Founders are *imaginative fictions*, characters in the specifically literary sense, whose circulation is essential for their constitution and whose significance in the narrative often results from narrative elements clustered around them. Narratological theory stresses this point by renaming characters "actants" to mark their structural position, an observation Adams approaches when he reflects on the "concurrence, if not a combination, of events" that links together Burr, Dayton, Miranda, Hull, and Wilkinson. This conjunction "strikes" Adams, as if he is unsure what this means, but he describes a process of overdetermination whereby characters draw semic material from the confluence of events. Here, it seems, one of the actants—perhaps Burr?—takes greater cohesion as it draws together the semiotic resources in circulation in late 1805. Instead of the usual historicist debunking (there are myths, but here are some facts that indicate the deeper truth) which reaffirms Founders Chic, Adams verges on formulating the reverse procedure: there are facts, yes, but here are some myths that indicate the deeper truth. The point, of course, is that we are not trying to get at an empirical phenomenon but rather at some very different kind of cultural manifestation, one requiring different methods and theoretical assumptions.

In this light, the very phenomenon of Founders Chic speaks to a disciplinary confusion that *The Traumatic Colonel* seeks to address. Rather than treating the Founders as actual agents who need to be more aggressively historicized with empirical data (true, but in a more limited sphere than often assumed), our starting point is that they are *primarily* imaginative, phantasmatic phenomena best explored from a broadly literary perspective—as a broad characterological drama whose plot often remains obscure. Accordingly, our approach in this work insists on a *parallactic* division of what we have been calling the historical and the literary. In recent theoretical work, the idea of the parallax has been most notably explored in Slavoj Žižek's *The Parallax View*. Žižek's immediate inspiration is the Japanese Marxist philosopher Kojin Karatani, who takes the term from Kant, who himself borrowed it from early modern astronomy. In its original formulation, "parallax" designated the change in position or direction of an object as seen from two different points: the parallax of a star or a planet was necessary for calculating its exact location. Used metaphorically, the term refers to the gap in perceptions of the same thing from different vantage points. Kant used the metaphor philosophically to denote the gap between common sense "from the standpoint of my own" and "from the point of view of others." Hugh Henry Brackenridge, in the final volume of *Modern Chivalry* (1815), used the same metaphor to describe the gap between the political-theoretical differentiation of humans and animals and, from a more remote perspective, their similarities. For Karatani, the parallax view becomes the foundation for the proper form of criticism—what he calls *transcritique*—which is *not* analysis from a priori systems of thought (i.e., the application of theory) but rather a movement between two different theoretical registers—resulting in an antinomy. Philosophy proper is this transcritical reading of parallactic contexts—in Karatani's project, a reading of Kantian philosophy alongside a seemingly incompatible Marxian political economy. Žižek expands this view of the parallax to propose it as the proper mode and orientation for cultural criticism. The parallax, understood as the constitutive rift in human perception, opens up the consideration of a host of theoretical aporia—he speaks of "an entire series of the modes of parallax in different domains of modern theory"—the most important of which is the parallax between Lacanian psychoanalysis and Marxism.[8]

In the most vulgar sense, the impulse to juxtapose these two theories aims to address the gap between the interior, psychic constitution of the subject and the objective, material forces of the historical moment. It is this gap that ideology always seeks to fill, stressing the continuities between the two spheres. A parallactic analysis, by contrast, resists such closure, insisting that the analysis of these two perspectives can only proceed if initially kept distinct. To take the Founding Fathers as an illustration, the problem with Founders Chic is that it collapses the distinction between the mythical-literary and the historical-empirical, as in the attempts to find the "man in the myth." A parallactic view of the Founders would instead emphasize their mythical stature and accept this as one perspective worthy of analysis and requiring careful juxtaposition with, say, biographical or sociopolitical details. The point is not to fold the one into the other in an effort at synthesis but to explore how the parallactic distance between the two better helps us identify what we are seeing.

For Žižek, Jacques Lacan's neologism "extimacy" best identifies this gap. The extimacy concept aims to solve the conundrum of theorizing "a cause that is both exceptional to the social field . . . and internal to the field."[9] As Molly Anne Rothenberg describes it in *The Excessive Subject*, the extimate addresses the aporia separating theories of immanent and external causation in the social field. The former, for which Michel Foucault serves as the most influential example, "treats causes and effects as mutually conditioning one another within the same field."[10] The latter, exemplified by certain kinds of Marxism, finds causes external to effects. Thus, an immanent account of the Founders might find a discourse of power unfolding and accumulating around a Thomas Jefferson, while an external account might posit a social system—say, the plantocracy—as the social cause for Jefferson's hyperbolic discursive status. The problem with each position is its failure to address the other, particularly by considering the shift of the phenomenon in question from intimate to extimate spheres. The bind becomes clear in the frustrated musings of Adams and Rush. At times, they want to stick with an immanent analysis, as when they discuss Washington's ten talents or his theatrical abilities: he is great because he performs greatness, has great skills, and so on. At other times, they opt for an external analysis—for instance in arguing that politicians decided to elevate the Virginian for political purposes. The inadequacy of these explanations comes through in their more complex attempts at commentary, as when Adams describes the mysterious aura of Washington. In this insightful argument, it is not that admirers of Washington perceive something properly within him, nor that he is puffed up by any particular social forces, but rather that Washington names an oracular site in which certain qualities are read and then received back again and so on in a constant feedback loop. Extimacy names this process, which is neither properly external nor internal and which exists precisely because "intimate" discourses must be externalized. In contrast to intimacy, which associates subjectivity with the private, interior self, extimacy, as Mladen Dolar puts it, names "the point of exteriority in the very kernel of interiority, the point where the innermost touches the outermost, where materiality is the most intimate."[11] Such is the point of Žižek's most fundamental claim: "the Unconscious is outside, not hidden in any unfathomable depths—or to quote the *X Files* motto: the truth is out there."[12]

The Traumatic Colonel ventures the first steps in an extimate history of the Founders, along the lines of what Adams called "*Character[s] of Convention.*" What is their history? When were they created and in relation to what narratives, what other characters? Chapter 1 begins with this task, offering a basic literary history of the formation of the four major figures: Washington, Franklin, Hamilton, and Jefferson. The emergence of this particular constellation was slow and halting and extends from a preliminary moment in the mid-1770s to the much more significant decade from about 1796 to 1806. As we outline this argument, it will become clear that we take the literary dimensions of our argument seriously, for we are convinced that imaginative works can help us better situate and understand the formulation of the Founders. Accordingly, we follow our initial speculations on the Founders with detailed explorations of two early American novels—Charles Brockden Brown's *Ormond* (1799) in chapter 2 and Tabitha Gilman Tenney's *Female Quixotism* (1801) in chapter 3—as further guides to this process. Brown's novel, we argue, predicts the dynamic operation of the Founders system, while Tenney's novel carefully and insightfully maps its emergence and political mobilization. Just as importantly, however, we want to insist on an expanded sense of imaginative literature that includes not just novels such as Brown's and Tenney's but the rich and significant political literature—the pamphlets, polemics, tracts, and biographies—of the early republican period. To that end, we try to reimagine a literary history that might accommodate works such as John Wood's *The History of the Administration of John Adams* (1802) or James Cheetham's *A View of the Political Conduct of Aaron Burr, Esq.*, of the same year. We even speculate that this flourishing of political writing may help us fill the notorious gap in US literary history, between 1800 and 1820.

But literary analysis is not an end in itself here. It is rather an exploration of a medium in which the dynamics of political fantasy are more easily grasped. Such dynamics are essential to our readings of the two proper novels, which we read as complementary explications of an emerging fantasy at the heart of US political culture, but this analysis allows us to take up the figure of Aaron Burr, the "traumatic colonel" of our title. The thing called Burr has a particular interest for us as the distinctively anomalous figure hovering at the margins of the Founders proper. So we will be arguing that the significance of Burr is precisely its resistance to incorporation in the semiotic system of the Founders. This is an argument broached in chapter 2 but explored in detail in chapter 4, where we outline the articulation of the Burr in the years between 1799 and 1804. In so doing, we try to make sense of those odd details that have proven so fascinating in contemporary literature of the Founders: Burr's electoral tie with Thomas Jefferson in 1800, the accusations of seduction, the assault waged by the New York Republicans, the duel with Alexander Hamilton, and the Federalists' odd courting of their hated antagonist to lead a secession movement. Chapter 5 examines the ramifications of this argument, as the uncertain fascination with Burr suddenly coalesced, between 1805 and 1807, into a major conspiratorial fantasy and a notorious treason trial that uncannily reassembled the former leaders of the Revolution. Burr's formation; his brief circulation through and around the symbolic field of the Founders; the repeated attempts to assimilate him as a Founder figure; the ultimate, violent repudiation and expulsion of this figure—together these reveal Burr to be the traumatic colonel of the Founders constellation. In this respect, Burr is indeed the cipher it was repeatedly described as being, with an emphasis on both meanings of that term, code and key.

This brings us to our third objective, namely, a new historical perspective on the early republican period informed by the Burr and the literary and phantasmatic elements it designates. Rush and Adams hint at this argument when they note the conjunctions of late 1805, though they miss the crucial reference: Toussaint L'Ouverture, dead in France in 1803. In short, we will be arguing that the history of Burr in relation to the Founders clarifies the complex processing of the great crime of slavery, its increased political institutionalization with the election of the "Negro President," its likely extension with the Louisiana Purchase, and through all this the enormous threat posed by the Haitian Revolution to the US South. This is an argument slowly developed throughout *The Traumatic Colonel*, first in a reading of the racial dimensions of the

Founders constellation, then in an insistence on the important racial sub-texts of *Ormond* and *Female Quixotism*. Chapters 4 and 5 then aim to situate Burr's rise and fall as a coded response to the consolidation of slavery, such that Burr, the imagined renegade conspirator of a breakaway empire, stands revealed as Toussaint in whiteface. The story of Burr, then, is one important story of the US engagement with Haiti.

This brings us, finally, to another reorientation central to *The Traumatic Colonel*—that of periodization. Scholarship of the early republic has remained firmly focused on the 1790s, that most historiographically privileged of decades. The 1790s, particularly among literary scholars, have been understood as the pivotal moment of intense ideological division between left and right, a brief moment of the flourishing of radicalism, and a literary boom period before the lull heralding the Era of Good Feelings. Such a focus has fit well with the field's recent emphasis on nationalist anxieties, the novel, and circumatlantic exchange, in which literary histories have foregrounded the national allegory and transnational affiliations in a cluster of novels from the decade. While we do not dispute the insights of this scholarship, it is worth considering the name that older anthologies gave to this decade—the Federalist Era—and how it may recontextualize our framing of the broader expanse from 1780 to 1820. For from the vantage point of 1808 and the official cessation of the Atlantic slave trade, the 1790s appear to be anomalous, an unusual hiatus in the long consolidation of power by the plantocracy in its alliance with northern workers. Washington's iconic preeminence guaranteed eight years of rule during which Federalism forged its uneasy compromise with slavery and partisan organization slowly emerged. The continuation of Federalist rule under Adams—facilitated by the still disorderly electoral system—was then the only presidency of a non-Virginian until the messy election of 1824. Given the solid rule by Virginian slaveholders, we might see the overall period as one of the consolidation of a slavery power, with the Louisiana Purchase a high point signaling the extension of human bondage to points south and west; with the Northwest Ordinance of 1785, ensuring a slave-free territory, a crucial exception, matched in foreign policy by the debates over the Toussaint Clause; or with the 1808 nonimportation legislation as the trigger for a doubling down of the slave powers.

To be sure, discussions of the 1790s have not been silent about race, whether in biographical accounts (e.g., discussions of Jefferson), local histories (such as the 1793 yellow fever epidemic in Philadelphia), or treatment of the world-historical impact of the Haitian Revolution. Indeed, much circumatlantic scholarship has followed Paul Gilroy and others in stressing a Black Atlantic, and we have been inspired by an impressive number of works exploring the centrality of enslavement to US cultural politics. These include older studies such as Winthrop Jordan's *White over Black* and David Brion Davis's writings, as well as such recent focused studies as Leonard L. Richards's *The Slave Power: The Free North and Southern Domination, 1780–1860* (2000), David Waldstreicher's *Runaway America: Benjamin Franklin, Slavery, and the American Revolution* (2004), Henry Wiencek's *An Imperfect God: George Washington, His Slaves, and the Creation of America* (2003), Gordon S. Brown's *Toussaint's Clause: The Founding Fathers and the Haitian Revolution* (2005), and Ashli White's *Encountering Revolution: Haiti and the Making of the Early Republic* (2010). As important have been such new syntheses treating slavery as Garry Wills's *Negro President: Jefferson and the Slave Power* (2003), Alfred W. Blumrosen and Ruth G. Blumrosen's *Slave Nation: How Slavery United the Colonies and Sparked the American Revolution* (2006), Matthew Mason's *Slavery and Politics in the Early American Republic* (2006), Peter Kastor's *The Nation's Crucible: The Louisiana Purchase and the Creation of America* (2004), Adam Rothman's *Slave Country: American Expansion and the Origins of the Deep South* (2005), Eva Sheppard Wolf's *Race and Liberty in the New Nation: Emancipation in Virginia from the Revolution to Nat Turner's Rebellion* (2006), Craig Hammond's *Slavery, Freedom, and Expansion in the Early American West* (2007), and Mason and Hammond's *Contesting Slavery: The Politics of Bondage and Freedom in the New American Nation* (2011). Also significant has been a wave of cultural-critical works including Dana Nelson's *The Word in Black and White: Reading "Race" in American Literature* (1992), Leonard Cassuto's *The Inhuman Race: The Racial Grotesque in American Literature and Culture* (1997), Jared Gardner's *Master Plots: Race and the Founding of an American Literature, 1787–1845* (1998), Philip Gould's *Barbaric Traffic: Commerce and Antislavery in the Eighteenth-Century Atlantic World* (2003), David Kazanjian's *The Colonizing Trick: National Culture and Imperial Citizenship in Early America* (2003), Gesa Mackenthun's *Fictions of the Black Atlantic in American Foundational Literature* (2004), Sharon M. Harris's *Executing Race: Early American Women's Narratives of Race, Society, and the Law* (2005), Andy Doolen's *Fugitive Empire: Locating Early American Imperialism* (2005), the roundtable "Historicizing Race in Early American Studies" published in *Early American Literature* (2006, ed. Sandra Gustafson), Sean Goudie's *Creole America: The West Indies and the*

Formation of Literature and Culture in the New Republic (2006), Robert S. Levine's *Dislocating Race and Nation: Episodes in Nineteenth-Century American Literary Nationalism* (2008), Agnieszka Solysik Monnet's *The Poetics and Politics of the American Gothic: Gender and Slavery in Nineteenth-Century American Literature* (2010), and the special issue of *Early American Literature* "New Essays on 'Race,' Writing, and Representation in Early America" (2011, ed. Robert S. Levine).

These works have variously attempted to expand our understanding of the workings of slavery as an expansionist economic force and political program, but they are perhaps as important for the ways in which they foreground the interpretive challenges of understanding the United States as a slave nation. The Blumrosens, for instance, recast the Revolutionary political narrative as one of often indirect responses to the Somerset case, from the early 1770s to the Northwest Ordinance and the framing of the Constitution: as such, they insist on a reprioritized hermeneutic at odds with the usual practices of intellectual history. Garry Wills similarly foregrounds a minority yet substantial political discourse of the "federal ratio" and "Negro President," clarifying what these terms meant for an antislavery analytic buried beneath a "national reticence."[13] Or, to take another example, Mason's account of political struggles pre-1808 simultaneously stresses the ways in which consideration of slavery "insinuated itself into a wide array" of issues but also ways in which the analysis of slavery remained incomplete and unarticulated, in many instances beyond agents' ability to formulate them coherently.[14]

What many of these works have in common, then, is a dual appreciation of the importance of slavery *and* a methodological awareness, even insistence, on its discursive elusiveness, which is variously explained through recourse to obfuscation, reticence, emergence, confusion, code, or even impossibility. Several years ago, the last term was something of the *doxa* in many US discussions of the Haitian Revolution, the discourse of which was simultaneously silenced or (in Michel-Rolph Trouillot's term) "unthinkable."[15] But a decade's worth of excavatory scholarship has perhaps confirmed that parts of the Haitian Revolution *were* thinkable, even if difficult to articulate, such that a major challenge we face today is not just the (historical) *thinking* about the moment but a better understanding of its distorted *articulation*. We thus follow the lead of Colin Dayan and Sybille Fischer, whose pathbreaking books have allowed critics to read for historical memory and agency beyond the textual record. For Dayan, vodou combines both intimate and communal religious enthusiasm to the political unconscious, while Fischer uses the psychoanalytic language of disavowal to make the gaps and absences of memory and cultural production legible.[16] Comparison may here be drawn to revisionist interpretations of American gothic literature, in which a racial subtext is regarded as constitutive of more explicit narrative and thematic aims.[17] It is in this vein that we try to read the political discourse of the era. Matthew Mason concludes his chapter "Slavery and Politics to 1808" with the observation that the Burr Conspiracy "engrossed Americans more than the slave trade debates did" and that "only thereafter" did it become "clear that slavery was the prime threat to the federal compact."[18] We would less dispute these claims, taken in their most literal sense, than note that the Burr Conspiracy was so engrossing *because* it was essentially a coded, indirect drama about slavery and slave revolution. And if slavery's threat to the federal compact became clear in the aftermath, it was in part due to the revelatory distortions of the preceding decade. In this respect, our study of the Burr phenomenon is offered as an attempt to explore the coded racialization of US cultural discourse, in keeping with the imperative presented in Toni Morrison's *Playing in the Dark*.[19]

Perhaps the best emblem of our project may be found in Aaron Burr's death mask, now in the Laurence Hutton Collection at Princeton University. Hutton had acquired the mask but was not sure of its provenance: "I had no special admiration for Burr—who once killed a Scotsman,—but I had all the collector's enthusiasm for Burr in plaster and I wanted to think my Burr was Burr."[20] But Hutton had met the person who had secretly made the mask, working as the agent for the best-known popularizers of phrenology, Orson Squire Fowler, Lorenzo Niles Fowler, and Samuel Roberts Wells. As Hutton noted, the Fowlers had found in the Burr mask evidence that his "destructiveness, combativeness, firmness, and self-esteem were large, and amativeness excessive."[21] Indeed, Orson Fowler, in his massive *Sexual Science*, dwelt on Burr's massive amativeness, adding this story about the crafting of the mask. The "posterior junction with the neck" was, in Burr, so large "that when his bust was taken after death, the artist took his drawing-knife to shave off what he supposed to be two enormous wens, but which were in reality the cerebral organs of Amativeness."[22] The excitement of discussing the death mask is such that it evokes anecdote after anecdote, two of which may be shared here. One is the story of Burr's experiment with a life mask, apparently following the example of his then British host Jeremy Bentham. The mask was taken by the Italian-Irishman Peter Turnerelli, who reportedly left a small stain on Burr's nose that he could not remove. The other is this story from Hutton:

A proud young mother once exhibited to me her new-born and first-born babe, now a blooming and pretty young girl. I was afraid to touch it, of course, and I would not have "held" it for worlds; but I looked at it in the customary admiring way, wondering at its jelly-like imbecility of form and feature. Alas! when I was asked the usual question, "Whom does she favour?" I could only reply, in all sincerity, that it looked exactly like a pink photograph of my death mask of Aaron Burr. And the young mother was not altogether pleased.[23]

The phrenological framing, belied by the "jelly-like imbecility of form and feature" of the unformed baby, may be read as the pseudoscientific codification, decades after its career, of the thing called Burr. And where "amativeness" looms ever larger—just as it does in racial discourse—there is a subtle constant concern with color through these details: the white mask, the dark stain caused by the life mask, the pinkish baby face. In Hutton's *Portraits in Plaster*, Burr is brought up near the end, immediately preceded by considerations of the masks of Washington, Franklin, and Jefferson. Discussion of Burr is then followed immediately by consideration of the masks of Daniel Webster, Henry Clay, John C. Calhoun, and Abraham Lincoln, as if Hutton is staging some strange theatrical version of the Civil War played out in masks. Two more masks remain—first, that of Lord (Henry) Brougham, a contemporary of Burr and active within British abolition, and then, finally, oddly yet not so oddly, the "Florida Negro Boy." Why end with this boy, "one of the lowest examples of his race"? Hutton insists that "his life-mask is only interesting here as an object of comparison," for "whatever the head of a Bonaparte, a Washington, a Webster, or a Brougham is, his head is not."[24] The boy from Florida thus emerges as the point of comparison, the uninteresting illustration so powerful that it must conclude Hutton's book, the puzzle and its own solution, the conclusion of the sequence that takes us from Washington to Burr and on to Lincoln.

1

The Semiotics of the Founders

Where did (or do) the Founding Fathers come from?

There are two default answers that seem to prevail. The first understands the elevation of the Founders as a natural phenomenon, the result of some determinable combination of moral or social complexity, political superiority, and/or practical efficacy. Thus, we remember Thomas Jefferson because of his leadership of the Democratic Party, his authorship of the Declaration of Independence, the hallmarks of his presidency, his exceptional intellect, his tortured grappling with slavery, and so on. Or we commemorate George Washington because of his military leadership, his combination of virtues, his special status as a "first" president, his Farewell Address, and the like. By this reasoning, the lesser status of second- and third-tier figures (the Patrick Henrys, Silas Deanes, or Light-Horse Harry Lees) simply reflects their lesser abilities or achievements. A second, more complex explanation for the Founders' status focuses on their construction by contemporary and subsequent cultural productions. We honor a Benjamin Franklin because of his thorough self-promotion and an extensive array of portraiture, poems, parades, and so forth, which have been glossed and perpetuated for more than two centuries. That both of these explanations—a quasi-Darwinian natural selection of great men or the concerted efforts of cultural hegemony—seem commonsensical and, often enough, compatible speaks to the tremendous cultural power of the Founders, so dominant that they corral nature and history to justify their genealogies.

The most basic objection one might raise to such explanations is their profoundly tautological nature. Is it not possible that we perceive the achievements of the Founders precisely to the degree to which they have already been elevated? That the gist of our explanations is already the fruit of their status, rather than the cause? One of the remarkable details about Washington is his symbolic elevation before he had really done anything—Washington Heights on Manhattan Island, for example, was named after the general in 1776, and he received an honorary LLD from Harvard the same year, as he arrived in Boston to command the Continental Army. Thus, by early 1777, John Adams (a perpetually baffled wannabe yet insightful reader of the Founders phenomenon) was addressing, in Congress, "the superstitious veneration which is paid to General Washington."[1] Or, to consider another example, in Richard Snowden's popular post-Revolutionary history of the war, *The American Revolution: Written in the Style of Ancient History* (and later sometimes subtitled *Written in the Scriptural, or Ancient Historical Style*), we find the Declaration of Independence buried in chapter 14, between the British military landing at New York City and the battle for Long Island: "Then they consulted together concerning all things that appertained to the provinces, and they made a decree"—here a footnote explains this to be the "Declaration of Independence"—"and it was sealed with the signets of the princes of the provinces. And the writing of the decree was spread abroad into all lands; and when the host of Columbia heard thereof, they shouted with a great shout" (101).[2] This scant attention—fifty-nine words in two volumes—not only registers the insignificance of the Declaration (at this moment a formal resolution of fleeting impact) but also anticipates how the Declaration achieved significance: through the elevation of Jefferson. We must resist, then, the natural-historical explanations for the Founders, as their status often preceded their so-called causes. We celebrate the Declaration not because it was significant but because Jefferson became important and secondarily elevated the Declaration. We know about Valley Forge because of Washington's significance, not vice versa: he became important not because of his military or political exploits—the debate about his military achievements catches a glimmer of this—but the other way around.

And yet we should also be wary of the cultural-constructivist explanation for the Founders—that they are creations. We would mention here a revealing counterfactual—the remarkable elevation of Nathanael Greene, at one time a major general with a reputation as Washington's most able officer. Histories of the Revolution written in the 1780s and '90s stressed Greene's achievements, a tremendous number of counties and towns were named after him, he was depicted in grand portraits by Trumbull and Peale, . . . and then his phenomenal status evaporated. The same is in fact true for many of the Revolutionary heroes or republican statesmen whose names we only vaguely, if at all, recognize today—Horatio Gates, John Stark, Benjamin Lincoln, William Heath, John Laurens, Henry Knox, Israel Putnam, Charles Thomson, and so on. Indeed, any survey of histories of the Revolution or early republican newspapers will reveal a constant, active attempt to construct iconic figures. Were the Founders culturally constructed? Of course, but the constructivist answer does not explain why some of these figures prevailed while others faded away. Indeed, the complementarity of these two explanations—naturalist-historical and constructivist—is essential to the gesture of "debunking" the Founders. One shows the "real" Benjamin Franklin (bawdy, manipulative, skeptical, or whatever) as if to reveal how "constructed" he is as a mythical Founder, but such debunking is in actuality the very constructivist process with updated historical content about sexuality, personality, private secrets, and the like.

Let us assert, then, at the outset that what we call the "Founding Fathers" was (and still is) primarily a literary and symbolic phenomenon—it entailed certain reading practices, narratives, relational logics, constellations, and genres. Given this textual formation, it is especially important to stress that the Founders emerged relationally, not as isolated instances of heroic figures. We discuss later the theoretical implications of the field in which the Founders arose but turn first to the unfolding, from the 1770s into the 1780s, of the first major Founders, George Washington and Benjamin Franklin.

The Royal Field

In a recent study of colonial royalism, Brendan McConville has outlined almost a century of a growing North American celebration of the monarchy, culminating in the intense "monarchical love" of the eighteenth-century imperial crisis.[3] In the aftermath of several decades of imperial neglect during the tumultuous years of the English Revolution, the restored Stuarts attempted, unsuccessfully, to transform colonial North American political administration. The Stuarts' error lay in the focus on royalization and consolidation of colonial charters and governments, attempts at which largely collapsed with the Glorious Revolution of 1688, marked in North America by a series of colonial rebellions in 1689–90. In the aftermath, a very different attempt to assert royal authority followed, with centralizing *institutional* reforms giving way to a very different "reorganization of political society, public life, and print culture" (48). In other words, the inability to reform political *institutions* gave way to reforms of political *culture*, starting with the introduction of annual rites bolstering a "cult of the British Protestant prince" (48). Thus, at the very moment when "parliamentary supremacy became firmly established in England," the colonies witnessed the emergence of a new political culture in which "the key imperial tie became the emotional one between the individual and the ruler" (50).

One sign of the effectiveness of this new political culture was the introduction of some twenty-six official holidays affirming this monarchical culture, and by 1740, McConville argues, "public spectacles celebrating monarch and empire, involving local elites and military display, occurred at least six times a year in the major population centers, while more modest activities occurred on twenty other days" (63–64). By the imperial crisis, colonial America evidenced a political culture grounded in an intense emotional investment in the king—what McConville at one point calls "the emotional structures" based on "the troika of love, fear, and desire" (106).

From our perspective, what is most notable about this symbolic formation is its relative isolation from other political and social institutions— this is the paradox emphasized by McConville again and again. Where royalist culture in Britain was integrated in "a political order dominated by extensive patronage ties, the state church, long established custom, and a tightly controlled land tenure system," in the colonies the royalist ties were compartmentalized and passionately intensified in "rites and print culture" (106) and, later in the eighteenth century, in a series of royally marked commodities, from medicines and tableware to iconography in prints and medals.[4] The result was a *more intense royalism in British North America than in Britain itself*, a point crucial to McConville's account of the imperial crisis.

After the initial imperial conflicts of 1764, colonials responded with "a flight to the king's love and justice" (251). Contrary to whiggish misinterpretations of the Revolution as the *gradual* repudiation of monarchical prerogative, colonials in the years before the rupture "completely abandoned the perception that strong kings tended to threaten liberty" (253), going so far as to articulate neoabsolutist arguments "relating the king's person to the entire physical empire" as fundamental to their interpretation of colonial charter rights (256). Thomas Jefferson, for instance, called for a return to the royal veto on parliamentary legislation—a practice unused since Queen Anne's reign (261). Thus again another paradox: "As counterintuitive as it may seem, the love of the king and country reached its zenith at the split second before imperial collapse" (251). That is, colonials *amplified* the symbolic position of the king until the monarch was the sole solution to the crisis into the 1770s. "By 1773, all that remained was faith in the king," as political theory and rhetoric were channeled through this symbolic conduit (250). When King George did not come to the rescue, when the links between king and imperial practices could no longer be denied, the peripety was sudden and dramatic. In fact, the emotional and symbolic investment in the king explains the long and passionate litany of accusations against him in the Declaration of Independence, which is as much a Declaration of Heartbroken Betrayal. Thus, the British colonies had, at the moment of the rupture with Great Britain, almost a century's tradition of cultic, symbolic investment in a political leader, unique in the empire in being institutionally unmoored and located primarily in print and pictorial representations.

This special iconic status, inherited by George III, anticipated the domain eventually to be occupied by the Founding Fathers. But a particularly North American occupation of this semiotic space also depended on the emergence of the king's negative composite during the years of the imperial crisis. Bernard Bailyn long ago noted the oddly persistent significance of John Stuart, the third Lord Bute, in pre-Revolutionary rhetoric, in which he was not only "the root of the evil" of the imperial crisis but also the "malevolent and well-nigh indestructible machinator" behind British politics.[5] If Bute is now largely unknown in popular Revolutionary lore, he appeared repeatedly in texts of the imperial crisis, from the Stamp Act controversy to the Declaration of Independence. Historian John Brewer has provided the most detailed account of the iconography of Bute,[6] trying to explain the strange "range and extent of hostility to Bute" by excavating the underlying "theory of politics" motivating this antipathy (*MLB* 5).[7] Indeed, Brewer, whose work belongs within the transatlantic "republican synthesis," argues that the fixation on Bute resulted from a conjunction of whig beliefs about monarchical prerogative, undue nonparliamentary influence, and fears of an unbalanced constitution, going so far as to add that such associations with Bute were unfair and somehow incorrect.[8] While one should certainly link the figure of Bute with related ideological positions, we should not let this prosaic translation exercise obscure Bute's tremendous symbolic composition, which Brewer elsewhere discusses. Two qualities seem most important. For one thing, Bute was a centripetal figure combining and channeling other figures. Indeed, other political officials were deemed Bute's "*locum tenens*"—his placeholders—in the parlance of the time, such that his distance or absence from the political scene simply provided more proper names to constitute his power.[9] These secondary figures—considered "'cyphers' or agents for the minions of Bute" (*FLB* 102)—were linked metonymically in discourse: Bute *and* this or that puppet. But in narrative, these connections were made through the emplotment of conspiracy, whereby secondary characters were metaphorical placeholders of the primary figure. In this framework, Revolutionary conspiracy theories may be read not so much as explanations of events, or indices of theories of historical causality, but rather as maps of semiotic layerings.

Just as important, however, was a countervailing centrifugal or splitting dynamic, whereby Bute gathered together traits, events, and qualities that could not initially be linked with King George. "Clearly, it was argued, responsibility" for absolutist tendencies in government "could not be placed upon a King who it was traditionally claimed 'could do no wrong'" (*FLB* 114). Thus emerged a theory of a secret "inner cabinet," or a "dual system of government"—a public or legitimate or monarchically constrained order, on the one hand, and, on the other, a secret, scheming, and prerogative-driven system (*FLB* 98, 102); thus also emerged the scandalous accusations that Bute had sexual relations with the Princess Dowager (*FLB* 111).

We see both of these dynamics in the North American versions of Bute, where he is the central figure in characterological clusters including other figures, most notably Lords North and Mansfield. Thus, we find John Leacock's satirical, mock-scriptural *First Book of the American Chronicles of the Times* presenting this composite vision: "Behold, yonder I see a dark cloud like unto a large sheet rise from the NORTH, big with oppression and desolation, and the four corners thereof are held by four great beasts, BUTE, MANSFIELD, BERNARD and HUTCHINSON."[10] When, in 1776, Leacock published his mock metadrama *The Fall of British Tyranny*, "Mr. BUTE" would top the list of "Dramatis Personnæ" as "Lord *Paramount*," with Mansfield, Dartmouth, North, and others in subordinate roles.[11] John Trumbull's 1775 *M'Fingal* opened linking its central character with a Scottish rebelliousness that "With Bute and Mansfield swore allegiance / . . . to raze, as nuisance, / Of church and state the Constitutions."[12] Hugh Henry Brackenridge's 1776 dramatic poem "The Battle of Bunkers-Hill" envisioned General Gage crying "Oh BUTE, and DARTMOUTH knew ye what I feel."[13] The popular pamphlet series *The Crisis*, collaboratively written in England but published serially and repeatedly in the colonies, was full of similar references.[14] Bute, for example, "sternly bids North lay another

tax," while anti-American "sentiments are Bute's by Mansfield's penn'd";
royal speech, in yet another installment, is "no ordinary composition, it
originates from Bute, is trimmed up by Mansfield, adopted by North, and
pronounced by a royal Orator."[15] Similarly illuminating is a 1776 pamphlet, published in Philadelphia, focused on persuading Quakers to join
the independence movement. In one scene, four of the main characters—
the Irish American "Pady," the Quaker "Simon," the Scottish American
"Sandy," and the New Englander "Jonathan"—have largely come to agreement about the imperial crisis but suddenly come to blows as they begin
to fantasize that one another are scheming counselors to the king: "*Simon*:
If you were lord North, I would—then fetches Sandy a blow and knocks
him over the bench, and breaks his arm;—whilst Jonathan and Pady keeps
struggling on the floor, Jonathan cries out if you were lord Bute, but I
would—and in striving to throw him, breaks his leg, and down he goes,
crying out for justice."[16] Apologizing for the broken limbs, Simon says,
"When I began to think of lord North, it put me all in a fume his laying
the Americans at his feet," while Jonathan answers, "That's what made me
think of Bute when you mentioned the other, and I thought they should
go together."[17] One last example: Mercy Otis Warren begins her *History
of the Rise, Progress and Termination of the American Revolution* describing "Lord Bute, who . . . had become the director of the monarch on the
throne of Britain" and by "secret influence" had made Parliament "the
mere creature of administration."[18] She later mentions Bute's retirement
in 1766, but adds "there had been an extraordinary variety and succession
of characters in the colonial department" who had subsequently "taken
the lead in this thorny path"—she mentions lords Grenville, Rockingham,
North, Hillsborough, and Dartmouth.[19]

Thus, the semiotic field, on the eve of the Revolution, was occupied by
two complementary figures: a positively valorized George III and the neg-
atively charged, aggregative figure of Lord Bute. George represented an
executive power, a royal prerogative, an ability to *act* on behalf of the colonists, though acting in silence. Bute, by contrast, represented deliberative
powers—suasion, rhetoric, manipulation, misinformation, and jesuitical
sophistry. What is important, from our point of view, is that this pairing
persisted even after the sudden emotional reversal toward the king, at which
point the pairing designated differently inflected qualities mobilized for
tyrannical purposes. The king still represented executive power, though in
the form of coercive actions and violence, and these were complemented
by the schemes and plans of Bute and his minions. Such a dichotomy is

implicit, for example, in *The Crisis* number 18, which suggests that "Fate hangs on Bute's proud will and George's brow. / Below, North represents absconding Bute, / Above, a Nation dyes by Roy le veut."[20] Here George is the exterior bodily expression—the brow—as compared to Bute, whose "will" speaks of intellectual, emotional, and religious interiority.[21]

Generating Washington

We pause here to discuss briefly the semiotic square theorized by the structuralist linguist and narratologist Algirdas Greimas.[22] Greimas argues that a given cultural situation will be structured around a fundamental opposition that expresses a logical understanding of that moment. In the mid-1770s, many British North American colonials perceived their political conflict as an opposition between a practical, politically active, yet nonintellectual kingly force and a deliberative, insinuating intellectual advisory force. What is important about this binary, for Greimas, is that, when it comes to be perceived as inadequate, its stalled logic generates its solution or transcendence—that is, a culture does not simply reset or shift to altogether different figures but attempts to develop a solution from within its semiotic constraints. What this means for the political conflict in question is that the Revolutionary response would be constrained by the terms of the initial pairing.

GEORGE III	LORD BUTE
Executive	Deliberative
Doing	*Thinking*
Body	Mind
Silence	Insinuation

We see precisely this phenomenon in the emergence of Washington as a figure. Washington, we should stress, did not simply arise as a replacement for George III; he was not the same kind of figure and was in fact defined in relation to—that is, in contrast with—George III's qualities. Remember that the king had been called on to exercise royal prerogative—executive action—on behalf of the colonists and against the evil counsel of the Butites. He had failed to act vigorously on America's behalf and had then pursued a number of aggressive actions—repressive financial measures, military expeditions, the incitement of blacks and Indians against good English colonists—in short, all the acts of aggression enumerated in the Declaration of Independence. When "Washington" finally emerged, then, it had to address and correct this characterization—it had to embody a reactive executive position, but with the very different inflection of restraint. This difference is evident in a number of key moments in Washington's mythological construction: his humility and hesitation upon accepting his role; his visitation of so many homes ("George Washington Slept Here"), whereby he relied on the hospitality of his "subjects"; his endurance of hardship at Valley Forge; his often defensive, evasive, and stalling maneuvers as a general; his reluctant execution of Major John André (an agonizing act of duty against his personal inclinations); his endurance of criticism and cabals. . . . In all these instances, "Washington" acts, but at the behest of the people, reluctantly, not for his personal power but in service to others. Even the famous cherry-tree anecdote from Parson Weems, which later adhered to the mythic figure, confirms this: young George's action (chopping down the tree) serves as something for which he must take responsibility and be humbled, and the crucial quality here is less simple honesty than the shameful admission of his infantile lapse into monarchical prerogative. We might thus translate "I cannot tell a lie" as "I actively chopped down a tree and will never act so aggressively again"—it is with this gesture that he is contrasted to George III, who remained silent about *his* actions.[23]

We must stress here that we are not showing how Washington gradually, biographically, historically, came to define and occupy his symbolic position. Rather, these details are selective emphases, fabrications, or distortions of the historical record, which reveal that a "Washington" position quickly took shape in contrast to the position of King George. For this reason, the insight often attributed to Washington Irving's "Rip Van Winkle" obscures as much as it clarifies—the American George was not simply a blue-coated leader figure substituted for a red-coated one but a different figure generated in response. The problem with many readings of Irving's story is that they see the Washington figure as *positional*—that is, they assume that Washington's special standing had to do with institutional or political power, and specifically with a hierarchy of positions of charismatic, political, or deific leadership which, when vacated, must be reoccupied. By this view, it seems quite natural that the commander in chief of the Continental Army might eventually become the president of the United States, as he moved from wartime leader to leader in peace. This spatial-positional framework also implies that "Washington" is the *central* cultural site in which a host of cultural issues are mediated. There are two related errors that follow from this assumption. For one thing, such readings tend to understand history as cumulative and gradualist—Washington is appointed to his military command in 1775, becomes extremely popular with his open letter demanding humane treatment of American prisoners, then becomes still more popular with his refusal of General Howe's informally addressed letters, and so on and so forth. It is as if each episode quantitatively adds to Washington's fame through some kind of natural progression, or as if symbolic importance is something that grows incrementally, like manufacturing output. Relatedly, there is a suggestion that "Washington" is somehow *homologous* to other mythological Founders. A "Thomas Jefferson" will be another variant in the master pantheon, while a "John Jay" must be read as simply a diminutive version of Washington's grand stature.[24]

In light of such assumptions, it is all the more important to insist that the significance of Washington is not positional but rather *relational.* That is, Washington's significance makes sense only relative to other symbolic figures and has no necessary relationship to his political or military authority. It is therefore misleading to suggest that "Washington" designates a particular abstract space in which cultural concerns—for example, nationalism—are negotiated: as we will demonstrate, this processing of cultural concerns requires a larger relational field attuned, like fictional narratives, to more complex problems. To put this differently, the symbolic figures that emerge will not necessarily serve the same abstract function any more than the knights of the Round Table all represent "chivalry": because they exist in a relational field, they may complement one another and may function differently from one another, as we shall see. What is more, because this symbolic field is relational, it is not subject to a steadily predictable, incremental dynamic. The configuration can undergo sudden shifts, and seemingly important figures may disappear, while obscure figures suddenly assume new significance.

Let us return for a moment to Nathanael Greene, who, as we mentioned before, experienced a similarly rapid and dramatic symbolic investment during the war. A nice summation of his signification is offered in Crèvecoeur's mosaic of Revolutionary-era mythology, in which he includes this anecdote about Greene:

> The history of the war in Carolina . . . is a eulogy for General Green more exact than anything one could say.—Among the many qualities

that distinguished him, I will mention only this one.—All the dispatches announcing reversals were always addressed to Congress in his capacity as commander in chief of the southern department.—But every time he gained any advantage, it was to general Washington that he made his reports, as an officer under the Commander in chief.[25]

Greene's outstanding qualities, then—the particular combination of military ability and humility, of taking on the burdens of the war while passing on the laurels to others—are precisely those qualities that underlay the symbolic development of Washington. And in Crèvecoeur's anecdote, we see with great clarity how Greene is not a separate figure but a parallel one—an alternative Washington much as Washington was an alternative Greene. In a similar fashion, Crèvecoeur describes a number of Revolutionary generals reluctantly drawn to war and then happily retiring to their farms: all of these formulations of the Cincinnatus myth speak to the development of a symbolic designation that transcends George Washington and that George Washington finally filled decisively.[26] In short, Greene was not a distinctive figure or even a homologous one—*he was the very same position*, a variant through which the Washington configuration, a necessary relational slot, was developed. One might imagine a counterfactual scenario whereby Washington, not Greene, had died in 1786: in that case, the symbolic work invested in Washington could easily have shifted to Greene.

Here we may turn to a different symbolic nexus, in fact the main configuration that was juxtaposed to the Washington figure—that of Benjamin Franklin. If we look ahead to the late 1780s and the ratification battles over the US Constitution, one finds that these two names—Franklin and Washington—are the two that have achieved and maintained a special status. What was the specific position of Franklin at this point? Here we must be careful not to confuse the "Franklin" of the 1770s with the "Franklin" that took shape in the 1790s and helped generate additional symbolic positions in the Founders' pantheon. In the mid-1770s, Franklin's significance was that of the intellectual or "philosopher": he was Doctor Franklin, scientist of electricity, theorist of the Gulf Stream, inventor, genius, and so on. None of these qualities was enough to determine his symbolic importance, which did not become clear until the Hutchinson affair of the early 1770s. Gordon Wood is correct when he writes that "this affair was the most extraordinary and revealing incident in his political life . . . [and] effectively destroyed his position in England and ultimately made him a patriot."[27] But where Wood makes this a biographical claim about Franklin, we read this as a claim about the symbolic construction of the "Franklin" position. In 1772, Franklin had received some private correspondence which included a now infamous letter in which lieutenant governor Thomas Hutchinson advised British administrators to pursue "an abridgment of what are called English liberties" in order to avoid the growing "anarchy" of the American independence movement.[28] Franklin passed these letters on to North American colleagues, who published them. All indications suggest that Franklin hoped to effect a reconciliation between the colonies and the empire by casting Hutchinson as a scapegoat, but the public drama cast Franklin very differently. With the 1773 publication of the Hutchinson letters, and relations inflamed by the Boston Tea Party, Franklin himself became the scapegoat and was famously called before the Privy Council—in the "Cockpit"—to receive criticism and insults from Solicitor General Alexander Wedderburn. Franklin famously received an hour of abuse in total silence, while the audience cheered and laughed. Two days later, Franklin was fired from his position as deputy postmaster general of North America; relations between Great Britain and the colonies continued to deteriorate. Meanwhile, as Michael Warner notes in his account, "The incident greatly recuperated Franklin's colonial reputation, which had suffered in the mid-1760s, and did much to inflame revolutionary sentiment."[29]

The Hutchinson affair—or the Wedderburn-Franklin exchange, as it was frequently presented in the early republican press—proved fundamental to the formation of "Franklin" not because of its biographical significance but because it took the famous figure of the intellectual and encoded it in relation to the figure of Lord Bute. The Cockpit humiliation made this distinction hard to avoid: Wedderburn was one of Bute's alleged minions and as solicitor general embodied the position of imperial intellectual—the schemer using his wits to insult, mislead, manipulate, and misdirect. In this confrontation, the intellectual Franklin's behavior was recast in a contrasting position: he had used his formidable gifts to *expose* the schemings of Bute and company. This use of his intellect—to bring bad political advising to light and therefore check it, rather than to obscure it further—was then doubly encoded as he refused to use his famous wit to respond to the Privy Council, opting instead for silence. In this respect, "Franklin" answers and corrects the figure of Lord Bute much as "Washington" answers and corrects the figure of the king. Where Bute was a figure of considerable culture and learning complementing, enabling, and amplifying the executive symbolic position, Franklin suddenly rises to significance as a corrective figure. A perfect illustration may be found in John Trumbull's 1774 poem "An Elegy on the Times," which Elihu Hubbard Smith featured prominently as the opening piece of his 1793 anthology *American Poems, Selected and Original*. The poem laments the "mock debate," "servile vows," "well-dissembled praise," and generally "fruitless offerings" of English politics (ll. 48–52)[30] and then transitions to this description of Franklin's encounter:

> While Peers enraptur'd hail the unmanly wrong,
> See Ribaldry, vile prostitute of shame,
> Stretch the brib'd hand and prompt the venal tongue,
> To blast the laurels of a FRANKLIN's fame!
>
> But will the Sage, whose philosophic soul,
> Controul'd the lightning in its fierce career,
> Hear'd unappal'd the aerial thunders roll,
> And taught the bolts of vengeance where to steer;—
>
> Will he, while echoing to his just renown
> The voice of kingdoms swells the loud applause;
> Heed the weak malice of a Courtier's frown,
> Or dread the coward insolence of laws? (3)

In the event, Franklin remains silent "While Infamy her darling scroll displays, / And points well pleas'd, oh, WEDDERBURNE, to thee!" (4). Characteristics later associated with Franklin—most notably his ribald humor and his expressiveness about wealth—are at this moment English vices one could never associate with the seemingly puritanical and disinterested scientist. Franklin stands an impassive scientific observer, his response to hostile questioning akin to his "unappal'd" assessment of the thunderstorm. Nonetheless, we may see glimmerings of mythical elements later to accrue to Franklin—for example, the adoption of the Poor Richard persona, in which intelligence assumes an assertive modesty; or the crucial figure of the printer (as distinct from the author), who publishes but also maintains a kind of modest silence; or the scientist, who tries to describe things as they are, as opposed to the political theorist describing how they should be; or the creator of the public library, trying to make information available to all. Indeed, the famous 1778 portrait of Franklin by Joseph-Siffred Duplessis—Franklin in simple coat, lips noticeably clamped shut—pictorially codifies this symbolic moment.[31]

Let us be clear about our argument. The symbolic relational pairing of George III and Lord Bute generated not one new position (Washington) or an infinite series of countersymbols (Washington, his generals, various political leaders, and so on) but a decisively answering pair: Washington-Franklin. Washington was not a substitution for George III but an important *correction* and therefore a new relational position, just as Franklin signaled a relational *corrective* to the Bute figure. Consequently, the emergence of these new figures retroactively confirmed and clarified the original generative roles of king and Bute. Aggressive action and shadowy insinuation were reworked as reluctant action and intellectual illumination, at least for the time being. If biographical behaviors provided raw material for these new positions, so much the better; but these symbolic configurations were not dependent on such data and drew easily on fictional and apocryphal embellishments, selective distortions of the historical record, and composite biographical details of adjacent and subordinate figures.

GEORGE III	LORD BUTE
Executive	Deliberative
Doing	*Thinking*
Body	Mind
Silence	Insinuation

GEORGE WASHINGTON	BENJAMIN FRANKLIN
Reluctant Action	Intellectual Illumination

Founders: The Next Generation

By the moment of the Constitutional Convention, these two mythological figures, Washington and Franklin, played parts on the political stage—the former called out of retirement to preside over the convention, the latter providing the most published written defense of the new system and the tactic of the unanimity resolution.[32] Alexander Hamilton, assessing the prospects for ratification, listed Washington's influence as the major advantage, and Luther Martin, an opponent, later published his convention notes in which he seemed to complain that "neither General Washington nor Franklin shewed any disposition to relinquish the superiority of influence in the Senate."[33] Noah Webster's October 1787 pamphlet concluded with a glorification of Washington and Franklin as "*fathers and saviors*" of the country; another piece in the *Massachusetts Centinel* warned anti-Federalists that Americans "will despise and execrate the wretch who dares blaspheme the POLITICAL SAVIOUR OF OUR COUNTRY."[34] If many essays did not refer to the two giants, they nonetheless suggest the tremendous influence of these figures in popular assessment of the Constitution. By November, Roger Sherman of Connecticut could write,

> It is enough that you should have heard that one party has seriously urged that we should adopt the *new Constitution* because it has been approved by *Washington* and *Franklin*, and the other, with all the solemnity of apostolic address to *Men, Brethren, Fathers, Friends, and Countrymen*, have urged that we should reject as dangerous every clause thereof, because that Washington is more used to command as a soldier than to reason as a politician—*Franklin* is *old*—others are *young*—and Wilson is *haughty*. You are too well informed to decide by the opinion of others and too independent to need a caution against undue influence.[35]

Washington and Franklin remained firmly iconic and still somewhat differentiated in their respective roles of executive actor and deliberative intellectual—useful formulations for supporters, dangerous ones for critics. When an early anti-Federalist piece, Samuel Bryan's *Centinel No. 1*, challenged the icons, then, it had to characterize Washington as naive (that is, so much an actor as to lack intellect) and Franklin as senile (his mind having succumbed to his bodily aging).[36] Most anti-Federalists, though, passed over the two in silence or tried to characterize the convention with reference to a noniconic figure, as in the preceding allusion to Wilson or when a piece in Philadelphia's *Independent Gazetteer* described the convention as a group of physicians directed by "John Adams, Esquire."[37]

With the Revolution receding, however, both "Washington" and "Franklin" drifted into a somewhat bland period when their significance seemed to lose definition. Perhaps the best illustration of this loss of symbolic force is the poem written by young Charles Brockden Brown, titled "Inscription for Benjamin Franklin's Tomb Stone." When Philadelphians circulated the poem and learned that Franklin wanted to write his own epitaph, Brown's brother apparently sent the poem to the *State Gazette of North Carolina*, where it appeared as "An Inscription for General Washington's Tomb Stone"—Washington's name was simply inserted in place of Franklin's. If the references to the "Shade of Newton" and "Philosophy's throne" today seem baffling, it appears that generalized platitudes about "American's favorite . . . / Whose soul for the want of due room, / Has left us to range in the skies" could fit the one as easily as the other.[38]

As the war continued into the early 1780s, there had been signs of the generation of new positions emerging. The strongest versions of new positions centered on the figures of Benedict Arnold and Major John André. If Richard Snowden's aforementioned *The American Revolution* ignored the Declaration of Independence, it gave great attention to Arnold, whose crucial turn is announced toward the end of the second volume: "And it came to pass, in the one thousand seven hundred and eightieth year of the Christian Hegira, in the ninth month, on the twenty-first day of the month, that Satan entered the heart of *Benedict*" (2.148–49). The final verses of the chapter speak of "the fatal fruit of treachery" and how "the monuments of thy victory on the plains of Saratoga, serve only to blaze forth the death of thy fame" (2.158). It is tempting to see in Arnold simply a crude evil counterpart to Washington, the Satan to the latter's Christ—self-promoting in contrast to Washington's self-denial and so forth. But again we must consider the Arnold position in relation to André, introduced by Snowden as "valiant in war, and where the brave were, there was he" (2.150). It is this positive coding that gives meaning to the full André narrative, in which two details were important. First, he was captured by American sentries who had misidentified themselves as Tories— "they spake in the subtilty of their hearts," as Snowden puts it (2.153). Second, when tried by the Americans, he maintained his integrity—"he answered with dignity, composure, and truth; his magnanimity did not forsake him, in the hour of extremity" (2.155–56). Perceiving the prisoner as "a shining model of all that was excellent!" the Americans want to save him but execute him from a sense of duty (2.156). This drama is still more pronounced in William Dunlap's 1798 play *André*, strongly declared a tragedy in the introduction: in Dunlap's drama, the ranking American figure, the "General," struggles to do his duty according to his larger cause and reluctantly orders André's hanging.[39] The André figure thus requires a more complex relational understanding of Arnold, for the concern of this tentative constellation of the mid-1780s was not crude demonization but a formulation of sin and treason in a framework of Revolutionary republicanism. André was on the side of evil, was himself a good man, showed signs of great culture, was tricked by the American sentries and abandoned by Arnold—in all these details, this figuration attempted to express the moral challenges of postmonarchical justice in a politically divided society of patriots and tories. André's position was important precisely because of its association with, and difference from, the

Arnold position. The problem posed by the pair, then, was not one of evil but an important revision of the Washington and Franklin positions. Washington signified reluctant action, but Arnold represented less its opposite, after the fashion of George III, than the dangers of the Washington position for the ambitious and valiant: Arnold was less Washington's antithesis than a figure generated from the Washington position, so constrained by the rigors of selflessness as to be driven to the enemy. André, meanwhile, signaled an important variant of Franklin—the cultured intellectual, a careful conduit of information, a figure of virtue . . . but for the wrong side. Relative to Arnold, André became the tragic traitor but perhaps more importantly allowed a vicarious staging of an encounter between Washington and Franklin. In any case, the historical persistence of these figures, especially of Arnold, should be read as a trace of this brief moment when the emergent Founders' constellation was still largely military in orientation and the nascent national semiotics were organized around questions of loyalty.

But if the Arnold-André pair marked a brief detour of the 1780s, a different and more decisive constellation was to emerge in the 1790s. Washington and Franklin were symbolically reinvested in important ways, and two different figures emerged. How did this happen? We would stress here three concurrent phenomena. The first Washington administration witnessed a series of political conflicts over national economic development and the related role of the government therein. In each instance, the stakes were high, while the terms of debate were abstract—concerned with constitutional hermeneutics, for example, or with the unintended consequences of state interventions in economic subsystems. The year 1790 witnessed a debate around Hamilton's February "First Report on Public Credit," concerned with the retirement of national debt; the following year saw this conflict extended to include the problems of banking and currency, this time focused on Hamilton's "Report on a National Bank" (submitted December 1790); and 1792 saw yet another conflict, this time over mercantilism and the interpretation of the Constitution's "general welfare" clause and triggered by Hamilton's "Report on the Subject of Manufactures" (submitted December 1791). Each of these conflicts was accompanied by a substantial body of print argument—not just Hamilton's theses but a number of essays, pamphlets, and editorials, not to mention internal Cabinet memoranda. Each conflict was narrowly decided in favor of the northern financial classes, and none of these conflicts could, in its own turn, activate the semiotic resources to mobilize mass political action, instead leaving the elites deadlocked. Consequently, these years also witnessed a series of interventions to break this deadlock and translate these conflicts into an iconic repertoire, whereby political disagreements could be reconfigured symbolically.

Critical here was the rise of a new form of political press. In the summer of 1791, for example, Jefferson and Madison, having led and lost the battle against the bank, began urging Philip Freneau to relocate to Philadelphia to launch a national newspaper capable of answering John Fenno's *Gazette of the United States*, founded at Hamilton's instigation in 1789; Freneau's paper, the *National Gazette*, began publishing in late October 1791. From that moment, print played an increasingly important role in ironizing political discourse. There had already been partisan newspapers, to be sure, but now competing discourses were coordinated and synchronized by national papers. Both papers continued to publish essays of political theory—indeed, Hamilton and Madison wrote scores of tracts during these years—but the classic essay of the deliberative public sphere was increasingly complemented by new forms influenced by Revolutionary propaganda. Freneau's satire "Rules for Changing a Limited Republican Government into an Unlimited Hereditary One" (July 1792) beautifully illustrates this transition. Presented as a series of proposals for subverting the Revolutionary heritage, the essay's main achievement was the construction of the persona of a devious conspiratorial monarchist. The essay concluded ominously:

> Should it be found impossible, however, to prevent the people from awaking and uniting; should all artificial distinctions give way to the natural division between the lordly minded few and the well-disposed many; should all who have common interest make a common cause and shew an inflexible attachment to republicanism in opposition to a government of monarchy and money, why then * * * * *—[40]

This abrupt conclusion not only confirms the semiotic priority granted to character over plot but typographically denotes the symbolic space to be filled in the next few years. Whatever the subject matter of public discourse, character would become a regular part of political debate. In 1791, the publication of *The Rights of Man* prompted a huge body of secondary literature not simply on Paine's arguments but on Paine himself, giving us the legendary caricature of the rabid, drunk womanizer.[41] A decade later, it was routine for the Federalist newspapers to publish long mocking analyses of the president's writing style, as if his character and policies could be ascertained by his elaborate and effeminate diction and sentence structure.

These same years saw a series of pamphlets written as political commentary and presenting an informal characterological theory of political partisanship—this is the moment we typically recognize as the birth of the US party system. From our perspective, the primary cultural work of the party framework was the translation of political disputes into characterological terms, as parties came to be defined not so much by political and theoretical positions or the economic interests of their member groups as by individuals or personality profiles. A good illustration of this emerging analysis can be found in William Laughton Smith's 1792 pamphlet *The Politicks and Views of a Certain Party, Displayed*, which began by marveling at the attacks from Freneau's paper on measures "sanctioned by the *Man* we all love and revere"—Washington, of course.[42] The ensuing narrative of votes translated the economic debates of 1790–92 into a tale of this congressman expressing shame and remorse, these congressmen voting in secret in committee, and those who "never openly avowed" their views (11). Hamilton's particular positions were recast as indices of his historic stature as a minister of state ("his reputation traversed the ocean and in distant climes his Name was mentioned among the great ministers of the age"); criticisms were therefore the result of "*Envy*" begotten from "*Fame*" (12). Deliberative disagreements over the duration clause in the banking bill were now described with reference to "solemn threats, sulky looks, big works and great Guns" (17). This political breakdown coincided with "*the arrival in this Country of a certain Personage*" (3)—Jefferson's return from France—and this "*personage*," later called "the *Generalissimo*" (with Madison, his "*second in command*," known also as "the *General*"; 22), is the subject of the final third of the essay.[43] In these pages, we find one of the first character sketches of this next moment of the Founders:

> Had an inquisitive mind in those days [1790] sought for evidence of his Abilities, as a Statesman, he would have been referred to the confusions in France, the offspring of certain political dogmas fostered by the American Minister, and to certain theoretical principles only fit for Utopia: As a Warrior, to his Exploits at *Monticelli*; as a Philosopher, to his discovery of the inferiority of Blacks to Whites, because they are more unsavory and secrete more by the kidnies; as a Mathematician, to his whirligig chair. (29)

Elsewhere Jefferson is cast as "a certain tall and awkward Bird which hides its head behind a Tree and supposes itself unseen tho' its posteriors are publicly displayed" (32–33), as "this philosophical Patriot, or patriotic Philosopher" (35), and as the devious sponsor of the "Poetaster" (Freneau) given a position as a translator in the State Department (33).

Contributing to this partisan polarization was the well-known international conflict between the two global powers vying for hegemony. The catalyzing role of the French Revolution provided a lexicon for accelerating and polarizing the semiotic unfolding. In early 1793, the execution of Louis XVI (January) and the declaration of war against Britain (February) set the stage for recurring crises with France through the next two decades. If students of American history even today have a hazy familiarity with a series of proper nouns from this period—Genet, the Jay Treaty, the XYZ Affair—it is because each name denotes a scandal that momentarily clarified and advanced the semiotic polarization, ostensibly around the polar terms of England and France. If events during the Jefferson and Madison administrations revealed the ephemeral nature of this distinction, this did not make it insignificant.

Finally, we must add that Federalist rule clamped down on popular political outlets. Popular instruction had already been discouraged during the first Congress (August 1789), but the crucial moment came with the formation of the Democratic-Republican Societies (spring 1793), concurrent with the arrival of Genet. These societies' association first with Jacobinism and then with the so-called Whiskey Rebellion led to their condemnation in Washington's Message to the Third Congress (November 1794) and a military expedition led by Washington himself, with Hamilton at his side. After the suppression of the insurrection—which itself had a tremendous chilling effect—popular political engagement was increasingly displaced to the press and the party. The frenzy over the XYZ Affair and the Alien and Sedition Acts of 1798 further stifled popular political activities, while increasing the political significance of the national partisan papers. Again, we miss the important structural and cultural transformations of the moment if we see these events as "tap[ping] into a widespread, deep-seated, and preexisting animus towards such ideas"; as Seth Cotlar has argued, the reverse is the case—this moment "led to the rapid crystallization of a xenophobic and explicitly anti-revolutionary vision of American politics."[44]

The extensive political conflicts and mobilizations, their complex and esoteric formulations, the international polarization, an electoral system consolidating a two-party complex, the rise of the partisan press and the diminution of vernacular political organization—all of these meant that the 1790s would see the reactivation of the Founders constellation. We should be clear: we are not arguing that the Founders were the inevitable cynical production of propagandists seeking to mobilize supporters. Propagandists were at work and accentuated the partisan inflections, to be sure, but the symbolic imperative and its effectivity betoken a cultural phenomenon beyond political manipulation. As the Arnold-André pairing showed, the symbolic constellation did not need to be confined to the macropolitical sphere, as the iconic portraiture of the later nineteenth century was to demonstrate, with constellations that incorporated Native Americans and prominent African Americans. But in the 1790s, this characterological activity was concentrated in the political sphere, as we saw with William Laughton Smith's 1792 pamphlet. For Smith selected and assembled many of the details that would allow for a range of different inflections—for example, the significant gendering and sexualization of the Founders evident in allusions to Jefferson's cowardice. If Hamilton, in 1792, was already privately writing that Jefferson and Madison *"have a womanish attachment to France and a womanish resentment against Great Britain,"* it was works such as Smith's that established this semiotic code firmly in public discourse.[45] It is equally worth noting that Hamilton (with whom Smith was in agreement) has only the vaguest contours in Smith's pamphlet—it was through the corresponding attacks on Hamilton that his positive and negative qualities themselves coalesced. Again, when contemporary works of Founders Chic excitedly declare that the great Founders were subject to vicious personal attacks, they obscure the very role of such attacks in *creating* the Founders as a system—it is not *despite* such personalized insults that the great Founders emerged but in part *because* of them.

WASHINGTON *Doing*	**FRANKLIN** *Knowing*
Cautious icon of government	Mobilizing public through culture via print, juntos, civic institutions

JEFFERSON *Doing → Knowing*	**HAMILTON** *Knowing → Doing*
PHILOSOPHER-PRESIDENT	INSTITUTION-BUILDER
Author of Declaration of Independence, Virginia Constitution, *Notes on the State of Virginia*; inventor	Orchestrates Constitutional Convention; guides establishment of military, Treasury, Bank, and Federalist Party
AVOIDS ACTION AND CONFLICT	SEEKS ACTION AND CONFLICT
Cowardice during war; slipper-wearing intellectual; withdrawal to Monticello	Military service, propagandist, and organizer

We may now spell out the constellation that emerged over the 1790s. Washington, who was originally a figure of executive restraint in contrast to George III, now took on partisan inflections—from a Federalist viewpoint, cautious, nonaligned government-building, or from a Republican viewpoint, Anglophilic passivity exploited by underlings. Franklin, originally a figure of republican illumination in contrast to Lord Bute, now emerged as a marker of radical cultural mobilization, either deluded or virtuous, depending on one's party. (The competition between these inflections, we may note, heuristically guides the attempts, in today's scholarship, to locate a figure such as Franklin politically—such attempts continue the posthumous constellational work of the 1790s.) These two positions could then generate two new positions using the semiotic material associated with the Jefferson and Hamilton portraiture. The former emerged as the embodiment of action rendered as knowledge—Doing becoming Knowing. He was the Philosopher-President, associated, increasingly, with the Declaration of Independence, the Virginia Constitution, *Notes on the State of Virginia*, the Kentucky and Virginia Resolutions, and eventually the forming of the Library of Congress and the University of Virginia. Ensconced in his hilltop plantation estate of Monticello, he pursued governance through retreat, again with positive or negative variants. For Republicans, he was the theorist of democracy who withdrew from the Washington (and later Adams) administrations, to direct an opposition through ideas. For Federalists, he was the coward of 1781 (the famous flight from the British), now ridiculously theorizing racial difference while exploiting slave labor, then shuffling about in his slippers playing with his inventions. Hamilton, meanwhile, embodied the reverse movement, as the enactor of intellectual mastery through active programs—Knowing becoming Doing. Thus, he was then known (and still is) as the builder of national institutions (the Federalist Party, the Treasury, banking, the military, tax policy, infrastructure, etc.). Far from withdrawing to bucolic isolation, he was a figure of the city and the office, commemorated for work as Washington's right hand and the behind-the-scenes orchestration of the Constitutional Convention. For Federalists, he was the very force of visionary energy itself, while for Republicans, he was the manipulative schemer. And we can see here how the Jefferson-Hamilton pair, generated from the reconfigured Washington-Franklin pair, fed back into the revision of the latter. From the Federalist perspective, Hamilton combined the intellect of Franklin with the achievements of Washington; from the Republican perspective, Jefferson combined the enlightened democratic commitments of Franklin with the careful restraint of Washington. And so too the reverse: for Federalists, Jefferson combined Washingtonian passivity and delay with Franklinian heterodoxy and immorality, while for Republicans, Hamilton pursued a conniving Franklinian system-building with a combination of Washington's Anglophilia and militaristic aggression.

In the Revolutionary moment, the Washington-Franklin pair emerged from a royalist cultic system to address and explore the question of political resistance, the affective combinatorics of republicanism. In the 1790s situation, still defined by the sense of republican intellectual hegemony, the problem was governance, not the challenge to government, and the consequent parsing of the problem took different shape. Because this symbolic system was not first and foremost about political *positions* but about affective fantasy, it matured in ways that paralleled other imaginative media of the time. We might note that the constellation of the '70s

WASHINGTON
Childless

FRANKLIN
Promotes illegitimate heir
Exuberant sexuality

JEFFERSON
Produces non-promotable
heirs with slave, Sally Hemings

HAMILTON
Fatherless
So-called Caribbean bastard;
tragic son killed in a duel;
scandalous affair with Maria
Reynolds

had more in common with the characterological portraits of heroic historiography (from which it drew and which it fed), whereas the configuration of the '90s inevitably drew more on the novel, in which women were often, if not always, central figures. Thus, the '90s witnessed a dual gendering and sexualization of the Founders, already prefigured in Judith Sargent Murray's portrait of the republican mother as commonwealth president—a female Washington. Again we may draw on our seemingly trivial and nonacademic knowledge of the Founders to sketch out their respective positions. Washington could emerge as the Father of the Nation not despite his apparent sterility and childlessness[46] but precisely because of it, a position affirmed by the complementarily vague status of Martha Washington: cautious and reluctant action found its sexual manifestation in surrogate parenting. By contrast, the "knowing" Franklin emerged as a figure of sexual activity, with his wife receding into the shadows, obscured by the more prominent William, the bastard son who became the royalist governor as a marker of sexual excess. The Jefferson and Hamilton positions played out these masculine variants—the Jeffersonian scandals of the day stressed his widower status but also his illicit sexual relationships (first the assault on Elizabeth Walker, his neighbor's wife; later the liaison with Sally Hemings). He was not quite masculine in a solid sense but still sexually active, and his nonpromotable heirs (slaves) signaled a variant of the childless Washington and Franklin's bastard. Meanwhile, Hamilton was himself the bastard son, and his tremendous intellect could not prevent him from entanglement with Maria Reynolds and her husband. In each instance, the gendered and sexual characterization rounded out the political portrait: Washington's restraint meant that his citizens (or, in some variants, his slaves) were his "children"; Franklin's ideological tendencies became manifest in excessive sexuality; Jefferson's focus on reflexive theorization meant that he produced not a solid republican family but property to be analytically assessed; and Hamilton's focus on aggressive masculine enactment led to a spectacularly self-destructive affair.

As this sexual encoding may suggest, however, the primary impetus of the expansion of the Founders constellation was, we believe, the encoding of the growing conflict over slavery. As we noted earlier, historiography has for a long time struggled to express the significance of slavery in the post-Revolutionary era, though it was central to debates about the nature of the Union, the admission of new territory, and the formation of new parties. Especially at the moment of the Haitian Revolution,

WASHINGTON *Doing* Benevolent slaveholder	**FRANKLIN** *Knowing* Abolitionist
JEFFERSON *Doing → Knowing* Slave-owner who theorizes race, knows slavery is evil, but sleeps with his slaves	**HAMILTON** *Knowing → Doing* Creole, who pursues an alternative to slavery

slavery was essential, if nonetheless obscured, in the very formulation of republicanism itself. And we see this significance in the Founders constellation, which articulates four positions on slavery. The first pair gives us two stark positions of the 1770s and '80s—Washington, the benign slave owner of Mt. Vernon, who treats his slaves with gentle compassion, and

Franklin, the urban abolitionist.[47] For or against, doing (using slave labor) or knowing (understanding slavery's evils)—the obvious incompatibility of these two positions in turn generated two more positions, those of Jefferson and Hamilton. The former (doing → knowing) was the slave owner who understood, even theorized, the evils of slavery while also asserting the inferiority of Africans and sexually reproducing (with) them; the latter was the "creole" of perhaps racially suspect origin who theorized and implemented a northern capitalist system (supposedly) inimical to slavery. One might say that the Jefferson position embodied a republican cynicism (*I exploit slave labor, but I know it is wrong*) while the Hamilton position embodied a republican denial (*I have grown up amid slavery, and I actively pursue its alternative*).

Literary Characters

Given our insistence on a "literary" reading of the Founding Fathers, we may pause here to consider how the Founders' constellation fits into a broader cultural history of the period. At one level, we might say that the coalescence of this constellation has clear literary markers to which we have already alluded—Mason Weems's biography of Washington, Franklin's autobiography, and John Marshall's multivolume biography of Washington (written before and while he presided over the Burr trial), among others. Thus, we might link this moment to the emergence of biographical writing that finds its most sustained expression in the career of Samuel Lorenzo Knapp, perhaps the first professional biographer in the United States. Knapp produced such general omnibus works as *Biographical Sketches of Eminent Lawyers, Statesmen, and Men of Letters* (1821) and *Female Biography* (1834) as well as a focused biographical sketch of Susanna Rowson affixed to her posthumous novel *Charlotte's Daughter*. But he also wrote book-length biographies of the notorious eccentric Lord Timothy Dexter and of such political figures as Daniel Webster and DeWitt Clinton, not to mention Aaron Burr.

But where may we locate imaginative fiction in relation to this biographical surge? Here Amélie Oksenberg Rorty's terminological distinction between "figures" and "persons" may be helpful.[48] "Figures" are exemplary idealizations, whether cautionary or heroic, as in the early US readings of Plutarch's *Lives*. Unlike earlier "characters," figures have an interiorized sense of themselves—they discover what they are (because of ancestry or tradition) and act accordingly. In the novels of the 1790s, it is "figures" who discover their affinity to Young Werther and then put bullets in their heads. "Persons," by contrast, appear as this sense of one's role becomes increasingly a matter of differentiated choice: the person chooses roles and is judged by those choices. A reader encountering a literary figure recognizes a certain destiny in its actions; a reader encountering a literary person considers him or her as a moral, legal actor with responsibilities and liabilities; intention and self-understanding displace social role and habit as foci for judgment. Though the *figure* does not have identity crises, the *person* does.

The Founders, as they take shape, first appear as figures and gradually—especially with the layering of sexual and racial components—become persons. That is, their characteristics steadily expand to include responsibilities and accountabilities. When the anti-Jefferson "Epaminondas," writing of Jefferson's machinations within the Washington administration, asks, "Did the Guardian Genius of Washington slumber for a moment that he should conceive the base design? Or was his unerring sagacity for once imposed on and made the dupe of others less virtuous than himself?" he at once casts Washington as a figure (synonymous with his "genius" and "unerring sagacity") and Jefferson as a person (imposing with his base design).[49] In imaginative fiction, too, figures gradually yield to persons, who in Rorty's account typically appear alongside legal thinking. The nineteenth-century volumes of *Modern Chivalry*, with their fixation on common law and juridical liberality; Caroline Matilda Warren Thayer's *The Gamesters; or, Ruins of Innocence* (1805), which introduces gambling as a problem originating from economic inheritance and bad lifestyle choices; George Watterston's *The Lawyer; or, Man as He Ought Not to Be* (1808), which makes immoral decisions and legal thought virtually synonymous—all register the growing significance of legal discourses and practices as the person becomes more and more established in novelistic plots. Not surprisingly, the same period gives us the first inklings of the bildungsroman, a version of which finds articulation in Watterston's 1810 *Glencarn*, with a stronger formulation in 1818's *Life and Adventures of Obadiah Benjamin Franklin Bloomfield*.[50] But we may note that generally, when it comes to characters, the novel lags behind the purportedly nonfictional works clustered around the Founding Fathers, making the ultimate union of these two currents in the historical-novel boom of the 1820s a somewhat logical conjunction.

Here, then, we would conclude with two observations. First, it would be best to think about the imaginative work surrounding the Founders as a literary track that for the time runs parallel to, or a bit in the lead of, the novel. Freed from the generic conventions with which many novels struggled, and impelled by the partisan divide and the greater career opportunities for writers in political-journalistic prose, the writings about the Founders constitute a compellingly innovative canon of character exploration alongside the relatively skimpy, rival novel production. But this divide should encourage us to think more creatively about the two currents' connections. For if the novel lagged behind in the expansion of character, it produced some amazing formulations of the structure of political fantasy. It is to two fascinating examples that we next turn.

2

Hors Monde, or the Fantasy Structure of Republicanism

This kernel of the REAL encircled by failed attempts to symbolize-totalize it is radically *non-historical*: history itself is nothing but a succession of failed attempts to grasp, conceive, specify this strange kernel.   —Slavoj Žižek, *For They Know Not What They Do*

Just because people ask you for something doesn't mean that's what they really want you to give them.
             —Jacques Lacan, Seminar XIII, March 23, 1966

As we showed in the previous chapter, the symbolic positions of the Founders were generated relationally. Though the structure has a certain (uncanny) coherence, each generative pair responds to a preceding pair only to reveal yet another iteration of conflict, a difference for which no synthesizing solution is readily available. The machinery of fantasy thus continues to rumble. For Jacques Lacan, this is the function of desire: it is the incessant movement around that minimal difference between a set of available options. Lacan named this minimal difference "object *a*," or the kernel of the Real. To this concept, we owe the inspiration for our title, *The Traumatic Colonel*. In chapters 4 and 5, we explore how something called Aaron Burr ends up occupying the position of object *a*, this strange kernel of the Real. But if the parallax and its remainder, this object *a*, may be described as "radically *non-historical*," each attempt to name it, to grasp it, to make it "practically assailable"[1] will necessarily be bound by the horizon of the possible *at that moment*. In the case of the Founders, we have argued, the vectors of sociosexual reproduction and slavery converge at that horizon. The pull of that point of convergence is the traumatic colonel.

The two novels that we turn to here in chapters 2 and 3 also aim to fill in that space in the collective, or political, fantasy of the era. Each novel, Charles Brockden Brown's *Ormond; or, The Secret Witness* and Tabitha Tenney's *Female Quixotism*, recognizes this gap, this something missing, this need to find the traumatic kernel. In *Female Quixotism*, the focus of the next chapter, Tenney explores the vicissitudes of crisis as a problem of regional incompatibility. In the absence of a credible, regionally compos-ite suitor, Tenney's heroine, Dorcasina Sheldon, is left heirless and under the charge of her black servant, Scipio. The fantasy of interracial repro-duction surfaces if only to be suppressed as comedy, and thus the result of the fruitless search to bequeath the estate and secure the future is static resignation. If Tenney's fantasy evokes a macroscopic dystopia, Brown's *Ormond* inhabits a much more cramped interior space. Whereas Miss Sheldon strives for an exogamous solution and ends up right where she began, Brown's Constantia struggles with a crumbling center. This cen-trifugal deterioration is displaced onto a composite figure, the semanti-cally overloaded Ormond, an agent of a vast international conspiracy but also an ever-present and supposedly quotidian black chimney sweep. That both Brown and Tenney propose an Africanist presence as the object cause of desire is a stunning insight that the political characterology of the moment can only circle and imply.

Let us begin with the subtitle of Brown's novel: *or, The Secret Witness*. It seems the perfect evocation of the Foucauldian panoptical paradigm, an allusion to a series of monitory and disciplinary institutions and dis-courses. All those representations of witness—spying from behind false walls, peeping through keyholes, entering homes in disguise—would seem to reference a plethora of well-known social anxieties of the period, from xenophobic fears of immigrant radicalism to the changing norms of eco-nomic exchange to the reconstituting of boundaries between public and private spheres. The driving force behind such metaphorical witness, it fol-lows, would be the dominant ideology of the period, the republicanism so thoroughly described by the leading historians of the past generation. The substance of this republicanism is clear enough, leaving the literary crit-ic's task that of an archeology of its corresponding modes of surveillance. Indeed, one seems to find confirmation for exactly this framework in the novel's prefatory epistle. "The distinctions of birth, the artificial degrees of esteem or contempt which connect themselves with different professions and ranks in your native country," writes S.C. to her mysterious European friend I. E. Rosenberg, "are but little known amongst us."[2] The apparent contrast here, between Europe's traditional hierarchies and artifices and the new and rational assessment of human worth in the United States, seems to capture the shift, so crucial to Foucault and his readers, from the hierarchical world of punishment to the bourgeois world of discipline.

But what if we read this seemingly simple passage differently? In Europe, it claims, esteem and contempt are already and predictably structured according to "different professions and ranks" (the nobility, the clergy, intellectuals, and so on). But in the United States, *artifice structures itself in different ways*, ways yet to be examined, ways still obscure in the new republic. In other words, the opposition here is not between European artifice and US clarity but between a familiar European artifice and an unknown artifice—which will be examined under the rubric of "secret witness." Far from a self-congratulatory diagnosis, then, the preface names the novel's crucial problem: if occupation and status give structure to esteem and contempt in Europe, what structures these feelings in the United States? We would go a step further and argue that the problem identified is that of *fantasy*, here understood as the formal structure through which ideology is experienced. Specifically, we suggest that "secret witness" now operates as the fantasy structure at the heart of republicanism. By this view, *Ormond* is not yet another instantiation of republicanism but rather stands alongside such novels as *Edgar Huntly*, which uses sleepwalking as a way to approach the question of actions divorced from conscious reflection, or *Wieland*, which uses biloquism to approach the question of expression divorced from the body. "Secret witness" does not denote social surveillance but rather a structure of consciousness, and *Ormond* is not a panoptical text but an astute critical reflection.

In light of Charles Brockden Brown's magazine sequences, *Ormond* may be read as a progressive series of fantasy studies, rather than a unified narrative. These sketches trace the progression of Anglo-American fantasy from the colonial period to the post-Revolutionary republic. Stephen Dudley embodies the earliest moment, while the latter is localized in the character of Constantia, whose name alludes to Judith Sargent Murray's celebrated pseudonym in the *Gleaner* essays, collected and published just the year before.[3] It is tempting to imagine that the name Constantia had an appealingly intrinsic irony, given that it was the mask for a character associated with honesty and forthrightness. In any event, *Ormond*'s exploration of Constantia proceeds through her pairing with Ormond, a very different entity, something *hors (du) monde*, outside this world. What is more, this relationship, like that between Constantia's father and the con man Craig, is defined by the fundamental importance of labor and specifically the tremendous problem of slavery. Indeed, the constitutive role of slavery in the republican fantasy structure helps explain the hyperbolic rhetoric of the Revolution, whereby colonists compared themselves to the enslaved. Our analysis, we should add, focuses on the Constantia-Ormond relationship, somewhat at the expense of the fascinating women characters that figure so prominently in the latter chapters of the novel, not to mention recent criticism. This decision reflects our sense that these characters mark the novel's preliminary attempts to think a way beyond republicanism, to consider the development of political fantasy at century's end. Consequently, we devote most of our analysis to the intricacies of the republican fantasy core itself.

The Baxter Episode

We begin with the brief subplot about Baxter, the husband of the Dudleys' washerwoman, Sarah, whose frenzied death from the yellow fever is presented in chapter 7. Baxter's neighbors, he thinks, are a Frenchman and his daughter. He hates the French—he had fought against them in the War of Austrian Succession—and suspects they are "exempt from this disease" (64/87). He shows sympathy, though, for the daughter, "Miss Monrose," and once encountering her in seeming melancholy, asks after her father. She answers in French, and "this, and the embarrassment of her air, convinced him that his words were not understood" (64/87). One night, as he leaves watchman duty, his concern leads him to the Monroses' door. Its shutters closed, no light is visible, and he "put[s] his eye to the keyhole" only to discover that "all was darksome and waste" (65/88). He retires to bed, resolving to inform the authorities the next day, when his wife awakens him to note "a certain glimmering on the ceiling" (66/89). Assuming a violent robbery in progress, he rushes to the window to glimpse a figure carrying a candle entering the Monroses' back doorway. Further alarmed—he now imagines "midnight plunderers"—he grabs his sword and rushes to the Monrose house. Again he looks through the keyhole. Again he sees only darkness. He runs to the back of the house and takes a position at the back fence. Eventually he sees a pale Miss Monrose in the doorway, a freshly dug hole in the backyard, the lady dragging a sheet-wrapped mass to the hole, and, at the last moment, sheet drawn aside, "the pale and ghastly visage of the unhappy Monrose" (69/92). Baxter starts with fear, Miss Monrose sees him and shrieks in turn, and he returns home only to sink into disease and death.

This seems at first a reportorial or realist account of Baxter's illness: he thinks thus and so, does such and such, and consequently, his imagination profoundly stricken, catches the fever. But many of the narrative's details suggest we would better read it *as a dream*—that is, as a compressed narrative of fantasy experience. Hearing words one somehow cannot understand, feeling as if one is not understood, looking and finding only darkness, sensing a nearby crime, watching but unable to move, dreading that which one knows one will inevitably see—are these not characteristically phantasmatic dream elements? Indeed, this dream state is confirmed in the description of Baxter watching in the Monroses' backyard, where, "raising his head above the fence, at a point directly opposite the door, [he] waited with considerable impatience." The next paragraph gives this description:

> Human life abounds with mysterious appearances. A man perched on a fence at midnight, mute and motionless, and gazing at a dark and dreary dwelling, was an object calculated to rouse curiosity. When the muscular form and rugged visage, scarred and furrowed into something like ferocity, were added,—when the nature of the calamity by which the city was dispeopled was considered,—the motives to plunder, and the insecurity of property, arising from the pressure of new wants on the poor and the flight or disease of the rich, were attended to,—an observer would be apt to admit fearful conjectures.
>
> We know not how long Baxter continued at this post. He remained here, because he could not, as he conceived, change it for a better. (67/90)

The passage's oddity lies in its conflation of Baxter's narration of events with an exteriorized description *of Baxter himself.* He lifts his head above the fence only to see . . . himself sitting on the fence watching the backyard. This is the true moment of terror: *his externalized perception of himself watching the Monrose house.* He is his own secret witness. All that he sees is his own fantasy, as Martinette / Miss Monrose later confirms: "The rueful pictures of my distress and weakness which were given by Baxter existed only in his own fancy" (210/208).

The scene thus suggests Zeno's paradoxes as they have been discussed by Slavoj Žižek. The paradox of Achilles and the tortoise, in which Achilles is never able to catch up with his slower competitor, actually "stages the relation of the subject to the object-cause of its desire, which can never be attained."[4] In a similar vein, the Baxter story is less an "objective" or "realist" description of how fantasy came to affect his perception than an attempt to convey the structure of that fantasy itself. Throughout the sequence, Baxter is simultaneously unable to perceive clearly (he cannot understand Miss Monrose's words, he sees nothing through the keyhole) *and* condemned to perceive all too clearly (intuitively knowing Mr. Monrose is dead, anticipating the dead man's face). This contradiction becomes clear when he finally sees not the dead man's face but *the terrifying sight of his own perception.* As in dreamwork, the scene's topography is carefully drawn. He is "perched on a fence," the boundary separating him from the seemingly terrifying object. Or he is at his "post," committed and compelled to watch—he is, after all, a night watchman. His earlier inability to perceive clearly thus seems a resistance to the desired encounter with the fever, but a resistance that drives him to that encounter. His sense of an intrusion next door likewise seems an anticipation of his own intrusion— his witnessing of his own death. The truly fatal moment comes when, to his horror, he at last realizes that he desires that which he dreads (seeing the dead man).

This subplot not only illuminates the novel's concern with fantasy but also sheds light on how the novel is structured. S. W. Reid long ago noted that the Baxter narrative was published separately before *Ormond*, in the *Weekly Magazine* of February and March 1798, almost a year before the January 1799 publication of *Ormond*.[5] He suggests the episode was merely used as filler in a novel otherwise concerned with Constantia and Ormond. But we would suggest a different relationship between these two texts—namely, that the Baxter episode, in its original context, formulated the central problem that *Ormond* would attempt to narrativize. The Baxter episode appeared earlier in the fourth and fifth installments of a thirteen-part series titled "The Man at Home."[6] The titular narrator is introduced, in the first piece, as a sixty-year-old man confined to a small, sparse room in order to escape arrest for debt. Without books, company, or scientific tools, he finds freedom and amusement only through reflection and writing. "My memory is, indeed stored, and my imagination never was a sterile sand," he writes, "but the power of deduction and arrangement are, to a certain degree, taken away by the consciousness of present difficulties."[7] The subsequent pieces accordingly offer different elaborations of this imaginatively rich but chaotically unarranged consciousness. His landlady, Kate, inspires a series of reflections—on the paucity of plebeian language, the obstacles to economic advancement, her childhood and emigration, and of course the death of her husband, Baxter. These are interspersed with a series of other reflections on—to name just a few topics—a locked chest sitting in his room, the history of his acquaintance Miss De Moivre, the possibility that love is a disease, and the "history of intestine commotions." In the latter case, the narrator reflects on a political revolution in one of the ancient colonies of "Magna Græcia," in which the newly dominant faction formed a "secret tribunal" to carry out nighttime executions and create a climate of "the utmost terror." One friend of the narrator insists this terror is "parallel" to the yellow fever epidemic of 1793—that is, of the Baxter episode's context.[8]

Does this reduce the yellow fever to a metaphor for social conflict? On the contrary, the narrator repeatedly suggests, in different ways, that the parallel lies in the fantastic dynamics of terror, of which social conflict is the material staging point. Indeed, the historical particulars cannot even be discerned. The annals recording the Greek terror convey "none of those general views which fill the reader's imagination, and translate him to the scene of action." All the better, for even "the dullest reader" may then "*circumstantialize* the picture" (11:320, emphasis in original). It is *not* the specific "scene of action," but rather the circumstantialization of the picture that is important—not Greece, but terror, not any particular social conflict, but fantasy. *Circumstantializing* thus denotes the imaginative reconstruction of the fantasy's coordinates, as opposed to the detailing of context. This process finds a more banal illustration earlier in the narrative, when the Man at Home muses about the mysterious chest in his room. Unable to move this "artificial receptacle," the narrator variously imagines it to be full of "Portuguese gold" and "white sand."[9] When he discovers it is nailed to the floor, he realizes it may be empty and recalls a childhood memory when his schoolteacher used a chest nailed to the floor to convert a habitual skeptic to belief in magic.[10] The chest can hardly be read as a metaphor of a reign of terror, but as an "artificial receptacle," it captures in usefully quotidian terms the program of circumstantializing fantasy. "Methinks I could sit here, occasionally glancing at it," he writes, "and find employment for years, for my mind and pen, in revolving and recording the ideas which it furnishes."[11] This point is reiterated one last time in the final "Man at Home" piece, which takes as its starting point Erasmus Darwin's analysis of love as a disease. The Man at Home adds to "love" both "laughter" and "sleep," thereby alluding to the three classic topoi of psychoanalytic theory: sexuality, jokes, and dreams. If this reformulation implies that "the world may, at present, be regarded as one vast hospital," the Man at Home nonetheless resists the pathologization of fantasy.[12] Because it is "interwoven with the very constitution of a human being," "men can no more hope to enjoy exemption from it than to increase the number of their eyes or legs." These universal diseases may be "deviations from the truth of things and the perfection of our nature," but they "are diseases whose tendency it is to exclude diseases still greater."[13] Fantasy is an inevitable and constituent part of human experience.

The Baxter episode, far from being an anomaly or a contextual reference to 1793, signals *Ormond*'s concern with the structure of fantasy. In the terms introduced in "The Man at Home," it is a masterful "circumstantializing" of secret witness, for which the fever is less a "scene of action" in some crude sense than an "artificial receptacle." If a number of elements of "The Man at Home" reappear in *Ormond*, then, they do so to stage the problem of fantasy.[14] In fact, this is apparent from the novel's opening account of Stephen Dudley's financial ruin, which culminates in a revealing episode surrounding a purloined letter.

Dudley's Con

We return, then, to *Ormond*'s first developed moment of secret witness, at the end of the opening subplot in which Thomas Craig, Stephen Dudley's apprentice, cons Dudley into abject poverty. When Craig is briefly absent, a letter arrives bearing an unknown superscription. Dudley leaves it unopened for a "considerable time" but eventually cannot resist reading the letter. He discovers that a Mary Mansfield of Portsmouth, New Hampshire, has become convinced that her wayward son resides with Dudley. She rebukes her son for his flight, which has left her to support herself as a washerwoman, "drudging for her livelihood" (13/46). Could Craig be the wayward Mansfield, Dudley wonders? He "dismisse[s] the affair from his thoughts" (13/46), leaving the letter on the mantelpiece. The moment of secret witness follows. Craig returns; the writing "immediately attracted [his] attention"; he reads the letter and mutters, "Damn it!" Dudley watches this scene, unobserved, from the next room, "screened from observation by his silence and an open door" (13/46). Twenty minutes later, Craig reappears, acting as if he has just arrived. He reads the letter as if for the first time and laughs as if it were a mistake. Within a week, Craig has absconded to

Jamaica, leaving the Dudleys in "total ruin" (16/48). Whatever the insights of this con narrative, a Foucauldian reading of it—that it speaks to contemporary economic pressures, capitalist discourses, and market practices—must inevitably ignore the odd length and fantastic complexity of Craig's con: he labors for no less than five years, continually intercepting and forging letters, even adding money to the common stock. What is he waiting for? In fact, the con awaits Dudley's moment of secret witness: only then can it play itself out. The letter on the mantelpiece is the return of the repressed, complete with its own frame—the silence and open door through which Dudley watches Craig reveal the letter's meaning.

We are not suggesting, then, that economic matters are irrelevant. On the contrary, *Ormond*'s analysis of republicanism begins with a fundamentally economic fantasy, encapsulated in the Dudley family history. Stephen Dudley's father, an apothecary, wishes to free his son from the burden of work. He is sent to Europe to study painting rather than learn the trade of his American father. If the father's wish is not fulfilled, the son nevertheless imbibes its spirit as his own. "Relieved from all pecuniary cares," Dudley acts not for economic gain but "without much regard for futurity" (5/39), developing an aristocratic sensibility ill suited to the challenges that await him. Forced to assume his father's profession upon the death of his parents, Dudley later denies himself the freedom to act solely in accord with his desires and must instead "regulate his future exertions by a view to nothing but gain" (6/40). These details constitute no more than the first page of Brown's novel but nonetheless offer a compressed example of the generational permutations of desire. The father cannot pass on to the son the *fulfillment* of the wish but only the *wish* itself. But while the elder Dudley looks to his son to achieve class mobility, the son in fact reproduces his father's frustrated dreams. "The longer he endured [the drudgery of work] the less tolerable it became," each day seeming more "humiliating and ignominious" (7/40). Dudley's disgust with his new life of labor is, of course, shame for his father's life and the direct result of the father's failed attempts to save the son.

Enter Thomas Craig, from the streets, presenting himself as the perfect apprentice, the ideal dependent. "All his propensities," we are told, "appeared to concentre in his occupation and the promotion of his master's interest, from which he was drawn aside by no allurements of sensual or intellectual pleasure" (8/42). The sentence at once captures the brutality and shame behind Dudley's fantasy. The elder Dudley had sought to rescue his son from labor: Stephen Dudley, by contrast, seeks the ideal dependent, labor devoid of any desires of its own, living to fulfill his duty. The proof of Dudley's desire is his refusal to impute the same desire to Craig. To admit any "sensual or intellectual pleasure" on Craig's part would be to reveal the violence of social life, the instrumentalization of the Other at the heart of the economy. Should Dudley acknowledge Craig's desire, he would then have to restrain or limit Craig to dependence—perhaps even by force. What this means, of course, is that the central element of Craig's con is not embezzlement but rather the hiding of his own, and the adoption of Dudley's, desires. Craig performs this absence of desire brilliantly by counterfeiting a fantasy family—his mother and brothers in England—to whom he is entirely devoted, for whom he toils. Of course, this family is also *Dudley's* fantasy, not Craig's. Its most insightful embellishment, indeed a structural necessity, is the creation of a younger brother, a mini-Craig who will serve his elder brother as Craig has served Dudley. This fantasy younger brother redoubles Dudley's position as patron, while reinforcing Craig's own position as dutiful laborer. In some way, this second Craig should reveal to Dudley the desires of the first Craig, for in the new business scheme, the younger Craig serves Craig much as Craig served Dudley. Thus, the con also requires Craig to be hesitant about, even opposed to, this opportunity for the younger brother: "His sense of gratitude was too acute to allow him to heighten it by the reception of new benefits" (11/44). It is only Dudley's insistence, after Craig "modestly requested Mr. Dudley's advice on this head," that carries the scheme forward, veiling Craig's desires.

Thus, the Dudley narrative offers an early republican analysis of what we have since come to call the American Dream. This fantasy is often misleadingly summarized as that of the individual who believes that, upon arrival in America, economic success will also be open to him or her. But the American Dream is at one remove from this: it is the fantasy that *others'* continued belief in economic success underlies the successes already earned by a preceding generation. In other words, it is the fantasy that the self-negating immigrant (Craig) will make possible the success of the truer American (Dudley). The dream of hard work in America is for the other and makes it possible to escape the contemptible world of work. We would note, as well, a not coincidental echo in Dudley's tale to the primal biblical scene of secret witness, that of Noah:

> And Noah began to be an husbandman, and he planted a vineyard: And he drank of the wine, and was drunken; and he was uncovered in his tent. And Ham, the father of Canaan, saw the nakedness of his father, and told

his two brethren without. And Shem and Japheth took a garment, and laid it upon both their shoulders, and went backward, and covered the nakedness of their father; and their faces were backward, and they saw not their father's nakedness. And Noah awoke from his wine, and knew what his younger son had done unto him. And he said, Cursed be Canaan; a servant of servants shall he be unto his brethren. (Genesis 9:20–25, King James Version)

Here the patriarch is seen drunk and naked, having loosed restraints of mind and body. The rewarded sons are those who cover up that which should not be seen—Noah's desire—while the supreme punishment falls on the son who has witnessed the father's secret. Here the target of wrath is Ham (and all his descendants), cursed with generations of servitude. Does this not begin to explain the special resonance of the Ham story for slaveholding America, in which the slave has special knowledge of the violent economic fantasy of the fathers? We will return to this Noachian insight later but here suggest that the story, which notoriously rationalized the enslavement of the Hamitic peoples, more fundamentally explained the threat the slave posed to republican fantasy. It is not that Ham was condemned to servitude because he saw his father's desire but that he saw his father's desire because of his servitude.

We return, then, to the moment of secret witness, triggered by the appearance of the letter from Craig's real mother. This letter has numerous destinations. To Dudley, it briefly shatters the illusion of Craig's fantasy family: not only has Craig not been serving his (English) family; he has in fact abandoned his (American) family to pursue his own desires. He quickly represses this reading as "no doubt, founded in mistake, though it was to be acknowledged that the mistake was singular" (13/46). To Craig, it is the potentially dangerous exposure of his desire. His outburst—"Damn it!"—is prompted not by the contents of the letter but by its "broken seal" (13/46). But the third and most important reading is that of the secret witness—of Dudley's silent observation of Craig's hidden desire. "Damn it!" is here the denial of the life Dudley has imagined for Craig. Dudley's repression of this insight is facilitated by Craig's replacement of the letter, earlier "thrust . . . hastily into his pocket" (13/46), to the mantelpiece, leaving it in broad daylight, where he will later laughingly dismiss its contents.

It is tempting to speculate that Edgar Allan Poe was inspired by this staging of a purloined letter, concealed by placing it in the open, where it is most easily hidden. But Brown's staging of this first moment of secret witness has a different orientation than we find in Poe, for it encapsulates a preliminary assessment of fantasy in the new United States. The elder Dudley had tried to remove his son from the dynamic of economic aspiration by providing freedom from labor. When this failed, the shamed and mortified Dudley had inverted his father's project. He denies Craig's desire, fantasizing that the young con man will be pure labor. The revelation of the con thus exposes this eminently masculine fantasy of the Other's dependence as a crime. In some sense, then, there are multiple cons: for Craig's con rests on Dudley's conning of Craig and, more fundamentally, Dudley's conning of himself. The moment of secret witness is the moment when, seeing the subordinate for what he is, all of these cons become clear. After this revelation, all will collapse. Dudley loses his business, his house, his wife. Finally he goes blind, an infirmity brought on, in Brown's apt phrase, when "his sight was invaded by a cataract" (20/51)— the intrusion of an opaque region on the eye or, alternatively, a deluge or flood. After witness and blindness, madness will loom.

Constantia's Madonna

But *Ormond* is ultimately not the story of Stephen Dudley but of his daughter, Constantia, whose name, that of Judith Sargent Murray's famous moralizing persona, would have unavoidably evoked the Revolutionary and post-Revolutionary configuration of *republicanism*. Recent historiography has so relentlessly treated republicanism as an ideological discourse defined by authenticity and sincerity that we may find it difficult to imagine that a late eighteenth-century novel set out to explore the fantasy structure underlying republican thought.[15] Yet this is precisely what *Ormond* sets out to do. At first glance, it may seem that Constantia is *Craig*'s substitute, entering the narrative as he leaves, occupying the place of the next generation that either succors or suckers the patriarch. But whereas Craig cunningly assumes a role crafted in Dudley's fantasy, Constantia emerges as a powerful fantasist in her own right. As a new iteration of the fantasy structure previously inhabited by her father and grandfather, Constantia is no Cordelia to Dudley's Lear but rather is *Dudley*'s substitute. Thus, republican fantasy will be defined in relation to, as the successor of, an older "colonial" fantasy structure associated with Stephen Dudley.

As a woman, Constantia simply cannot occupy the same position of apprentice to master as Craig: she is kin, the only survivor among sixteen children.[16] But the parallels are clearest in the details of her education. Following a Wollstonecraftian plan, Stephen Dudley educates his daughter with an eye to "the gratification of all her wishes" and "to make her, not alluring and voluptuous, but eloquent and wise" (21/52, 33/62). In place of the romance languages, she learns Latin and Milton's English; in place of music and art, considered merely sensual and ornamental by Dudley, she learns Newtonian physics, mathematics, anatomy, and philosophy. Given Dudley's own infatuation with the arts, this may appear incongruous. However, we see a more fundamental or formal doubling: both father and daughter have been educated outside norms that discipline and manage social reproduction and inculcate conventional class and gender values. Is not Constantia the recipient of a formally similar transference in which aspirations of gender equality take the place of a desired class transcendence? Dudley is *not* trained to continue the father's labor, and Constantia is *not* trained to attract the most favorable husband. By design, she has been fashioned to enjoy both economic disinterest and a mind tuned to the score of enlightened reason. Thus, she is even "less fitted than her father for encountering misfortune" (21/52). Yet misfortune she faces, again and again. Her father's debt, blindness, despair, drunkenness, and ultimately murder will be the testing ground for a new fantasy formation—as if Brown can conceive of no truer republican example than a woman so situated.[17]

Here we must turn for a moment to the yellow fever, the historical catalyst of the properly US fantasy structure: it is during the fever epidemic that Constantia is essentially formed. Again and again, the fever is described in fantastic terms: "symptoms of terror" (35/64), "general panic" (40/68), "cruel prohibitions" (55/80), "useless disquietudes" (57/81), and so on. The role of the fever as an imaginative phenomenon is most clearly revealed at its termination, when the "theatre of suffering" (61/85) smoothly gives way to the "public entertainments" of an actual "new theatre" of "overflowing" audiences (72–73/94). The parallels between fever and theater are reiterated with this observation: "Such is the motley and ambiguous condition of human society, such is the complexity of all effects, from what cause soever they spring, that none can tell whether this destructive pestilence was, on the whole, productive of most pain or most pleasure" (73/94). That the yellow fever is not clearly a painful phenomenon is something Brown had considered earlier in the "Man at Home" pieces, in which the narrator's friend Wallace attributes his happiness to the fever. His forced relocation and the suspension of his business result in "a lovely wife, a plentiful fortune, health, and leisure"; "for all these," he says, "I am indebted to the

Yellow Fever" (11:323). But if the fever is simply a screen against which our fantasies play out, what determines the survival or death of the fantasist?

The paradigmatic victim of the fever seems to be the Dudleys' neighbor Whiston. He announces its arrival and obsessively and almost joyfully recounts a "tale of the origin and progress of the epidemic" until he has "thoroughly affrighted and wearied his companion" (35/64). Whiston's "mind appeared to be disburdened of its cares in proportion as he filled others with terror and inquietude" (43/70)—that is, he finds pleasure and avoids pain by projecting the horrors of the fever onto his listeners. The destructiveness of this fantasy structure is revealed, however, in Whiston's death. He arrives at the Dudleys' apartment, "silent and abstracted," "his eye . . . full of inquietude" and "wander[ing] with perpetual restlessness," to announce "his belief that he had contracted this disease" (43/71). Unable to further fantasize the death of others—his eye now wanders and cannot settle on anyone—he believes the fever must now strike him. His eventual demise in the countryside follows from this isolation—his inability to use others to process his terrors. Abandoned, he dies, and his body "decay[s] by piecemeal" (48/74).[18]

Constantia's fantasy structure emerges in contrast to the plebeian Whiston's. Whereas Whiston's selfishness, exemplified in his abandonment of his sick sister, finally leads to his destruction, Constantia's self-sacrifice, illustrated in her care for Whiston's sister, guarantees her self-preservation. Whereas Whiston evacuates his fears to take a surplus pleasure from compulsively recounting terrifying stories, Constantia, following the Žižekian injunction, learns instead to *enjoy her symptom.* Whereas Whiston verbalizes the death of others in order to avoid the fantasy of his own, Constantia repeatedly envisions her pending death. Stephen Dudley encourages this fantasy structure by repeatedly predicting the Dudleys' destruction, a "perverseness" expressed as the desire "to undermine her fortitude and disconcert her schemes" (36–37/65–66). The paradoxical result, however, is her greater strength, not because she resists the fantasy but because she embraces it. "Death, as the common lot of all, was regarded by her without perturbation," we are told: "it excited on her own account no aversion or inquietude" (42/69–70). Indeed, it is the suffering of the fever and its related ills—threats of eviction, hunger, the death of neighbors, the increased melancholy of her father—that seems to enable her to come into her own.

More than a response to the fever, this fantasy structure transforms the household economy and virtually all of Constantia's interactions with others. After Craig's embezzlement, she had already suppressed her own desires to "devote herself, with a single heart, to the alleviation of her parents' sorrows" (23/53). During the epidemic, this self-sacrifice becomes extreme and systematic—the very mode of fantasy. She "refused no personal exertion to the common benefit" (23/54), selling her music and books and hiring herself as a washerwoman. Indeed, she thrives while managing the household economy under these adverse circumstances. The discovery of the frugal economy of hasty pudding produces a surfeit of pleasure (56/81), and even the painful sale of treasured objects (the miniature portrait of Sophia and her father's lute) are experienced, in the language of desire, as "irresistible" (76/96). Self-denial becomes gratifying.

We see here the basic contours of republicanism—its stress on self-denial, service to others, frugality and industry under any circumstances, and so on. But whereas contemporary scholarship sees republicanism as a conscious value system, *Ormond* sees it as a fantasy structure crafted in response to catastrophe. More precisely, it is a structure in which basic social ideals—prosperity, self-fulfillment, social prominence, and the like—are systematically bracketed in such a way that the means to such ends are satisfying in themselves. But we must explore the social structure of this fantasy, and above all its relationship to witness, in more detail. Let us turn then to the moment when Constantia, on the brink of eviction and destitution, must visit the pawnshop to sell the portrait of her dearest friend, Sophia. There she encounters Martinette (the Ursula Monrose of Baxter's encounters) for the first time. The sight of Martinette inspires a feeling of reverence: "It was not the chief tendency of her appearance to seduce or to melt. Hers were the polished cheek and the mutability of muscle which belong to woman, but the genius conspicuous in her aspect was heroic and contemplative. The female was absorbed, so to speak, in the rational creature, and the emotions most apt to be excited in the gazer partook less of love than of reverence" (77–78/98). One might follow recent criticism in locating, in passages of this type, a homoerotic charge; indeed, the substitution of Martinette/Monrose for the miniature of Sophia Courtland suggests a same-sex erotic circuit. But missed in these analyses is the point to which that circuit ultimately runs. For Sophia reports that the description later conveyed to her by Constantia—gifted with a "sixth sense" for the "vividness and accuracy with which pictures of this kind presented themselves to her imagination"—was ultimately "suited, with the utmost accuracy, to herself" (77–78/97–98). That *Constantia sees herself* is confirmed by the language of the preceding passage,

which contrasts an erotic connection of seduction and "love" with a "polished" and "contemplative" object of "reverence." This is not the same
externalization we witnessed in the Baxter episode, for in Baxter's dream,
he sees an exteriorized self that he cannot distinguish from his position as
observer: as is common in dreams, the boundaries of dreamer-as-viewer
and dreamer-as-viewed are so entangled as to be inseparable. In the
pawnshop episode, by contrast, the polished and revered image of her self
is distinct, if unrecognizable, to Constantia. It is only through the written description to Sophia that the identity of Constantia and Martinette
becomes apparent. Constantia herself remains "unconscious" of the connection (78/98).

We would note here, as well, that this symbolic circuit, linking
Constantia, Martinette, and Sophia Courtland's portrait, illuminates
Ormond's ostensibly religious subtext. As Constantia prepares to sell the
portrait, we are told that she viewed it, with "a species of idolatry," as a
kind of "beautiful Madonna" (75/96). As Sophia later explains, she herself served as "a model for those who desired to personify the genius of
suffering and resignation"—or more precisely, for "those whose religion
permitted their devotion to a picture of a female" (242/234–35). We may
now appreciate the complexity of the symbolic circuitry at the pawnshop, where Constantia, selling her personal Madonna, transfers her
"reverence" to Martinette, though actually, unconsciously, seeing herself. At first glance, we would seem to be suggesting that Constantia,
through the circuit of Sophia → Martinette → Constantia, is somehow
worshiping herself. But the Madonna figure is less an object to worship
and more a formal model of worship oddly suitable to republicanism.
After all, the Madonna figure stages a reverence toward something (the
infant savior) which is in some sense the product of her own actions and
virtues. Thus, the Madonna deserves worship not only because of her
worshipfulness but because she has given birth to that which she worships. What does this iconic figure of Roman Catholicism have to do
with Constantia, who is "unacquainted with religion," even regarding
it "with absolute indifference" (179–80/182)? The link is a formal one.
Constantia, as Judith Sargent Murray well understood, is the US republican version of the Madonna. She deserves republican worship not only
because of her worshipfulness of republicanism but because she has
given birth to that which she worships. Whence another of the insights
of *Ormond*'s analysis of republicanism: as a fantasy structure, it is a
form of *unconscious reverence toward oneself.*[19]

The pawnshop scene may also be contrasted to a contiguous episode in which Constantia is rescued from a sexual assault by Balfour, the chaste and proper merchant. After this romantic scene of knight-errantry, Balfour "could not overlook" the suitability of Constantia for his bride. What attracts him to her? "Not even the graces of person, or features, or manners, attracted much of his attention. He remarked her admirable economy of time and money and labour, the simplicity of her dress, her evenness of temper, and her love of seclusion. These were essential requisites of a wife, in his apprehension" (82/102). Balfour's fantasy is decidedly republican, preferring careful management of polenta over beauty. Does this not make Balfour the perfect husband for Constantia? On the contrary. To be Constantia's match, Balfour would need to have the same fantasy structure as Constantia—that is, rather than focusing his fantasy on Constantia, he would need an indirect fantasy of *himself*, as a man sacrificing his immediate satisfaction for his wife and family and so on. Without such a fantasy, Balfour would also threaten Constantia's fantasy, which requires not an overt and external observer (the admiring husband) but a covert and internalized observer—Constantia herself, but hidden from herself. This is the important lesson of the brief Balfour episode: it confirms that Constantia *is, and must be, her own secret witness*. Republicanism cannot sustain itself by serving as the object of admiration or fantasy for others: such a structure would reduce republican virtue to a cynical performance to earn others' respect, thereby becoming a performative contradiction. Instead, republicanism assumes that we secretly, unconsciously, observe ourselves acting as perfect republicans—perhaps by displacing our witnessing eyes onto a stranger in a pawnshop. It is no surprise, then, that Constantia rejects a marriage that "would annihilate this power" (84/103). "So far from possessing property, she herself would become the property of another," we are told, and we need only pluralize the object of this declaration to appreciate the stakes for her fantasy. So far from possessing (republican) properties, she herself would become the (nonrepublican) properties of another.

Republicanism's Voice

What we have described so far, in the passage from Dudley's to Constantia's fantasy, is a historical argument about the mutation of US fantasy. Dudley's fantasy—that a servant will surrender his desires to serve the patriarch—is, as we earlier suggested, a *colonial* fantasy, one particularly suitable to the phenomena of immigration and especially slavery. Its moment of secret witness—the glimpse of subaltern rage, the Other's "Damn it!" as the traumatic kernel of one's desire for economic independence—illustrates why this fantasy cannot be sustained. The fantasy structure of Constantia, by contrast, betrays a growing political unease with the ideology of human servitude. In the context of Revolutionary discourse, within which colonists increasingly decried their own servitude, this colonial fantasy mutated into the more ostensibly virtuous and self-negating dynamics of republicanism. In the new fantasy structure, the generational exploitation of the servant/slave was reworked as the exploitation of oneself. Industry, temperance, modesty, public service— these forms of self-denial and service to others had the double virtue of further suppressing the crime of slavery while rendering oneself worthy of reverence. One might say that the United States was thus founded on a fantasy structure that, eager to suppress chattel slavery, fostered a form of self-worship later given the label "nationalism." We will have more to say about slavery in relation to republicanism but must first return to *Ormond* and its deployment of free indirect discourse (FID).

Ormond dabbles in FID at several points, as when the narrative of Baxter describes him as having "too much regard for his own safety, and too little for that of a frog-eating Frenchman," to enter the Monrose house (64/87). Here the indirect narrative voice, recounting Baxter's story, assimilates elements of Baxter's xenophobic direct discourse ("a frog-eating Frenchman"). Another example occurs when Constantia, pursuing Craig, inquires after him at the Indian Queen Tavern. The waiter's reaction is described this way: "How was he to know where gentlemen eat their suppers? Did she take him for a witch? What, in God's name, did she want with him at that hour? Could she not wait, at least, till he had done his supper? He warranted her pretty face would bring him home time enough" (93–94/111).

Again we find the combination of the indirect narrative voice and the direct voice of the waiter, though the insulating use of quotation marks suggests the still tentative quality of Brown's use of FID. Constantia's response to the waiter is similarly revealing. Dismissing this address as typical "base and low-minded treatment," she asserts the distinction of status, threatening to report this rude speech to a superior. "You had better answer me with decency," she says: "If you do not, your master shall hear of it" (94/112). The response, in Constantia's words, demonstrates the stylistic return to narrative order, as the plebeian's speech is reduced to the more properly delimited sphere of direct discourse: "He began to perceive himself in the wrong, and surlily muttered, 'Why, if you must know, he is gone to Mr. Ormond's'" (94–112).[20]

We read this moment of FID and its immediate "correction" as acutely attuned to the social dynamics underlying FID itself. In its initial appearances (most notably with Jane Austen, for example), FID signals the combination of an ostensibly neutral and controlling literary language—that of the narrator—with an idiosyncratically marked direct discourse, often betokening a marginal ethnic, occupational, or class distinction. Thus, Baxter's slur ("frog-eating") or the waiter's impudence ("What, in God's name") stand out in an otherwise "neutral" narrative style. But Constantia's rebuke, and the corresponding reversion to direct and indirect discourses, betrays a fear that the normative, pseudoneutral mode of indirect discourse is itself destabilized or problematized. This should not surprise us. In the historical development of literary narration, FID is succeeded by first-person narration increasingly marked by the characteristics of direct discourse. Eventually FID may combine two idiosyncratically marked discourses, that of the narrator and that of the narrated voice. This development is under way in *Ormond*, in which the indirect discourse is initially the normative republican voice of Sophia Courtland. But with the formation of Constantia's character, this indirect voice becomes more relativized, less neutral. Let us offer two consecutive paragraphs in which Constantia muses about how to persuade Helena Cleves, Ormond's mistress, to leave Ormond. We are told these "were the meditations of Constantia on this topic" (142/152):

> P1
>
> But, alas! what power on earth can prevail on her to renounce Ormond? Others may justly entertain this prospect, but it must be invisible to her. Besides, is it absolutely certain that either her peace of mind or her reputation will be restored by this means? In the opinion of the world, her offences cannot, by any perseverance in penitence, be expiated. She will never believe that separation will exterminate her passion. Certain it is that it will avail nothing to the reestablishment of her fame. But, if it were conducive to these ends, how chimerical to suppose that she will ever voluntarily adopt it! If Ormond refuse his concurrence, there is absolutely an end to hope. And what power on earth is able to sway his determinations? At least, what influence was it possible for her to obtain over them?

P2

Should they separate, whither should she retire? What mode of subsistence should she adopt? She has never been accustomed to think beyond the day. She has eaten and drank, but another has provided the means. She scarcely comprehends the principle that governs the world, and in consequence of which nothing can be gained but by giving something in exchange for it. She is ignorant and helpless as a child, on every topic that relates to the procuring of subsistence. Her education has disabled her from standing alone. (141/151)

The second paragraph is more straightforward, its FID resulting from the combination of Helena Cleves's direct discourse and Constantia's indirect discourse. The resulting reflections show Constantia carefully imagining Helena's objections to her plan (Helena's direct discourse: *What mode of subsistence should I adopt?*) before gradually distancing herself from Helena (Constantia's indirect discourse: *She is ignorant and helpless as a child*). How then do we read the preceding paragraph? It, too, utilizes FID, but with different constituents. Here the direct discourse is Constantia's (*Others may justly entertain this prospect, but it must be invisible to me*) combined with an indirect discourse of moral censure. In other words, the FID is constructed using the fantasy position of Constantia under observation. What is striking about the two paragraphs, side by side, is the manner in which they demonstrate the odd state of Constantia's consciousness, as she becomes *distanced from her own thoughts*. As a result, her republican moralizing with herself becomes, at this moment in the text, one discrete voice alongside another, that of Helena's objections. Consequently, when Constantia finally settles on the moral case she will make, we are given this sentence—"The lady, of course, would be its fervent advocate" (142/152)—again, in FID. Here the direct discourse (*I will be its fervent advocate*) is combined with an indirect discourse in which Constantia marks herself with her social position: she will assume the position of a "lady," a position marked by class and gender exceptionality.

We would suggest, then, that *Ormond*'s experiments in FID incisively illustrate the dynamics of republican fantasy, such that the republican consciousness is split between a direct expression (Constantia's discourse in the first paragraph) and an indirect expression (Constantia's discourse relative to Helena in the second paragraph). It is this duality—a consciousness at once direct and indirect—that constitutes republican fantasy precisely as a fantasy about one's own moral position. That is, the republican

TABLE 2.1   *Free Indirect Republicanism*

P1	{	— Normative voice of republicanism		
		— Constantia	}	Republican Fantasy
		— Constantia		
P2	{	— Helena		

fantasy is one of a relationship of moral self-supervision and self-enjoyment. Or to put it more tendentiously, pleasure consists in the fantasy of depriving oneself of pleasure through the imposition of moral restrictions. Thus, *Ormond*'s refiguration of Judith Sargent Murray's archetypal republican seems to magnify the position implicit in her name: the standing-with of *Con-stantia* is precisely a standing-with-herself.

Significantly, it is at this moment—when the republican fantasy structure is clearly elucidated in Constantia's discourse—that the novel stages the encounter between its two main characters, Constantia and Ormond. Constantia makes her case: Ormond should act justly and marry Helena. But instead of a moral debate, the ensuing scene depicts a new figuration of republican consciousness, as the focus shifts from Helena, "the subject of discourse," to a more unsettling metadiscourse. "Come," Ormond declares,

> proceed in your exhortations. Argue with the utmost clearness and cogency. Arm yourself with all the irresistibles of eloquence. Yet you are building nothing. You are only demolishing. Your argument is one thing. Its tendency is another; and is the reverse of all you expect and desire. My assent will be refused with an obstinacy proportioned to the force that you exert to obtain it, and to the just application of that force. (154/162)

What does this claim—that Constantia's argument is at odds with its tendency—mean, if not that republicanism contains an internal rift separating its moral claims (here the advocacy of Helena) from its essence as moral argument? Such is the radical insight provided in the form of Ormond's external witness of Constantia, and the narrative reveals the inadequacy of her resistance. Though she insists on "construing [her] motives in [her] own way," she is, within paragraphs, modifying her "calculation" (157/164). Why? The "image of Ormond" now "occupies the chief place in her fancy . . . endowed with attractive and venerable qualities" (157/164), and their time seems a "doubling of existence" (158/165). She now feels such "a sufficient resemblance" in their thinking about "virtue and duty" that differences of opinion are minor. Let us be clear: the fate of Helena, the two options of marriage or sexual exploitation, is a minor matter relative to the "resemblance" in their thought—or to put it another way, the distinction of *content*, in the form of antithetical moral claims, is secondary compared to a similarity of *form* as those moral claims are made. The introduction of Ormond, then, enables a further crucial step in the analysis of republican fantasy.

Ormond's Function

To understand Ormond's role in the novel, we must return to the problem of witness. It seems incontrovertible that Ormond is the "secret witness" of the novel's title. Not only does he secretly spy on the Dudleys in the guise of the chimney sweep, but during his first overt encounter with Constantia, the narrative repeatedly calls attention to his gaze: "He fixed his eyes without scruple on her face. His gaze was steadfast, but not insolent or oppressive. He surveyed her with the looks with which he would have eyed a charming portrait. His attention was occupied with what he saw" (152/159). But any emphasis on Ormond as witness is incomplete if it does not consider his equally important status as an object to be witnessed. The first substantial description of Ormond characterizes him as a cipher difficult to see accurately. "No one was more impenetrable than Ormond," we are told: "To the vulgar eye . . . he appeared a man of speculation and seclusion, and was equally inscrutable in his real and assumed characters. In his real, his intents were too lofty and comprehensive, as well as too assiduously shrouded from profane inspect, for them to scan. In the latter, appearances were merely calculated to mislead and not to enlighten" (117/131). Ormond's appearance is every bit as important as what Ormond sees, and indeed these two things are irrevocably entwined. The description of Ormond as one who "carefully distinguished between men in the abstract and men as they are" not only identifies Ormond's two ways of looking at the world but also affirms that, in looking at him, *one looks at how he looks at others.* So, too, in the first encounter with Constantia, when Ormond fixes his sights upon her, he simultaneously challenges her to "be a looker-on" (151/159). How do these two roles fit together?

Perhaps the most revealing reference comes during Ormond's first overt meeting with Constantia: "His attention was occupied with what he saw, *as that of an artist is occupied when viewing a Madonna of Rafaello*" (152/159, emphasis added). We have already suggested that Constantia not only is a republican Madonna but also, in the circuit of displacement and misrecognition in the pawnshop, emerges as the unconscious object of her own self-worship. In this first encounter with Ormond, we see an externalization of this phenomenon: if Constantia was earlier unable to witness herself witnessing and worshiping herself, she now finds in Ormond—an entity who simultaneously gazes at her and demands to be witnessed—a figure who reveals the dynamics of her own fantasy structure. Ormond is the novel's "secret witness," yes, but specifically in the sense of revealing Constantia's secret of self-witnessing. Put most bluntly, Ormond is an embodiment of fantasy itself and is thus essentially a *function* within the novel. If his numerous characteristics add up to nothing and to everything, it is because he exists at the intersection of "men in the abstract and men as they are"— where the Imaginary brushes up against the Real. Like the "meaning full" chest described in the "Man at Home" pieces, he is an "artificial receptacle" necessary to the structuring of Constantia's republican fantasy.

Another Brown text, known as "A Series of Original Letters" and also published in the *Weekly Magazine* in 1798, helps us approach this puzzle. The letters purport to be the correspondence between Henry D— and his sister, Mary. At one point, Mary makes a brief reference to lawyers as those who make "a trade of weaving together subtleties and sophisms calculated to mislead that consciousness of justice implanted in the mind of every rational being."[21] Henry, a law student, is outraged. Had not Mary previously told him law "was the road to honour," "the regulator of the claims and conduct of men in society," a path to wealth and even government? Yet she now criticizes the law.[22] "Pr'ythee explain thyself," he demands. To justify her comments, Mary resorts to "a two-fold point of view." From one perspective, justice is an absolute good "due from every human being to his fellows."[23] Were all moral problems resolved by simple expression and discussion, legal institutions would be unnecessary. The "profession of a lawyer"—a guide to basic moral values—would be unneeded, even a preposterous fantasy. But in "relation to things as they are," justice is rarely realized, and "all men [are not] imbued with a just reverence" for moral precepts. Behavior follows from "circumstances" with negative results and "the most poignant miseries." Laws become "multifarious and unintelligible" in these conditions. Consequently it is "unquestionably *right* that some one should be capable of interpreting [the law]."[24] This portrait of the Law anticipates Ormond's distinction "between men in the abstract and men as they are" but more importantly captures the relationship between Constantia and Ormond. As a virtuous republican, Constantia should embody and contain the Law and should not need or accept the Law as an external reality. But circumstances make the clear apprehension of the Law impossible, and she must resort to an external figure—Ormond—to interpret it. Like a lawyer, he is a despicable figure of sophistries and subtleties. And, again like the lawyer, he is the virtuous and structurally necessary interpreter of the Law as well. Thus, during Constantia's moral confrontation with Ormond (when she urges him to marry Helena), it is Ormond who demands that she "proceed in [her] exhortations" and "argue with the utmost clearness and cogency." It is Ormond who reveals that her moralizing is conflicted, its argument (Law as it should be) at odds with its tendency (Law as it is). If the "image of Ormond" comes to occupy "the chief place in [Constantia's] fancy," it is because his clear and brutal immorality is fundamentally constitutive of her moral demand. This dual role explains Constantia's seemingly odd reaction to Ormond's announcement that he has dismissed Helena and in fact loves Constantia. "I hope, in every vicissitude, to enjoy your esteem, and nothing more," she says, adding, "You have disappointed me. . . . I have always condemned the maxims by which you act" (167/172–73). Here Constantia testifies to her moral superiority over Ormond, whose failings enable Constantia to stage her Imaginary ego ideal. *You disappoint me; I want nothing but your esteem*—in this odd formula, we see how Ormond gives Constantia's virtuous republicanism its stability and consistency, not to mention a sense of autonomy. Because he watches her, she knows she does right. In political terms, republicanism is thus defined as an ideology dependent on a secret external witness, at once aware of an ideal morality and the brutal violence of the actual world. Only this necessary secret witness can create an ideological coherence in the witnessed republican.

It should be clear, then, that Ormond is to Constantia what Craig is to Mr. Dudley—an other around whom a particular fantasy is structured and an other through whom the fantasy breaks down. In Dudley's colonial fantasy, he imagined a subordinate slave figure, Craig, suppressing his own desires to Dudley's benefit. This fantasy not only structured Craig's con but also determined the moment of Dudley's secret witnessing of Craig's desire, the traumatic "Damn it!" that Dudley glimpses and quickly represses before he sinks into blindness. Constantia's post-Revolutionary fantasy mutates into the fundamentally feminine fantasy of republican self-denial, in which one watches, admires, and worships one's embodiment of republican virtue. This is the self-congratulatory modesty we find performed by the Founding

Fathers, from Washington and Franklin to Adams and Jefferson. But as this fantasy extends to encompass Ormond, as an externalized secret witness, its structure is briefly revealed. Indeed, if there is any doubt that Ormond is the post-Revolutionary version of Craig, we need only remember Craig's dual position as con man and lowly apprentice. Do we not find these same two roles—schemer and subordinate—amplified in the figure of Ormond, who is both global conspirator and black chimney sweep? It is to these two manifestations that we now turn.

Ormond is frequently and misleadingly described as the novel's conspiratorial figure, but this characterization actually comes quite late in the novel.[25] As various critics have noted, the Bavarian Illuminati scare had erupted in the United States in late 1798, as Brown was drafting *Ormond*. The text invites the association, describing Ormond's career as a mercenary for Potemkin and Romanov, his "secret and diplomatic functions at Constantinople and Berlin," his involvement with projects of "new-modelling," his time spent among Native American nations to the northwest, and so on.[26] How should we read these conspiratorial allusions? Might one not venture the familiar argument, extending from Richard Hofstadter to today's Foucauldians, that conspiracy theory imposes a classificatory coherence on the world, with a corresponding disciplining of the Other? On the contrary, the chaotic conspiratorial references surrounding Ormond suggest otherwise. Not only do they never cohere; the proliferation of geopolitical allusions and insinuations verges on parody. Their late appearance too—as if an afterthought of the final chapters—similarly belies the equation of conspiracy and systematicity. Rather, Ormond's transition from quasi-lover to threatening rapist and conspirator depicts the destiny of the secret witness. As that witness becomes increasingly overt and unavoidable, as its function intrudes more and more, it becomes necessary to repress that site and place it back where it belongs: *hors du monde*, outside this symbolic world. The best means to dematerialize this threatened encounter with the Real is not by insisting on its unreality but rather by covering it with as much semic material as possible. In this view, the most baroque conspiracy theories are littered with absurd references and connections not because the overwhelmed theorist has sought to place these terms in some kind of order. Rather, to expunge the threatening kernel, it must be buried beneath disparate details referencing as much of the symbolic order as possible. In this context, the geopolitical references draw our attention away from Ormond's greatest success as a conspirator: the creation of the ideal republican, Constantia. Such success is partially thematized in comments about Ormond's efforts "to govern the thoughts of Constantia, or to regulate her condition" (177/180–81). And of course "his providence" (178/181) rewards Constantia with an income, a house, and even her father's sight in order to make her a comfortable republican. We would venture to suggest that this plan goes still further, beyond even the murder of Stephen Dudley, to the staging of the final conflict that results in Ormond's own death and Constantia's expulsion of the conspirator figure.

When it comes to conspiracy then, *Ormond's* greatest insight concerns not the Bavarian Illuminati but the fantasy structure of future conspiracy scares. Indeed, the novel offers an uncanny prediction of the rise and fall of the next decade's most significant traumatic colonel, the Burr. As we will outline, he bursts onto the national political scene in 1801, appears as Jefferson's strange double, and is briefly wooed by Federalists and Republicans alike until the attacks of 1802–3. After that point, the signals are mixed: he is the murderer of Hamilton and on the lam but the object for whom senators weep as late as 1805, after which he, too, become the kernel/colonel of a gigantic conspiracy fantasy—so laden with references to Spain, France, Mexico, Britain, and western yeoman separatists as to remain incoherent today. A spectacular treason trial, gathering a historical assembly of Revolutionary leaders, simultaneously acquits Burr while finishing his career, sending him *hors du monde*, to exile in Europe. Thus, Ormond rehearses the fantasy career of Aaron Burr, as Burr becomes the Ormond of American political fantasy.

But Ormond is not solely the master conspirator, and his first face-to-face encounter with Constantia is as a black chimney sweep. Undergoing what the novel calls "the most entire and grotesque metamorphosis imaginable" (134/145), Ormond "exchange[s] his complexion and habiliments for those of a negro and a chimney sweep" (134/145). In disguise, he witnesses Constantia's spotless dwelling, so clean as to have walls of "glistening white" (134/145), and marvels at Constantia's "graceful condescension" (135/146). Having completed his work, he returns with a note from a secret benefactor (himself), promising just enough money for the Dudleys to continue living in this fashion. He presents a "talkative disposition" and a demeanor of stupidity (135/146). When questioned, he insists that he must not reveal his master's secret but, acting the fool, deliberately drops hints in order to witness Constantia's response: she "saw that the secret might be easily discovered, but she forebore" (136/147).

One could certainly read the episode as an articulation of late eighteenth-century racial discourse, a revelation of certain attitudes about black inferiority and US race relations. But it seems more fruitful to read this episode as a symptomatic materialization of the fantasy of secret witness, in which the crucial details are there on the surface. Take the chimney sweep's task, for example. What are we to make of Ormond's marveling at the "glistening white" cleanliness of the place he has been hired to clean? Is this not an admission that whiteness is dirty enough to require a black man to clean it? Or consider Ormond's overdetermined disguise: not just blackface but blackface covered with the chimney sweep's soot. Though the text ostensibly presents the black sweep as the antithesis of the worldly (and white) observer, is not the slave—granted access to all domestic spaces as the invisible companion of white people—the ultimate eighteenth-century expression of secret witness? And what about Constantia's reluctance to question the black man: instead of "graceful condescension," does this gesture not reveal the profound fear of the white person when given the chance to discover the "secret" of black people? What if this forbearance is less a refusal to take advantage than a refusal to admit that republican society is built on regularly taking advantage of the enslaved, physically *and* culturally? In fact, the episode, in constantly referring the reader to the underlying secret of Ormond's spying, enacts one of the novel's central insights: that the best way to hide something is to place it out there in the open space of fantasy.

Here we note the care with which Constantia's forbearance is drawn: "She disdained to take advantage of this messenger's imagined simplicity" (136/147). Not once but twice does this sentence highlight the white fantasy about the black man's inferiority: in the seemingly redundant but actually self-negating depiction of black "simplicity" as "imagined" but also in stressing that Constantia disdains not the man himself but taking advantage of his "imagined" quality. Like Craig, to whom all of Dudley's ledger books had been open, the blackface chimney sweep has had untrammeled access to assess how Constantia manages her home. But here we note a crucial difference: whereas Craig's performed subordination had inspired Dudley to impose a more extensive communication under the assumption that the apprentice was uncomfortable and meek, Constantia, assuming superiority over the lowly black slave, cuts the exchange short: "she dismissed him with some small addition to his demand and promised always to employ him in this way" (136/147). From one perspective, Dudley's intrusion into Craig's private life may be conceived as a form of patriarchal violence (the extension of domination by doubly extracting a surplus from Craig's labor) masquerading as benevolence (the offer to apprentice the younger brother). But does not Constantia's forbearance paradoxically replicate the same structural violence? Is not her seemingly kind refusal to trespass on the black slave's secret a refusal to engage with the structural violence that makes him—supposedly, in her imagination—less intelligent? By not engaging him, the republican can more easily maintain the fantasy of abstract equality. We would suggest, then, that this moment of secret witness stages, for all to see, the secret of Ormond, the secret of witness. It is not that Ormond is a white man momentarily disguised as black but that he is the black man disguised throughout the novel as white.

There is one additional dimension to this scene: Ormond's response. Seeing the impoverished Constantia, he muses from behind his blackface, "Was it possible that such an one descended to the level of her father's apprentice? That she sacrificed her honor to a wretch like that? This reflection tended to repress the inclination he would otherwise have felt for cultivating her society, but it did not indispose him to benefit her in a certain way" (136/147). If Ormond is indeed the novel's black slave, how is it that he is put off by *Constantia's* debased condition? As we have insisted, the proper answer to this question must return to the structure of Constantia's fantasy and Ormond's role as secret witness. Ormond's appraisal of Constantia is therefore her sense of another's vision of herself and specifically the vision of the lowest member of society. This reaction begins with marvel at the acceptance of debasement; then comes an appreciation of the self-sacrificing gesture that transforms victimization into virtue; and finally there emerges a reverential desire to serve. As with the Madonna, whose image is the fulfillment of a future sanctification of which the subject is yet unaware, Constantia's performance of servitude anticipates not only the revulsion she will prompt but also the higher estimation that awaits her. Is this not how North American colonials deployed the metaphor of enslavement in their move toward independence from Britain? In other words, when the republican Revolutionary plays the slave, we must acknowledge this fundamental gesture of bad faith: this republican performance not only escapes servitude but serves as a lesson to the actually enslaved about how they should subordinate themselves.

Fantasy's Future

If we have insisted on a formal reading of *Ormond*—examining both its structure and style but also its own series of formal analyses—it has been in the spirit of Roland Barthes's well-known observation that "a little formalism turns one away from History, but . . . a lot brings one back to it."[27] Thus, we have sought to avoid the familiar mode of analysis focusing on cultural discourses mapped through ostensibly realist plot developments. Our insistence on a formal analysis has been furthermore motivated by our conviction—confirmed, we think, by the Baxter episode—that Brown was more interested in problems of cultural form than in realist description,[28] hence our progression through *Ormond*'s various stagings of secret witness and our account of Brown's formal analysis of republicanism's fantasy structure. Thus, we have come back to history through the puzzle of what has motivated Brown's formal analyses of fantasy: the observation that *black slavery is the fundamentally repressed problem of republicanism.*

Clifford Geertz once recounted a variation on a well-known parable of the world's foundations: "There is an Indian story . . . about an Englishman who, having been told that the world rested on a platform which rested on the back of an elephant which rested in turn on the back of a turtle, asked, . . . what did the turtle rest on? Another turtle. And that turtle? 'Ah, Sahib, after that it is turtles all the way down.'"[29] For Geertz, as for many of his Foucauldian admirers, the story illustrates the tremendous difficulty of getting "anywhere near to the bottom of anything" he had "ever written about" and thus serves as a warning to stick to the "hard surfaces of life—with the political, economic, stratificatory realities within which men are everywhere contained."[30] But this story seems to illustrate a very different point, namely, that these "hard surfaces" cannot be appreciated unless one considers the symbolic system that gives them their structure. Such, anyway, is the insight of *Ormond*, which seems to suggest a lateral variant of this story: the United States rests on a republicanism that in turn rests on secret witness, which also rests on secret witness, and so forth, "all the way down." What one discovers, however, is that there is a great deal to learn about these turtles, namely, that the black slave plays a fundamentally important role in this fantasy structure.

This insight brings us back to our initial question, announced in the preface to *Ormond*: if in Europe, esteem and contempt had been mapped onto legible signs of social stature, how were these feelings structured in the post-Revolutionary United States? *Ormond*'s answer to this question is that US republicanism has coherence only through the phenomenon of secret witness and specifically witness by the enslaved. We conclude, however, by noting that Brown, as in other works from this period of his career, appears inclined to explore these phenomena by transferring them from the sphere of labor to that of sexual reproduction.[31] In this vein, the positions taken by the women so prominent in the final third

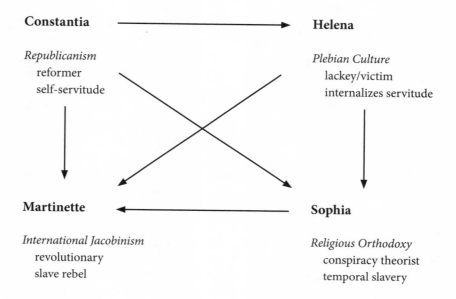

of the novel seem to present a semiotic constellation, a kind of sampling. If Constantia's assumption of servitude is an article of bad faith, Helena is her most obvious antipode, thoroughly accepting her subjection. Having sacrificed everything to her master, Helena is the complete dependent, existing as the appendage to her patron. Under Ormond's care, she had conceived herself as "happy, infinitely beyond [her] deserving" (171/176) and in her suicide note to Ormond had written, "No body more desired to please than I have done" (171/176). As the figure who accepts and adopts servitude, she stands as the distinction to Constantia, a reminder of the very different structure of the latter's fantasy: whereas Helena embodies the dynamics of actual servitude, Constantia's gestures of subordination signify what might be called "self-servitude." If Helena evokes the beauty object around whom epic struggles are fought, the remaining two women embody two structured responses of the late 1790s: Sophia obviously evoking the backlash of religious orthodoxy particularly evident in New England, while Martinette conjures a more militant radicalism. The details of these character portraits and their overt associations—Sophia with a conservative revivalism, Martinette with French and Haitian revolutions—have been discussed in recent criticism, but what are *Ormond's* insights about the *formal* quality of these emerging formations?

We have described the republican fantasy of secret witness as one in which that observer provides the very structure for republican virtues. The religious orthodoxy of Sophia, by contrast, short-circuits this support by singling out and repudiating this figure of the witness. Sophia's narrative interventions, which shift from a shared fascination with Ormond to a creeping anxiety about atheism, express the insight that republicanism depends not on God's purely external judgment but on judgments grounded in society—in turtles, we might say. For Sophia, Ormond is the incarnation of the arrogant human aspiration to reshape the world, the desire "to wander into untried paths" and "to positions pregnant with destruction and ignominy" (253/243). The presentation of Sophia thus sees conservatism for what it is: not an older, more traditional fantasy formation, as it might imagine itself to be, but rather a denial of a contemporary fantasy structure. Thus, Sophia represents not a *return* to religion but an exploration of what a postrepublican orthodoxy might look like after its negation of secret witness. The history of Sophia's mother's conversion reveals the surprising instability inherent in religion's ostensible commitment to stability. Politically, such a position produces a particular paradox. On the one hand, temporal concerns are bracketed as the temporary "sufferings . . . of terrestrial existence" (265/253), as Sophia notes in relation to Constantia; but on the other hand, the apparently unworldly believer emerges as the obsessive conspiracy theorist, as in Sophia's growing narrative fixation on Ormond. The result is a fantasy position abjuring transformational politics while at the same time betraying a growing need to classify and order all the details of the political sphere. In the terms we have here presented, we would say that Sophia embodies a position that rejects the role of the secret witness precisely by burying it in semic details.[32]

Brown's portrait of US conservatism through Sophia is matched, of course, by a corresponding portrait of a global radicalism most associated with France and, in the late 1790s, Saint-Domingue. If Sophia comes to religion between an absent father and the figure of a repentant mother, Martinette is driven from it by a lasciviously overbearing father figure (the rakish Father Bartoli) and a hypermutable mother figure (Madame Roselli, who converts back and forth from Protestantism to Catholicism). This amplification of Sophia's background creates, in Martinette, a definitive "abhorrence to deformity and age" (196/197) that more importantly signals hostility toward conservatism and the active pursuit of the glorified first principles of freedom and equality. If Sophia's fantasy is defined by the demonization of an earthly secret witness, Martinette takes the same insight and embraces it. If Constantia's republicanism is structured around a secret witness that is in fact an extension of one's fantasy, Martinette's radicalism openly asserts the subject's authority as its own secret witness. So Martinette fights in the American Revolution, then the French, and finally assumes an uncertain association with Haiti, from which she and Signor Roselli presumably arrive at Philadelphia amid the yellow fever's outbreak. As Constantia aimed to tame the conspirator figure of Ormond, and as Sophia avowed her hostility, Martinette adopts Ormond's conspiratorial activities and lays them in the open air of military conflict—hence her necessary association with Saint-Domingue, for in contrast to Constantia's self-servitude and Sophia's temporal servitude, Martinette defiantly rejects any form of servitude.

These concluding observations can only hint at *Ormond*'s final speculations but may at least suggest a different reading of these characters in relation to the novelistic framework—as potential variations on a fantasy structure that might, in turn, shed light on possible directions of US politics. We end, then, with this final question and reflection: what might have led Brown to imagine that one could anticipate the emergence of new ideological fantasies through fictional characters? In fact, there are intriguing ways in which the novel's final development of these female figures reiterates the broader semiotic unfolding of political figures of the preceding years, discussed in the previous chapter. But the novel seems oriented less to its immediate past than to the crisis of the late 1790s and the looming election of 1800, as the semiotics of the Founders were under increasing pressure. Brown's exploration of Constantia sought to explain why that was so. The exploration of Ormond, which interestingly predicted the emergence of Burr, sought to explore how that crisis might unfold.

3

Female Quixotism and the Fantasy of Region

In contemplating the causes which may disturb our Union, it occurs
as matter of serious concern, that any ground should have been
furnished for characterizing parties by *Geographical* discrimina-
tions—*Northern* and *Southern*—*Atlantic* and *Western*; whence
designing men may endeavour to excite a belief that there is a real
difference of local interests and views.
—George Washington, *Farewell Address*, 1796

In *Ormond*, Brockden Brown explored the fantasy structure
generated under republicanism with the explication of the figure of the
secret witness, which there designated an external—or more precisely extimate—position from which subjects could unconsciously imagine themselves being seen behaving just as their idealization of self ought to behave.
Ormond's fascinating achievement is to imagine the structural necessity of
the secret witness stepping out of fantasy to become a social figure. While
still a figure whose ideational content is obscured by an overabundance
of associations—Ormond signifies wealth, radical sexuality, conspiratorial manipulation, and doubling—he occupies the position of secret witness by adopting a racialized disguise: blacking up and taking on the role
of a chimney sweep—hence Brown's insight that republicanism gins up a
plenitude of fantasy Others to obscure what is unspeakable, namely, that
the omnipresent but overlooked black (slave, servant, underclass) is the final
arbiter of the republican subject's coherence. Brown suggests that the black
subject operates on three levels simultaneously: as an impure presence, as
the identifier of structural impurity in the republican schema, and as the
agent for cleansing those impurities. If we may hazard a politics here, the
struggle to the death at the end of *Ormond* seems to endorse the Jeffersonian view of the inevitability of race war (see *Notes on the State of Virginia*,

"Laws"). Ormond offers up to Constantia a series of possible obstacles to self-actualization at the end of the novel. He trades sexual debauchery for sentimental companionate love, restores the father's blindness, ameliorates the Dudleys' poverty, and ultimately kills off the paternal superego when it challenges the new equalitarian basis for sexual union. Finally, Ormond disposes of the fraudulent Craig, the gravest economic threat to the fantasy of transparent republican codes of virtue, benevolence, and order, the sign of excessive personal self-interest. But this is not enough. In the end, the novel reinstates Sophia, whose role has been both to reveal and partially to obscure Ormond's various conspiratorial associations. Looking through the keyhole, Sophia offers Constantia the key, albeit the wrong one, for unlocking Ormond. As Constantia sways toward Sophia's views, there are but two viable (and compatible) solutions—escape to Europe and the death of Ormond—for no reconciliation may be imagined.

Brown's was one literary approach to the problem of republicanism, focused as it was on the extimate dynamics of virtue. Tabitha Tenney's *Female Quixotism* (1801), however, serves as a useful counterpoint, for while it also explores the fantasy structure of republicanism, it shifts the focus to the broader coalitional logic of republicanism as a binding force in the United States. Written as Federalism moved from the institutional core to the periphery of the nation—that is, at the moment when the partisan conflicts of the 1790s give way to the more far-reaching regional divisions—Tenney's novel offers an insightful analysis of the limitations of partisan analysis. The novel's first significant episode is the thwarted marriage plot of the northerner (Dorcasina) with the southern slave owner (Lysander), while the remainder of the novel is a series of episodic explorations and repetitions of the aftermath of this failure. As in Brown's novel, such an exploration necessarily entails the symbolic enhancement and elevation of the black slave, Scipio, who from a conventional point of view seems to hover comically on the novel's margins but who actually, we argue, provides a necessary suturing of the novel's multivariate marriage dramas.[1] To put this differently, our burden is to show how the well-known scene of interracial desire—the garden scene in which Dorcasina and Scipio caress each other with love talk—is far from a simple moment of comic relief and is rather the novel's key episode. Indeed, this is the moment akin to the sudden transformation of Ormond at the end of Brown's novel, where the logical structure of Aaron Burr is mapped out and predicted.

But let us first begin with a few more general reflections on *Female Quixotism*.[2] The novel entered the early American literary canon with the

1992 *Oxford Early American Women Writers* edition and has frequently been read as a confirmation of the dangerous qualities of the early US novel—the paradigmatic "how-not-to-read-a-novel" novel. Cathy Davidson succinctly describes this formula as the "liberation from fantasy," as Dorcasina is purportedly purged of her obsession with fiction in a feminist-realist conclusion.[3] In this view, the novel ends with Dorcas drawing her fantasy life to a close, resigning her imagined identity as Dorcasina, and putting novels in their proper, subordinate place. The Quixote is correctively transformed into an exemplary citizen,[4] and readers are to ridicule—to disassociate themselves from—Dorcasina and to recognize themselves in her only at the novel's conclusion. Given the insistent simplicity of this argument, the novel is repeatedly described as "episodic," a label that implies that it is one damn subplot after another, a serial repetition of anecdotes that essentially reiterate the same point but with variations on character type (the Irish immigrant, the prankster, the class-climbing soldier, etc.). Far from being progressive, Dorcasina never learns from episode to episode and only achieves a stunning conversionary realization with the novel's conclusion. "I now find, and most sensibly feel the consequences of my ridiculous romantic and absurd conduct," she writes, as if to affirm the lack of a progressive plot: she renounces novels, advising Harriot Barry (née Stanley) to protect her children from the influence of such "pernicious volumes."[5] Within such a framework, the episodes are understood as serial retardations of (a much simpler) plot.

Such readings thereby deny the novel its intensely diachronic logic, and we want, at the outset, to stress the carefully historical structure of the novel, woven throughout with strategic temporal allusions. The novel is divided into two books separated by a seven-year gap. This hiatus, revealingly, ranges from 1784 to 1791—in other words, it skips over the framing of the national government, as if to assert the temporal irrelevance of this era's intricacies. Instead, it presents two books, the first corresponding to a colonial or imperial framework and the second to the illusory period of Federalist hegemony in a national context.[6] We would stress that we are not speaking of literal dates but of a conceptual periodization that identifies a prenational moment contrasted to a national one. Many of the dates and allusions of book 1 are imperial—Dorcas is born in 1751, the year Prince George (the future George III) became heir to the throne; Lysander is born in 1745, the year of the Jacobite Rebellion; Mr. Sheldon and Lysander's father end their close friendship in 1755, the year of Braddock's expedition (and thus the year that Washington becomes a potential military leader), and so on—as if to suggest that the colonial and Revolutionary eras' approach to the problem of political unification must be understood from a monarchical perspective. For that reason, the ascendance of George Washington, whom we see sketched in the Lysander figure, is properly speaking a *colonial-imperial* episode, an anachronistic moment that postpones the fundamental regional divide that is increasingly realized and foregrounded in book 2. Here we must refer once more to Brendan McConville's insight into the fundamentally monarchical framework of political thought before 1776, which in part explains the persistence of the royal-imperial hermeneutic into the nineteenth century. One may usefully recall that Judith Sargent Murray's long *Gleaner* series, which focused on the republican mother's education of her daughter, included a series of exercises about the British monarchy. At one point, the mother asks her daughter to undertake "an exercise from which will result obvious advantages," which included composing one essay on "whom you esteem most of the monarchs who have swayed the British scepter, from the year eight hundred and twenty-seven . . . unto the accession of George III to that throne" and another on the question, "What were your sensations as you read, and what are your sentiments of Mary Stuart, Queen of Scots?"[7] The daughter's answers to the Mary question alone—a long explication of the Mary-Elizabeth dichotomy—amounted to six *Gleaner* installments, affirming that in the early 1790s, the ideal republican mother could still be formed through an engagement with the figures of monarchical history.

Tenney's argument is in that sense more radical: it is not that monarchical figures might be pedagogically relevant to, or indirectly illuminative of, US history but that US history had its properly monarchical-imperial moment and was struggling to transition to something postimperial. The critical political task was to envision the transition from the monarchical-imperial-colonial moment to the 1790s, appreciating both the parallels *and* the differences. The marker of continuity and difference in *Female Quixotism* is the St. Clair expedition of 1791, with which book 2 begins. As a western military expedition marked by defeat by Native American forces, it amounted to the sharpest post-Revolutionary parallel to the Braddock expedition that became the mythological origin point for the figure of George Washington; in 1791, the disastrous military foray not only blasted the mythology of the US military associated with the first president but prompted a congressional investigation of him—the first such inquiry into the executive branch and one in which Washington claimed executive privilege in withholding information.[8] In this sense, the St. Clair expedition was the farcical repetition of Braddock's expedition, transforming Washington from a royal figure to a political one. We explore Tenney's historical narrative of US politics further later, but what we offer here is a parallactic reading of *Female Quixotism* alongside historical events. It is not that the novel contains historical references to real historical events or is to be unlocked and deciphered by such allusions or is even a commentary on those events but rather that it operates as a parallel narrative seen from another perspective.

With this insistence on the parallactic nature of *Female Quixotism*'s plot, we might point out as well the fundamental parallax of the novel's central character, Dorcas, whose name epitomizes this phenomenon. The source of the name is biblical. Here is the relevant passage from the Book of Acts (9:36–42):

> Now there was at Joppa a certain disciple named Tabitha, which by interpretation is called Dorcas: this woman was full of good works and almsdeeds which she did. And it came to pass in those days, that she was sick, and died: whom when they had washed, they laid *her* in an upper chamber. And forasmuch as Lydda was nigh to Joppa, and the disciples had heard that Peter was there, they sent unto him two men, desiring *him* that he would not delay to come to them. Then Peter arose and went with them. When he was come, they brought him into the upper chamber: and all the widows stood by him weeping, and shewing the coats and garments which Dorcas made, while she was with them. But Peter put them all forth, and kneeled down, and prayed; and turning to the body said, Tabitha, arise. And she opened her eyes: and when she saw Peter, she sat up. And he gave her hand, and lifted her up, and when he had called the saints and widows, presented her alive. And it was known throughout all Joppa; and many believed in the Lord.

At first glance, it appears that Dorcas is reborn as Tabitha—"Tabitha, arise"—suggesting that Tenney might have viewed herself as the reborn, corrected version of the deluded Dorcas; a milder interpretation might see Tabitha and Dorcas as two names—one Aramaic, the other Greek—for the same person. But the biblical story argues for a different distinction between the names, for Tabitha is the intradiegetic name of the good woman used by Peter and the woman herself, whereas Dorcas is her name extradiegetically—"*by interpretation*." May we not say that Tenney's choice of names reinforces a crucial parallax between history (Tabitha, the understanding and nomenclature of lived experience) and literature (Dorcas, the understanding and nomenclature of interpretation)? After all, in Acts, it is the authoritative narrator who interjects the name Dorcas, and for no apparent reason (e.g., a baptismal renaming) other than to emphasize two different perspectives. And this expansion of perspectives is itself reiterated in the names: Dorkas, a name of Greek origin, means *gazelle* and is related, perhaps because of the large bright eyes of those animals, to δέρκομαι (*derkomai*), "I see clearly." This clear vision through two perspectives seems almost an insistence on the parallax, structured into the presentation of *Female Quixotism* itself.[9]

With this point in mind, we may return to the novel's framing device, specifically the preface composed by "The Compiler," in which the distinction between history and fiction occupies prime importance. At first glance, the preface, addressed to the "*Columbian Young Ladies, Who read* Novels *and* Romances," seems to confirm the conventional reading of *Female Quixotism* as an antinovel novel. Dorcas's romantic adventures are to be compiled in the form of a "history," a "very singular and extraordinary piece of biography," a "true picture of real life," as opposed to the "mere romance" or "caricature" full of "whimsical and outré" "particulars" so productive of "baneful effects" (3). But an unironic reading of the preface seems a surprisingly naive gambit for literary critics, and a more critical reading might note that the veracity of this "true uncoloured history of a romantic country girl" is confirmed via comparison with the "authentic history of the celebrated hero of La Mancha, the renowned Don Quixote" (3)—in other words, verified by appeal to a novel treated as *history*.[10] If, as the didactic critic might argue, Tenney uses her novel to demonstrate how history should displace romance, how odd that the historical model for the exercise is itself a fiction. And here we might reflect on the novel's interesting title, which changes the well-known Quixote (deployed, as well, in Charlotte Lennox's *The Female Quixote*) to the processual noun, replete with ideological connotations—such as the "Jacobinism, atheism, and illuminatism" mentioned at the novel's conclusion (316). We suggest not only that quixotism here signals a parallactic fantasy dynamic defined by the distinct yet mutually informing relationship between history and fiction but also that this challenge to the conventional history-fiction distinction, on which so many readings of the novel hinge, models equivocation about a number of other social and political distinctions (Federalism/Republicanism; master/slave; elite/folk; North/South). Indeed, it is tempting to think of the novel as an engagement with

Jefferson's notorious inaugural assertion, "We are all Republicans, we are all Federalists," a sentiment vigorously mocked by the Federalist press as an unwarranted transcendence of the partisan conflicts of the 1790s. But *Female Quixotism* may be exploring the parallactic coexistence of these and other terms under the rubric of a quixotism in which we are all Dorcases, we are all Tabithas.

The Lysander Episode

The foundational episode of *Female Quixotism* is the first marriage sub-plot, the Lysander episode which explores the split national imaginary, the contest between the North and South. During a visit from an old Virginian friend of Dorcasina's father, she encounters his son, Lysander; Lysander falls in love with Dorcasina, but she does not feel a reciprocal passion—"that violent emotion, at first sight of you, which always accompanies genuine love," as she puts it (13). The marriage is not consummated, ostensibly because Dorcasina's mind was "so warped by the false and romantic ideas of love" (11). But much about this episode demands a more complex reading, for at the heart of this first apparent maladjustment is Dorcasina's resistance to marrying a southern slave owner. In other words, contrary to the view of her as a lover naively seeking romantic marriage, Dorcasina proceeds with a sobering confrontation with history—specifically the history of enslavement. Some critics have found Dorcasina's sentimental response to the plight of slaves a ridiculous parody. The sentimental heroine is overwrought in her grief over slave suffering and overextended in her fantastic solution—if she marries Lysander and frees his slaves, his neighbors will free theirs, "and all the blacks [would] be emancipated from bondage, from New-Hampshire even to Georgia" (9). But Dorcasina's reaction to the foreseeable consequences of a romantic connection actually shows us how her fantasies are calibrated to register and not to avoid the Real. Far from being a silly sentimentalist, she envisions the slave owners themselves learning the evils of slavery through their own bondage by the Algerines. Here Dorcasina may be reworking the well-known sentimental speech of Joshua Atherton (in 1800, New Hampshire's attorney general) against ratification of the US Constitution. Atherton began his remarks expressing skepticism about the 1808 nonimportation clause and had then proceeded to imagine "manstealers" seizing "the whole or a part of the inhabitants of the town of Exeter," Tenney's home.

Parents are taken, and children left; or possibly they may be so fortunate as to have a whole family taken and carried off together by these relentless robbers. What must be their feelings in the hands of their new and arbitrary masters? Dragged at once from every thing they held dear to them—stripped of every comfort of life, like beasts of prey—they are hurried on a loathsome and distressing voyage to the coast of Africa, or some other quarter of the globe, where the greatest price may await them; and here, if any thing can be added to their miseries, comes on the heart-breaking scene! A parent is sold to one, a son to another, and a daughter to a third! Brother is cleft from brother, sister from sister, and parents from their darling offspring! Broken with every distress that human nature can feel, and bedewed with tears of anguish, they are dragged into the last stage of depression and slavery, never, never to behold the faces of one another again! The scene is too affecting. I have not fortitude to pursue the subject![11]

Dorcasina's resistance to the marriage—the "greatest pain" of the potential match—is grounded in the fact that she "shall be obliged to live in Virginia, be served by slaves, and be supported by the sweat, toil, and blood of that unfortunate and miserable part of mankind" (8). The personal romantic fantasy occasions a guilt-ridden emotional distress, for Dorcasina's response inspires an empathetic identification not with Lysander but with his slaves. She rejects as fantastical the southern conceit that slavery is compatible with happiness and instead insists, via a quotation from the sentimental novelist Laurence Sterne, "disguise thyself as thou wilt, still, slavery, though art a bitter pill" (8). Again, let us reiterate the crucial point that sentiment stages not the treacle of unrestrained feeling but a crisis of identification and desire. The invocation of love, a pact of mutual recognition and reciprocal exchange of feelings, triggers its reversal: incomprehension and disgust. Of the southern slaveholder (and by metonymy, of Lysander, too), she says, "They complain of the idle, thievish, unfaithful disposition of their slaves" (8), but what do they know of the condition of the slave? Thus, Dorcasina's retributive fantasy sends back to Lysander the charge leveled at her by her critics—Dorcasina supposedly cannot distinguish fiction and reality, but this is precisely the error of the slave owner, who patches together an image of human bondage with necessary fictions. And, contrary to the reading that the marriage is not realized because of Dorcasina's delusions, we should foreground a counterstrain in the narrative, whereby the marriage is not realized because of *Lysander's* delusions. Indeed, this reversal of terms seems to find enactment in Dorcasina's two fantasies—in the first, she

imagines her encounter with Lysander as a scene requiring *his* heroic intervention (she is saved from falling off her horse, she is rescued from assault
by a rival), but in the second, *her* heroic intervention (she frees his slaves,
thereby triggering emancipation of all slaves) is central.

Such utopic agency crumbles when Lysander is actually encountered.
Governed more by rationality than passion, he greets Dorcasina with a
"style of easy politeness" that undermines her expectation of "piercing him
through and through at the very first glance" (10). With "no trembling,
no emotion, no hesitation in speaking to her," Lysander quickly abandons
Dorcasina, preferring to listen to the old men discuss the imperial "adventures of their youth" (10). So commences the courtship, and readers may
recall the scene as one in which Dorcasina succumbs to romance against
Lysander's level-headedness. Yet the reverse is arguably the case, for several pages later, Lysander is awake all night composing a marriage proposal, having spent the preceding weeks admiring Dorcasina's sensibility
(her "sweetness of temper, condescension to the servants, and duty and
affection to her father"; 11–12). How do we explain this odd inversion of
roles? We may first note that Lysander is himself a parallactic figure, as his
name suggests. On the one hand, his name evokes the Elizabethan figure
of the pastoral swain (as in Shakespeare's *A Midsummer Night's Dream* or
the poetry of Aphra Behn), and on the other, it suggests the Spartan general, treated in Plutarch's extremely popular *Lives*, who united the Aege-
ans against the Athenians' colonial empire and brought the Peloponnesian
War to a close. From one perspective the object of romance, from another
the practical political unifier, we see in Lysander a figuration of George
Washington, who as the Federalist northerners' southerner enacted, as we
have argued, a symbolic compromise on slavery. In this light, the running
debate on slavery between Dorcasina and Betty reads like the northern
antislavery debate about Washington: it is an outrage to live off the labor
of the enslaved; but perhaps they are well treated; maybe, but such treatment is hypocritical and rests on unfair caricatures of Africans; but even
the slaveholders admit it is an evil they cannot fix. . . . A more fascinating
depiction of Washington as northern Federalist icon, explicit in its convolutions, appeared in Sally Wood's 1800 novel *Julia, and the Illuminated
Baron*, in which one of the characters finds himself shipwrecked on the
Virginia coast, where he is rescued by black slaves:

> I never had entertained that narrow prejudice, that affects some people,
> that a dark skin, cannot cover a fair heart. It is the complexion of the

mind that stamps the man, a wretch or an hero; but still I was surprised, at the kindness and attention of these slaves. Upon enquiry, I found we were upon the estate of the best and greatest man, in the world; and that these kind protectors were the servants, or rather humble friends, of the Illustrious WASHINGTON; from him they had learnt to follow the dictates of humanity, to obey the impulse of benevolence, and to treat the broad paths of philanthropy. See, my dearest JULIA what the example of the great and truly noble, may do; these people are in a state of hostility with all civilized nations; the love of self preservation teaches them so to be; in general, more at variance, with their masters, than with any others; nor is this to be wondered at; for their masters are their tyrants. Yet behold them here performing every kind office; nor is this surprising, they are the servants of WASHINGTON; this wonderful man has made them happy, and learns them to make others so.[12]

We see here a variant of the fantasy outlined in Brown's novel, in which the republican dynamic includes the slave as a necessary position—here the fantasy of Washington as the republican father creating perfect US citizens finds its crucial intermediate position: Washington's perfect citizens are *slaves*, and it is their humble service to us that makes them potential citizens. It is their noble service, instead of the perfectly appropriate resentment of "their tyrants," that makes them the paradigm of republican virtue—in short, they are ideal republicans not *despite* being slaves but *because* they are slaves. In the context of such rationalizations, *Female Quixotism*'s critique of the Lysander figure is all the more stunning, and we may pause to appreciate that, when it comes to slavery, we see Dorcasina learning all the moral lessons that she supposedly can learn only after thirty or more chapters of mortifications. The novel's final pages present Dorcasina's illuminative confession to Harriot: "I find that, in my ideas of matrimony, I have been totally wrong. . . . I imagined that, in a happy union, all was transport, joy, and felicity; but in you I find a demonstration that the most agreeable connection is not unattended with cares and anxieties" (320). And have these lessons not been learned, as well, in the very first chapters—that union is never without pain and that romance always entails the cares and anxieties of history?

The rejection of Lysander/Washington by Dorcasina is overdetermined in these opening chapters by her very intimate relationship with her father, the aptly named Mr. Sheldon. Unlike Dorcasina, for whom "novels were her study, and history only her amusement," for Mr. Sheldon the reverse is true: "History was his favourite reading; and next to that (a singular taste for a man) he delighted in novels" (6). Sheldon is also shelled in by past "disappointments and mortifications," withdrawing from the bustle of the city to L—, some thirty miles from town; his isolation is heightened with the death of his wife, as he comes to devote himself with increasing affection to his daughter, "the only fruit of this connexion" (4). To reiterate: some painful experience leads to Sheldon's retreat, to a compensatory domesticity, to an incomplete effort to produce a male heir, and ultimately to social seclusion with only his daughter and his bifurcated library. In fact, we learn that "his affection for his infant daughter increased, till it engrossed almost every thought of his mind; and his very existence seemed to be bound up in her's" (5). In all but sexual matters, Dorcas comes to replace Sheldon's wife, and even the provenance of her name—taken from her paternal grandmother—underscores this aura of incestuous substitution. Sheldon is figuratively attempting to shack up with his past, while Dorcas's fondness for her father is sublated in her domestic role, in a "marriage" destined to be nonreproductive. In this respect, then, the Sheldon-Dorcas relationship illuminates the competing positions on history and romance. For Sheldon, the subordination of literature (a delight) to history (his favorite) implies a traditionalism or conservatism with secondary embellishments—the pleasurable status of novels confirming the retreat from the social. For Dorcas, however, novels represent not a turning from the world but a displacement of worldly matters onto the plane of sexual-romantic desire. Desire, seeking another object cause, turns to the "violent passions" of romance, absent a sanctioned sexual outlet. It makes sense, then, that Dorcas, reaching the milestone of her seventeenth birthday, wishes for a "romantic termination" to the domestic arrangement, a desire she cannot speak or effect but must articulate through a demand to alter her name. The change from Dorcas to Dorcasina fulfills in letter, if not in spirit, her break from the economy of her father's domestic fantasy—the break as yet incomplete, the name cannot be changed (Tabitha?) but only altered. Her attachment to her novels remains the means by which the frustrated political and domestic desires are shifted and allowed to play out through the screen of an alternative fantasy. If romantic love signals an intimate dynamic, the romance novel marks its extimate form. It is in this context that we ought to assess Dorcasina's "novel-mania": novel reading is not the cause of Dorcasina's crises but rather a symptom of the psychic struggle to balance intimate and extimate desire.

The Lysander episode is practically entwined with the introductory tableau of the Sheldons' domesticity and allows us finally to consider *Female Quixotism*'s assessment of the Federalist Washington cult and the moment of the so-called founding. However good, meritorious, and estimable the figure of Lysander/Washington, the poison pill of slaveholding weighs more heavily on the scale of potential happiness than a Mr. Sheldon will admit. Thus, Sheldon is content to live in the past with his old Virginia friend, pathologically displacing his need for pleasure on fiction, just as Americans glorified the imperial Washington, ignoring slavery in favor of the happy fictions of republican virtue. To glorify Washington is to insist on the general of the old colonial days rather than the political conflicts and compromises of the present—Washington stands revealed as an anachronism, as absurd perhaps as a shipwreck on the shores of Mt. Vernon. Thus, Dorcasina's harsh indictment of Lysander's proposal letter—"your letter was such as I suppose your grandfather might write, were he, at the age of eighty, to take it into his head to marry" (13). Lysander/Washington is out of date and does not answer the needs of the present—these are to be found in the "violent emotions" evoked by novels, through which the present is more directly engaged and processed, leaving history in its proper place as a reserve of "amusement." This reading, we think, suggests a different consideration of the novel's remaining episodes. They are not simply reiterations of the stupid errors associated with novel reading—one damn subplot after another, all belaboring the same antiromantic point—but rather a series of phantasmatic engagements with different political formulations, in what is essentially a novelistic rendition of the various ideological formations of the post-Revolutionary period.

In this respect, the reading of *Female Quixotism* as an antinovel novel is at once misleading and correct. Insofar as critics assume that Tenney was formulating a critique of fantasy or romance in favor of a more realistic history, they ignore the lessons of the Lysander episode. For Tenney insists that the experience of history is novelistic—it is a naive historical sensibility that is dangerous and therefore the real target of the condemnation of romance. The cure, accordingly, is to read one's way through the various "romances" popular in the period—the Washington-as-founder romance, the Democratic-opposition romance, the Federalist-critique romance, and so on. *Quixotism* is this process of working-through, and it quite naturally must be *Female*. For Tenney's novel, like Brown's *Ormond* or Murray's *Gleaner* pieces, endorses the sense that the paradigmatic republican subjectivity is feminine and that the drama of politics is one of marital fantasies.

From Suitors to Suture

After the brief Lysander episode (chapters 1 and 2), which, we have argued, offers a compressed hermeneutic for a racial-political reading of the novel, book 1 is largely devoted to the romance plot with O'Connor, from his introduction in chapter 4 until his punitive removal from the novel in chapter 18. The O'Connor plot is itself the seemingly straightforward story of a con artist. Son of an Irish nobleman's steward, O'Connor has immigrated to Philadelphia to seek his fortune at the expense of gullible Americans, unacquainted with his notoriety as a gambler, cheat, and thief. Learning of Dorcasina's penchant for romance, he plays the part of a disowned child of noble origin; having rejected the woman his father wants him to marry, he tells Dorcasina, he fled to Virginia, where he met the distraught Lysander and learned of Dorcasina's virtues—he has finally come to declare his passionate love for her. Although Dorcasina, who has waited fourteen years for another suitor, falls in love with O'Connor, the narrator lets readers in on the ruse from the beginning, making clear that O'Connor represents both the extravagant and sentimental European (in his demeanor) and the European underclass immigrant (in his motivation). As such, the O'Connor episode is the most straightforward—as many critics have noted, O'Connor represents the rise of a democratic opposition in the 1790s, with its combination of European ideas and affects with the grubby pursuit of power and wealth. The relationship between Dorcasina and O'Connor, then, captures the ideological dynamics of political affiliation. For instance, once Dorcasina has committed herself to O'Connor, her beliefs cannot be shaken until the "strong hysteric fit" of chapter 14, itself prompted by witnessing O'Connor's "public whipping" (144, 142). All the arguments of Mr. Sheldon, the suspicions of her servant Betty, or the beating by the African servant Scipio, cannot disabuse Dorcasina of her romantic attachment. Instead of confronting her own errors of judgment, Dorcasina must assume that her father has been duped, that Betty and Scipio are too ignorant to appreciate love, and so on. Truth is no antidote to a fantasy structure: ideology inoculates itself against just this form of attack. Once the romance has been written into the heart, it will take "struggles" and "time" to "erase . . . an image so deeply engraved there" (149). In sum, political ideology is structured extensively like a romance novel—with conventions, twists and turns, ironic episodes, conflicts and adversaries, and the like.

Furthermore, the (political/literary) romance to which we are committed is defined in part by its relation to other forms or genres. O'Connor understands this in introducing himself with reference to Lysander—he alludes to the earlier episode but with obvious and important generic improvements (his father's condemnation, his intensely passionate avowals, etc.). Likewise, when O'Connor absconds in chapter 12, in part because of Lysander's epistolary exposé, Dorcasina can reaffirm her commitment to her lover *because* of Lysander's intervention: "It is Lysander," she notes, "who is at the bottom of all the mischief"—that is, the clash between her father and O'Connor and the flight of the latter. So it is that the Democratic-Republican opposition is itself an ideology that necessarily defines itself in relation to Washingtonian Federalism—every democrat of the 1790s had to formulate a relationship to Washington that might explain his disapproval of the opposition (e.g., he was becoming senile, he was misled by his advisers, etc.). Furthermore, the best critique of an ideology emerges from its immanent contradictions and tensions. The best illustration here is the cross-dressing episode of chapter 14, where, with O'Connor on the lam, Dorcasina manages the "most grotesque appearance" of Betty dressed up as O'Connor (98). The plebeian servant's attempts to imitate the con man produce ridiculous ravings ("Dear soul, intoxicating charmer"; 98), public humiliation ("an immoderate fit of laughter"; 99), and a diagnostic misrecognition (the sham suitor, wearing Mr. Sheldon's clothes, is perceived as attempting to displace the father figure).

Less noted in readings of the novel has been Tenney's insight into the generation of the opposition to the opposition, here represented by the brief Philander subplot embedded at the end of book 1 (chapters 15 to 17). A "native of Connecticut, that hot-bed of American genius," and specifically a young graduate of Yale (104), Philander arrives on the scene *not* to pursue a romance with Dorcasina but to mock and parody her relationship with O'Connor by playing on Dorcasina's fantasy of O'Connor's subjectivity. Thus, his first gesture is not a romantic approach to win over Dorcasina but a mock affirmation of the O'Connor-Dorcasina relationship: encountering the name *O'Connor* carved on trees in the Sheldons' arbor, he carves the name *Dorcasina* underneath, on all the trees. Having revivified Dorcasina's love for O'Connor, he then enters into a more explicit relationship that repeatedly references the O'Connor relationship: he concludes his first letter, "O happy O'Connor! wretched, wretched Philander!" (108). After these remote encounters, he stages three physical meetings. In the first, instead of meeting Dorcasina himself, he arranges for an aggressive female rival to meet at the same spot; in the second rendezvous, Dorcasina meets with a plebeian barber, Mr. Puff, "set quite above his business" (118); and in the third, the anticipated wooing is displaced by a forced abduction. Thus, the Philander subplot is not akin to the O'Connor story, for not only does Philander never attempt to pursue a relationship with Dorcasina but Dorcasina's reaction to Philander is to reassert her love for O'Connor—the postscript to her letter to her father explaining her abduction by Philander ends with an appeal for news about O'Connor.

What Tenney offers here is a critique of the Connecticut (or Hartford) Wits, and specifically of their ironic political strategy. For the Wits, from this vantage point, pursued not a substantive ideology of their own but rather a mock rendition of the democratic opposition (in such mock epics as "The Anarchiad" or "The Democratiad"). To put this differently, this ideological current of Federalism did not appeal to citizen subjectivity but rather preferred to ironically mock it for fellow believers. The Wits could only approach the status of a significant political romance through the subtlety of their parodies—hence their spectacular failure: all the ironic combinatorics of the trysts staged by Philander ultimately strengthen Dorcasina's delusions. We see this ineffectuality in the final abduction scene—Philander is at one point "weary of racking his invention for extravagant speeches" and thus "remained silent" (134), and he leaves the novel "laugh[ing], till his sides were ready to burst, at this new instance of the vanity and credulity of Dorcasina" (136). So the Connecticut Wits offer not an interventionist or conversionary ideological strategy but one of ironic distance, and they exit, laughing. It is for this reason that the Philander story should be read as a subplot of the O'Connor story rather than a sequel, for Philander offers not a different romance but the pleasure of reading democratic kitsch. This is the gist of Tenney's ideological critique of the Federalist Wits: they do not constitute a successive episode, an alternative narrative to the Democratic-Republican romance of an O'Connor, but are formally derivative of, and generated from, the romance of opposition.

This formal subordination, we should note, is confirmed by the subplot of Mr. Puff, the plebeian barber whose sham romance with Dorcasina is orchestrated from a distance by Philander. Can the same be said, however, for the other fleeting romance of book 1—the crucial scene in chapter 9 that finds Dorcasina caressing the "tall stout negro, called Scipio"

(52)? This remarkable scene of misrecognition, race mixing, and violence occurs when O'Connor has arranged by letter to rendezvous with Dorcasina at night in the summer house. The family servant Scipio stays on guard against predators on the family melon patch but also awaits his own lover, Miss Violet, a black woman from town. By accident, Dorcasina finds Scipio asleep at his post and, mistaking him for O'Connor, "approached him softly, sat down by his side, and, putting one arm round his neck and resting her cheek against his, resolved to enjoy the sweet satisfaction which . . . in his waking hours, her modesty would have prevented her from taking" (53). Dorcasina will rarely, if ever, be shown in such a state of unselfconscious pleasure: "with a heart thrilling with transport, she blessed the accident, which, without wounding her delicacy, afforded her such ravishing delight" (53). Meanwhile, O'Connor professes his love to Miss Violet in the style most suited to Dorcasina's fantasy. The mistake is finally revealed, and in the ensuing scene, Dorcasina faints after jumping from the summer-house window, Scipio beats O'Connor (as a presumed melon thief), and Dorcasina, awakening to the conversation of "African lovers," is mortified by the whole affair. For her part, Miss Violet is unperturbed; she "could as easily exchange a white lover for a black" (54), and Scipio promises future beatings should anyone intrude on Miss Violet or his melons. By contrast, Dorcasina has a sleepless night, in distress for the well-being of O'Connor and uncertain how to "reflect on her familiarity with her father's servant": she wants to conceal it from general knowledge yet not lie about what was "strictly true" (55).

Here, then, is the distinguishing feature of the garden scene. Mr. Sheldon has not prohibited Scipio's courtship of Dorcasina. It has not even crossed his mind! But Scipio is an unthinkable romantic object for two reasons. He is, of course, black, but he is also too close to occupying the same position as Mr. Sheldon. Scipio is a paternal surrogate, deputed to guard the melon patch. He stands in for the father. Here, we note Tenney's awareness of the parallax inherent in Scipio's name via his ancient namesake, Scipio Africanus (236–183 BC), the Roman general who successfully conquered Carthage by defeating Hannibal during the Second Punic War.[13] This master of Africa was also renowned for his sexual continence, a theme captured in several Renaissance and eighteenth-century paintings, which feature his forbearance, resisting a captive maiden offered to him as the sexual spoils of victory. Thus, Tenney's Scipio is both Scipio Africanus and Scipio the African slave, both master and slave and, significantly in both avatars, able to suppress the sexual drive. We can now appreciate how sexual contact with

Scipio is the barest displacement of that illicit, unnamable, and incestuous desire for Sheldon for which O'Connor and the other suitors are exogamous alternatives. Scipio's special status seems to be confirmed at the end of the novel when Mr. Stanly returns Dorcasina to his care.

Yes, Dorcasina thinks it a "disagreeable situation" when she recalls that, with her "snowy arms, she encircled Scipio's ebony neck" (59). Nevertheless, we only hear about this particular, eroticized trauma in comparison to another much more disturbing assault—when she is mistaken for a prostitute, grabbed around the waist, and verbally assaulted by yet another Irishman at the Inn. This second assault is, in essence, the truth of *O'Connor's* veiled behavior, not of Scipio's. Thus, while Dorcasina views the two Irishmen through either violent attachment or repulsion, her "accident" with Scipio is only attended by concern that *others* would think poorly of her for it. The inexpressible wish here is to be the treasured melon, safe under the protection of this "tall stout negro," who prides himself on "keeping [the garden] in excellent order" (52). This identification of Dorcasina with the garden is underscored at the end of the episode, when, fleeing from the Inn, Dorcasina is chased by the same boys who have been responsible for theft and despoliation of the melon patch, trampling down everything in their way, "to [its] great detriment" (52). *Detriment* comes from the Latin *de* (away) and *terere* (to rub, wear), and in legal terms, it is the loss of a thing to which one is entitled.[14] As with the garden, Dorcasina is "stript . . . to some tattered remains [of her gown]" (60). We must note, too, that at the end of the novel, Mr. Stanly conveys Dorcasina back to L—, where she is greeted by Scipio with tears of happiness in his eyes for her return. These joyful tears shed for Dorcasina take us, as well, to the garden and its consequences. Then, it was Dorcasina whose eyes were "swoln with weeping" and O'Conner's face so "swelled that one eye was entirely closed" and the other mostly so (55). Dorcasina's anxious tears and O'Connor's eyes disabled by violence are both supplanted by Scipio's credible affection. If, as Mr. Stanly has told one suitor, Mr. Sheldon placed Dorcasina under his care and protection, his last act of restoring her to her estate is to hand this responsibility over to the former slave.

Ruptures in the Republic

Book 1 operates within the colonial, imperial, monarchical schema, and this is so right up to the end, when Mr. Sheldon's authority is restored.

Thus, the mode of book 1 is conservative, in that each movement toward exogamy ends in failure and takes the plot back to the beginning again. And what enables the return of the father but two methods resolutely imperial in form. O'Connor is disciplined in a public spectacle, and his history is suppressed with threats of further violence. We thus transition to book 2 with the abrupt revelation that Dorcasina has not, despite these imperial tactics, been "radically cured." The imperial solution in its American form (John Adams's Alien and Sedition Acts) is implicated. Adams's spectacular failure as heir to Washington reveals that what made the Virginian so effective was his service not as a ruler superseding party but as a *southern* monarch sustaining regional power under the guise of equanimity. The New Englander is but a pretender to this throne, an aberrant detour from the Virginia dynasty resumed with Jefferson's election in 1801. This may be why Adams's critics could so easily represent him as an aspiring monarch. Absent interest in the material conditions needing protection by force (slavery), Adams could only dress up as king and enact the form of monarchical authority. In contrast to Adams's will to power for power's sake, Washington's function was materially necessary. This, then, explains what the Federalists most rejected about Jefferson—not his soft Jacobinism and Francophilia but his fortification of slave power. He is the "Negro President," elected by a southern majority secured by slave representation and a sign that northeastern Federalism was nearing extinction, never to gain sufficient support in the Congress to protect itself from the "Virginia influence."[15]

It is with this politics of renunciation that Tenney resumes her narrative in book 2. What options did Federalism have to answer the Jeffersonian ascendancy? It was clearly not a return to the mythico-heroic general. Lysander had already shown that figure's limitations, and the imperial solution of violence and censorship had failed. Instead, Tenney directs our attention to the west, which by 1801 was read in two ideologically charged ways. In the positive Federalist fantasy of the west, the national government had by 1785 restrained individual states' claims to territories to the west and paved the way for the Union to allocate the land for the creation of new states. The first exercise of the Union's new powers was the enactment of the Northwest Ordinance, within which the states of Ohio, Indiana, Illinois, Michigan, and Wisconsin were eventually incorporated. In 1787, the prime mover of the Northwest Ordinance was the current president of the Congress, General Arthur St. Clair. A delegate from Pennsylvania and staunch Federalist, St. Clair envisioned the new

states to be carved out of the Northwest Territory as free states inclined
to northern Federalism. The Ordinance banned slavery from the territories, promising a counterforce to southern slave representation. St. Clair
became the first governor of the new territories. Thus, in the late 1780s, as
Federalists were drafting the Constitution and arguing for its ratification,
a northern Federalist was positioned to secure the west for the expansion
of Federalism. In book 2, Tenney even disabuses us of this recourse. This
is why book 2 begins with the wounded and weakened veteran of the St.
Clair expedition against the Indians in 1791, Captain Barry. For the second ideological coding of the west was the dystopic reversal of permanent
northern rule. This was the state of affairs for Federalists when Jefferson
was inaugurated, Tenney's occasion to write the novel. Jefferson was the
opposite and overwhelming force to Federalist dreams. He would counter
the incorporation of the Northwest Territories with a new sublime object,
Louisiana. And Federalists were sure that Jefferson would use the west to
extend southern influence by creating new *slave* states in the west. The
fantasy of a Federalist hegemony to be extended westward was now really
closed and the symbolic meaning of Washington clarified.

Tenney's stunning insight was to identify the true horror of Jefferson's election: Federalism had actually already died, swallowed the bitter pill, when Washington replaced Arthur St. Clair and became the first
president of the new federal government in 1789. It was less a political
revolution than a regionalist correction. By 1803, when the scope of the
Louisiana Purchase was being digested and interpreted, some Federalists had even begun to talk of secession as the only way not to sacrifice
northern interests to the Virginia Influence, an early iteration of the Virginia Dynasty.[16] As this idea makes clear, Jefferson's election was not just
a political reversal of Washingtonian Federalism but also an extension of
Washingtonian regionalism, its dynastic coattails. Thus, while the arrival
of Captain Barry, the veteran of St. Clair's ruinous defeat on the Wabash
in 1791, doubles the arrival of Lysander and signals another chance for the
Washingtonian military lover to prevail, it also represents the symbolic
death of Federalism in its inaugural moment, the so-called bitter pill of
slavery. We must recall here that Dorcasina's original fantasy in book 1
is that the heroic lover, Lysander, will arrive wounded and become reli-
ant on her care. But Captain Barry *is actually* wounded, debilitated at that
infamous defeat of whites by nonwhites on the frontier. This is where the
politically opposed views of the west converge. The extension of slavery
was likely to realize the calamitous dystopic fantasy of slave rebellion

presently being modeled for them all on Saint-Domingue. St. Clair had been humiliated by the Indians; Jefferson would also fail with racial Armageddon.[17] And here we must reiterate the apparent leapfrogging of the Washington administration in Tenney's imagination. For St. Clair is himself a parallactic object; structurally, he replaces Lysander at the point of departure for the second book (the young Washington), but, wounded and weakened, he is also the diminished product of the entirety of book 1. He is what remains of Federalism after Philander's wholly ineffective and self-absorbed gamesmanship and Sheldon's equally feeble exercise of imperialist paternal agency. The beginning of book 2, then, structurally goes "back to the future." We see now how the Federalist project crumbled even before it had begun.

The sexual economy of book 1 is also repeated with a difference in book 2. Not "radically cured," Dorcasina awaits but a "proper object" to excite her quixotic desire that had lain "dormant," or repressed, for the past seven years (152). We should read "proper" to contrast the incestuous sterility of Dorcasina and Sheldon in isolation at L—. In this sense, both O'Connor and Philander were *proper* objects, while Scipio, who in action most reproduces the father's role, is likewise *improper*. Book 2 introduces a new series of suitors/sutures: Captain Barry and his steward, James; Mr. Cumberland, John Brown, and Harriot Stanly in the guise of Montague; and Mr. Seymore. But instead of ending with the imperial patriarch, as in book 1, the novel concludes with an inversion. Since Mr. Sheldon has died, his contrary double, Scipio, welcomes Dorcasina home, where he and the other servants will take care of her and manage the estate. What is the logic of this series?

We recall that Philander used a proxy, the plebeian Puff, to stand in for him and to challenge O'Connor. Captain Barry and James, his steward, invert the previous paradigm. For in this inaugural suture of book 2, it is James who initiates the scheme to insert himself in place of the master. He uses Captain Barry as his tool to win access to Dorcasina, and it is only after he has fulfilled the protocols of her fantasy figure that he can reveal his true identity and hope that Dorcasina will transfer her affections to him, the agent if not the original object of her desire. As in the Philander/Puff subplot, the Barry/James storyline requires not one but two characters to occupy the function of the suitor. In both cases, what necessitates this complication is the move from the direct agency of Lysander and O'Connor (repulsion from or exploitation of Dorcasina's fantasy) to the metacritical agency of these later pairings, Philander/Puff (ironic play to gain solipsistic pleasure) and Barry/James (strategic manipulation to win economic benefit). James is comparable to O'Connor in that both represent themselves as something they are not. But James's plot is more complex. O'Connor identified the object of Dorcasina's fantasy and fashioned himself to occupy that place. That place, or position, is a mythic construct and relies on Dorcasina's naiveté. James also identifies the object of Dorcasina's desire, but that object is real (Captain Barry). James's self-fashioning, while still false, nonetheless requires that he replace a figure already occupying the position of object-cause. While O'Connor expresses no concern about what will happen once his fraud is revealed—he will have absconded with Dorcasina's fortune—James depends on the free-floating quality of Dorcasina's desire. He knows that his ruse is temporary, and he plans to reveal the truth as part of the plot itself. Having convinced the mortified captain that he can "wean Dorcasina's affections from his master, and fix them on himself" (165), he aims to kill two birds with one stone, freeing the captain while gaining his own social mobility. He will use the captain as a mask to draw Dorcasina in and will later reveal his stratagem to demonstrate how desperately he longed for her from his otherwise socially invisible, subaltern role. As one might expect, the plan does not unfold smoothly.

Before James has had the chance to transfer Dorcasina's love from the captain to himself, his ruse is nearly found out. At one point, mimicking the captain in a darkened hallway, James has to prevent Dorcasina from entering a chamber where the real captain is hosting Mr. Sheldon and his guest, Mr. Stanly. When Betty arrives with a candle, a second threat to his true identity, James dashes it and Betty to the ground, and he threatens to cut her throat if she does not remain silent. But Betty had already sounded the alarm—"Thieves! murder! fire! robbers!" (184)—and drawn the attention both of the gentlemen in the captain's chambers and the servants in the kitchen. What follows is the closest the novel comes to realizing race warfare. Sheldon, Barry, and Stanly find themselves "fastened in" and suppose "that some villains had entered the house and were murdering all below," while at the same time the "servants, . . . imagining that some terrible disaster had happened above, were coming, in a body, up the back stairs with Scipio at their head." A violent confrontation between the "gentlemen from the chamber and the squadron from the kitchen" is avoided only by Betty's body discovered in the hallway still sprawled on the floor (185). The subaltern body lying low with no apparent cause to explain her condition provokes laughter from the other servants and rage from Mr.

Sheldon, who is upset to have been alarmed so unnecessarily. As in earlier episodes involving Betty, Tenney once again uses her to demonstrate that the subaltern cannot speak. Her words, no matter how prescient or insightful, will be dismissed as superstition or ignorance. Her suffering body will only be attended to as a source of entertainment. James, too, fails to communicate effectively across class lines. He ultimately fails to woo Dorcasina; she is not swayed to accept his suit once his identity is revealed. His plans foiled, he rejoins Captain Barry eastward and suppresses his most recent adventures from his master. Thus, we see one final inversion of the Philander/Puff episodes: while Mr. Sheldon had to pay off Puff to keep Dorcasina's misadventures from publicity, James silences himself to remain in the captain's service. Is this not a political solution? The subaltern cedes his revolutionary aspirations voluntarily.[18]

Tenney's interest in class relations continues with the next two suitors, Mr. Cumberland and John Brown, each an extension of the critique of the impoverished northern response to southern power. A wealthy merchant from Philadelphia, Mr. Cumberland is the first suitor that has the formal endorsement of Mr. Sheldon, who had certainly not disapproved of Lysander. Lysander, however, was a southerner, whose wealth came from plantation slave labor. Mr. Cumberland earned his wealth by trading commodities. The shift is notable not only for these regional and economic distinctions, for we must note here the passing of the baton from military to civilian credentials. Tenney underscores this by marking the distinction of this Cumberland's character from his namesake, Lord Cumberland, who was general in chief at the Battle of Culloden, which ended the Jacobite Rebellion of 1745 against the Hanoverian dynasty and so guaranteed the smooth transition to the rule of George III. While Mr. Cumberland is in place to secure the paternal estate from further assault, he will almost certainly convert it to fluid money.[19] Cumberland does not intend to inhabit L— but to take its resources and trade them for merchantable commodities. Mr. Sheldon's treasured daughter becomes, for Mr. Cumberland, an immaterial value, a thousand pounds a year, and even a laborer "not likely to be so expensive a wife as one bred in the city" while being more "industrious" (205). While the estate will not be stained by association with the foreign or lowly, it will not remain intact in form.

Unlike the foreign deceiver O'Connor, then, Cumberland is an emblematic American character, the model capitalist. While O'Connor feigns a signification to hide his real identity, Cumberland takes his name as his bond. There is little superfluous or extravagant about him. Marriage is an economic transaction. This should remind us of Betty's warning at the end of book 1, where she advises that before Dorcasina commits to falling in love with a stranger, she ought to "first find out what sort of man he is." Dorcasina cannot suppress a patronizing smile and corrects Betty's "simplicity and total ignorance" of romance. "Why, surely," she said, "you do not think people can fall in love by design, or when and with whom they please?" (148). Mr. Cumberland is, of course, the very sort who can "fall in love by design." To him, marriage is strategic, and love an afterthought. He dismisses Dorcasina's frivolous and romantic conceits and tells her that he will commit to the "ceremony" of love only after the deal is sealed. He will not consider romance before he knows whether they "were like to make a bargain or not" (206). Here we see that Betty had stumbled on a truth of the governing elite that, when she tries to realize it for herself, excludes her by design. Noting Dorcasina's lack of interest in Cumberland, Betty sets her own sights on the merchant. With Scipio scheming in the background, Betty even comes to view herself as the object of Mr. Cumberland's affection. She ceases to work and demands to be called Mrs. Cumberland. But, as in the other episodes that feature middling characters gettin' above their raisin', Betty will be utterly humiliated for these pretensions. Dorcasina, for her part, finds Cumberland's market rationalism cold and disgusting. Lest we lose sight of the inaugural problem that Dorcasina had foundered on with Lysander, the owning of slaves, Dorcasina's penultimate suitor, John Brown, draws us back to the issue of the slave trade and once again raises the specter of northern complicity in the peculiar institution.

Brown is an illiterate farmer from Rhode Island. He has been hired just before the pivotal death of Mr. Sheldon. With Mr. Sheldon's passing, Dorcasina's repressed desire for her father becomes a more manifest search for his replacement. Brown is the first to capture her imagination in this new mode. Perhaps most distinctive about Brown is that, unlike each of the previous suitors, Dorcasina wholly initiates her entanglement with him. Brown does not pursue Dorcasina as had O'Connor, Puff, James, or Cumberland. Instead she *finds* him herself. Having been reading *Roderick Random*, Tobias Smollett's popular novel, Dorcasina once again conflates romance and history. Since noble Random, the titular character of the novel, has masqueraded as a servant under the name John Brown, her own servant must truly be a nobleman in disguise. We may also see Dorcasina's mistake in light of her rejection of the two-dimensional Cumberland. Reacting against Cumberland's depthless directness, she assumes that one's true identity must be veiled to be authentic. Thus, Brown's plebian ignorance is taken as a sign of its opposite. Once Dorcasina fixes her fantastical attention on Brown, she views it as her task to restore him to his place. So anxious is Dorcasina to place Brown in the position of Mr. Sheldon that she brings him into the home and has him dress in her father's old clothes. Brown here is the unwitting imposter. Unlike James, who adopted the guise of his master, Brown involuntarily is repositioned in that role in Dorcasina's fantasy. What is the significance of this truth of the Rhode Island plebian, John Brown?

It is unlikely that Tabitha Tenney picked up the name John Brown out of some random eighteenth-century novel and used it as a marker of simple plebian blankness. That is not how names work in her imagination. This we have demonstrated severally from Dorcas/Tabitha to Scipio Africanus the African slave. One does not have to wander far to find a historical referent for John Brown from Rhode Island. We will drag out the suspense a bit. John Brown may be the most tenacious of Dorcasina's suitors. Both Betty and Scipio desperately want John Brown displaced. They try to frighten Dorcasina by telling her that the ghost of her father is haunting the place. They lock him in closets and chase him across the landscape trying to hound him out. Scipio fears that "massa John Brown" will be no good for any of them, expecting the Rhode Islander to be the harshest of overseers. Scipio joins forces with Harriot Stanly, who thinks she can save Dorcasina by cross-dressing as *her own* father and, professing love for Dorcasina, threatening to run John Brown through with *his* sword. When Brown gets suspicious and tries to discover where this Montague (the name Harriot Stanly has adopted) comes from, Harriot and Scipio set a trap to spook Brown with another ghost. Brown chases Montague toward a supposedly haunted lane and, as Harriot Stanly quickly jumps out of sight, Scipio, dressed in a white cloth, pops out, prompting Brown to run home in abject terror. As the referent John Brown will reveal, this may be the most realistic event in the novel: the slaveholder confronted by the ghost of his victims.

When Samuel Tenney joined the Sixth Congress of the United States in 1800, he became a colleague of one John Brown, representative from the state of Rhode Island. *This* John Brown, a founding trustee of Brown University (then the College in the English Colony of Rhode Island and Providence Plantations) in 1764, made his fortune trading slaves. In 1796, he became the first American tried and convicted under the Slave Trade Act of 1794, which legislated that "no citizen or citizens of the United

States, or foreigner, or any other person coming into, or residing within the same, shall, for himself or any other person whatsoever, either as master, factor or owner, build, fit, equip, load or otherwise prepare any ship or vessel, within any port or place of said United States, nor shall cause any ship or vessel to sail from any port or place within same, for the purpose of carrying on any trade or traffic in slaves."[20] Brown's ship *Hope* had been equipped for the slave trade, and in 1797, following his conviction, his ship was confiscated. Brown represented northeastern complicity in the continuation of American slavery. It makes sense, then, that Scipio would object to serving a "massa John Brown" if he were to supersede Mr. Sheldon at L—. John Brown is the horrifying reminder that the southern institution depended on northern merchants to survive. The punishment for the "barbaric traffick" in slaves is telegraphed in the novel when Scipio, responding to a physical assault from Brown, tosses him out into the street. To the narrator, this episode proves the "instability of fortune" (283). The master may swiftly and shockingly be reduced by the slave. Brown, who "thought himself master of Dorcasina and all her possessions," was summarily "robbed of his mistress, stripped of all his possessions," and thrown out into the street "by a negro servant" (283).

Tenney may have also had another John Brown in mind, further underscoring the parallax of northeasterner/slaveholder. First serving Virginia in the Continental Congress of 1787–88 that drafted the US Constitution, the southern John Brown later became a senator from Kentucky. In 1792, Brown had introduced the petition leading to Kentucky's bid for statehood. Having studied in Thomas Jefferson's law office in the 1780s, Brown ran as a Democratic-Republican, serving Kentucky from 1792 until 1805. The ironic fusion of a slaveholding John Brown from Rhode Island *and* a Jeffersonian John Brown from Kentucky suggests how a corrupted Federalism might end up the support of Jeffersonian policy.[21] In the end, it takes a remnant of the Federalist past, a decorated veteran from Massachusetts, to intercede and separate Dorcasina from a Federalism clearly tainted with slavery. Scipio and Harriot (dressed as her father) fail, and only the authentic Mr. Stanly's intercession brings the John Brown episode to a close; the *real* father of Harriot Stanly and the deputed guardian for Dorcasina must abduct her to an even more rural retreat.

Critics have generally understood the ending of the novel as a correction of Dorcasina's misplaced credulity in novels. The end of the novel, in this view, gives us the reformed Dorcas, who resumes her real name and settles into a more sober and accurate accommodation to things as they are. For these critics, Dorcasina's adventures are fantastic excursions from reality and not, as we have argued, a formal reckoning with the fundamental contradictions of reality in post-Revolutionary America. In our view, then, the novel concludes not with the end of fantasy but with its resumption, a return to a fantastical stasis and isolationism which the episodes throughout have shown to be but a pasteboard mask veiling the real. Dorcas, like her father before her, now inhabits a rural estate on the very margins of modernity and still supported by an ambiguously free servant class, an unsustainable state of affairs at the time that regional divisions over slavery were polarizing the nation. But before Dorcasina can sequester herself once more at L—, she must suffer once more, this time via Seymore, the supposed schoolteacher from South Carolina.

Seymore—like Philander, whom he mirrors in inverted form—learns about Dorcasina secondhand. Philander was privy to the local gossip about Dorcasina and her affair with O'Connor, and this is confirmed when he visits the grove and sees that Dorcasina has carved her lover's name into several trees. Seymore also learns of Dorcasina through the rumor mill. Among the differences between them, though, is that while Philander was indeed a scholar, Seymore is only playing the part of a schoolteacher to cover his flight from his wife, his family, and his numerous creditors. While Philander indicates the Connecticut Wits, the Federalist satirists of Jacobinism in America, Seymore has spent years in France, where he had "imbibed all the demoralizing, and atheistical principles of that corrupt people" (297). Philander's plot comes to a close when the wit is thoroughly satisfied with the pleasure his cunning has given him. Unconcerned about the implications of his intervention, Philander returns to Connecticut. It is up to Mr. Sheldon to force Dorcasina to see O'Connor imprisoned in the town square. By contrast, Seymore leaves under duress. Thus, Seymore's demise parallels that of O'Connor, as both are made subject to the law. Books 1 and 2, then, end similarly with a symbolic closure enforced by the father or his surrogate. In each case, Dorcas/ina is removed from circulation and reinscribed in the patriarchal idyll.

John Brown's arbitrary promotion to master and overseer performed an important function, creating a transition from Lysander, the ennobled slaveholder, to Brown, the slaveholding master by fortune alone. Scipio and Betty feared Brown precisely because he represented the truth of master and slave, an arbitrary hierarchy sustained by force. Recognizing the emptiness of Brown's claim to mastery, they were certain he would exercise his authority most vigorously. Implicit here is a critique not only of the benevolent slaveholder, Lysander, but of Mr. Sheldon as well, the complacent slaveholder. Mr. Stanly's intervention to act in the name of the father (Sheldon) functions to hide the metonymic links connecting three modes of mastery: benevolence, complacency, and autocracy. And Seymore, hailing from the South and full of the radical egalitarian ideology of Revolutionary France, must also be displaced because he represents the base hypocrisy of each of these positions. To Dorcasina, he appears to be what he is not: he is not benevolent (he has abandoned his family), he is not complacent (he seeks to profit from chance encounters), and he evades legal jurisdiction (he imagines himself beyond the law). In 1801, all of these qualities point to a single character: Thomas Jefferson, the southern schoolmaster (advocate of public education), enamored of France, reputed adulterer with his own slaves, and hypocritical author of the Declaration of Independence. The name Seymore could signify that, though this guileless imposter is deposed, the republic will *see more* of his type as the Jefferson administration adapts to control of the government.

Our final task in this chapter is to explore the final disposition of Dorcas. Exposed to "the disagreeable truths" of her fanciful expectations of reality, Dorcas returns to L—, where she will live out her days in charitable work in the company of Scipio and Betty, the full witnesses of her history. Scipio and Betty occupy the position of the analyst much as the minstrel chimney sweep Ormond had in Brown's novel. Dorcas's cure, in Lacanian terms a somewhat irrelevant or secondary concern, brings her closest to the traumatic kernel of the Real. The disagreeable truths have a "strange effect" on her. As with her biblical namesake, her "eyes seemed to be opened" (317) such that she began to look on her past with disgust and see all men as "false, perfidious, and deceitful" (315). Her views of romantic felicity also take the fall. She learns of the struggles that have faced her friend Harriot after her marriage to Barry, most significantly of the death of her son within a month of his birth. After Dorcas has been embraced by Scipio and Betty upon her return to L—, she experiences another sobering sensation: "Her dearest friends being separated from her by death or removal, she found herself alone, as it were, on the earth. The pleasing delusion which she had all her life fondly cherished, of experiencing the sweets of connubial love, had now entirely vanished, and she became pensive, silent, and melancholy" (322). To Harriot, she writes, "I have passed my life in a dream, or rather a delirium; and have grown grey in chasing a shadow, which has always been fleeing from me, in pursuit of an imaginary happiness, which, in this life, can never be realized" (323). The reality principle governs; but is this not also the doctrinal position of her colonial forebears, that is, a religious code? It seems that God has finally assumed his place as the ultimate patriarch. Life is to be devalued for the life to come; stasis has become the rule. We might end our discussion here with the conclusion that Tenney accomplished her aim in reducing Dorcas to the proper scope of Christian suffering and longing.

4

Burr's Formation, 1800–1804

The opposite Party too are divided into many Sects, as the World
will see, if they succeed in their Choice. Their Man will not be
found to be the Man of all their People: No nor a Majority of them.
He is not thorough going enough. He is not daring and desperate
enough. In short one half the Nation has analyzed itself, within 18
months, past and the other will analyze itself in 18 months more.
By that time this Nation if it has any Eyes, will see itself in a Glass. I
hope it will not have reason to be too much disgusted with its own
Countenance.
　　　　　　　　—John Adams to Abigail Adams, November 15, 1800

The Empty Ballot

We turn now to the moment when that thing called Aaron Burr emerged
on the scene of US politics, its coordinates so well mapped and anticipated
by the likes of Charles Brockden Brown and Tabitha Tenney. We must
resist several historicist impulses here—for instance, giving the story of
how Burr's life and career unfolded, bringing him to the vice presidency,
or the political, "behind-the-scenes" narrative that reveals the true machinations the public could not perceive. This is particularly true with our
somewhat arbitrary starting point, the election of 1800. It is all too tempting to immerse oneself immediately in the details: Thomas Jefferson and
Aaron Burr found themselves tied at seventy-three electoral votes apiece,
the victory to be decided by the House of Representatives; in Congress,
the states split their votes eight to eight, and the politicking for a changed
vote began to unfold. But we would do much better to view the event from
the clarifying distance of the newspapers, which struggled to report what
was happening. In Pittsburgh, for example, the Democratic-Republican
newspaper, the *Tree of Liberty*, only published news of Jefferson's election
at the end of February, and while there were a few short accounts of balloting, it was only on April 11 that the local bookseller Zadok Cramer began

advertising the sale of *Proceedings of Congress While Balloting for a President of the United States, Which Continued for 6 Days, with the Speech of Thomas Jefferson, on His Inauguration as President, of the U.S.*[1]

This delay reflected not only the slowness of communication but also a very different perception of the election controversy itself. For through the months preceding the election, the victory or even significance of Aaron Burr was never imagined or acknowledged, and it was assumed that Jefferson's election could only be thwarted by Federalist perfidy. When the tie occurred, it was again assumed that under normal circumstances, it would be resolved by the election of Jefferson as president, Burr as vice president—unless the Federalists conspired to thwart the outcome. Republican newspapers accordingly carried stories about a conspiracy hatched in "Sam[uel] Chase's house in Baltimore," to maintain the tie until the resolution of the election became, of necessity, extraconstitutional.[2] In the event, John Jay was to be declared "a perpetual President or Dictator."[3] In the same vein, the anti-Federalist polemics continued, detailing John Adams's last-minute appointments, a mysterious fire in the Treasury and War Departments (where, it was alleged, papers detailing illegal arms deals and shady Treasury transactions were destroyed), and the election results coming in from other parts of the country. Burr was absent, a nonentity, in all this reportage. We might even say that, outside New York, he barely even existed in public discourse. As early as October 25, 1800, advertisements began to appear for a special print of Thomas Jefferson, to be mass produced as "a match for [Gilbert] Stuart's print of General WASHINGTON"—a logical project, given Jefferson's firm establishment within the semiotics of the Founders.[4] It was not until January, by contrast, that this same advertiser, "by the advice of several citizens," published an accompanying notice for a portrait of Burr, "as a companion to that of THOMAS JEFFERSON."[5]

To repeat: Burr barely existed at the moment, especially when viewed alongside the extensive and rich semiotic portrait of Jefferson, by supporters and enemies alike. We might usefully compare the two verbal portraits presented by Morgan J. Rhees, delivered as an Inauguration Day oration and again widely reprinted in Republican newspapers.[6] Addressing the charges of Jefferson's deism or atheism, Rhees begins with a detailed defense of the new president's religious views (concluding, "It is enough that he believes in the divinity of the Christian doctrine, as delivered by JESUS"), but the focus is on Jefferson's political and philosophical greatness. "It is HE who drafted the charter of our rights and the declaration of our independence," Rhees notes, and "as a philosopher, the fame of JEFFERSON cannot be shrouded." The portrait of Jefferson runs three detailed paragraphs. And then comes this paragraph about Burr:

> Of our worthy *vice president*, it may not be amiss to say a few words—Although we have not heard, read nor know so much of him as we have of the "Sage of Monticello," yet some of us, and no doubt all the electors were sufficiently acquainted with his talents and republican integrity. HE fought with *Washington* in the field, and has displayed his wisdom and attachment to liberty, in the great councils of the nation. Few men, if any, in the United States have done more to produce the late change in the representation of the people, than colonel BURR. His Eagle eye penetrated thro' every scheme, of the adverse party, and he has combated with success the "*evil genius of America.*" While some were distracting their brains, with jarring elements and component parts, the capacious soul of Burr, conceived the harmony of the *great whole*. While others were collecting their materials, he erected his fabric. A man whose active genius is every where & whose goodness of heart and purity of morals have never been impeached, is an admirable *second* and may be a suitable *successor* to the sagacious *Jefferson*.

Burr appears again as an enigma of sorts—"we have not heard, read nor know so much of him"—whose significance revealingly comes via association with the semiotically rich Washington (with whom he fought), Jefferson (whom he will succeed), and Hamilton (the "*evil genius*" he has battled): perhaps, Rhees suggests, Burr may eventually become what James Madison was actually to become—a second, mini-Jefferson. But the most interesting detail of this portrait is its emphasis on form—for where political observers "distract[] their brains, with jarring elements and component parts," the "capacious" Burr expresses the "*great whole*" in which these collected "materials" will find their place. If Burr has no substance, he nonetheless emerges as an encompassing field, "every where," in which meaning might eventually be fixed.

This capacious emptiness even persists a year later, in John Wood's late 1801 *History of the Administration of John Adams, Esq.*, a 506-page partisan tract ostensibly laying the Federalists in their grave.[7] We will say more about the vexed history of Wood's publication later, but here we note that this rambling chronicle-like collection of Democratic-Republican details, news reports, and insinuations also ventures characterological readings of Federalists and Democratic-Republicans alike. Accordingly, in its concluding account of the 1800 election, it offers a chapter titled "Lives and Characters of Thomas Jefferson, Aaron Burr, and Charles Cotesworth Pinckney," the latter a Federalist rival of Adams. The Jefferson portrait, not surprisingly, is extremely detailed. We are given a precise physiognomy, accounts of Jefferson's major writings (including a host of private letters, the Declaration of Independence, and even a pamphlet Jefferson had not written), a refutation of his alleged cowardice as Virginia's governor, the high points of his diplomatic career, a summary of his service as secretary of state, his personal real estate history, and his theories on paper money. The account concludes with a romantic, grandiose portrait of Jefferson from the Italian Philip Mazzei, which should remind us of the increasing European literary influences on such semiotic work.

This account of Jefferson—some thirty pages long—stands in marked contrast with eight pages devoted to Burr. We are given some details, most notably about Burr's military career, though these seem to rely on associative proximity—Burr has such and such qualities because of his affiliation with Montgomery, Putnam, Wayne, Washington, and so on. A telling anecdote, about a dying British soldier whom Burr had encountered during the war, is particularly revealing. The soldier laments his "charged musquet," saying, "had I discharged my piece I should not have regarded my life, but would have died with satisfaction" (460). This anecdote of emptiness, of nonexistence and lack of definition, in some sense sets the tone of the full portrait. We are told that, upon Burr's retirement from the army (for vague health reasons), he "gave his mind entirely to literary pursuits" (461), but these are never enumerated, suggesting less matter than mystery. A list of legislative achievements in the US Senate seems more substantial, and it is worth noting that five of the seven summarized bills concern publicity and openness.[8] Yet such details will only seem paradoxical for a figure so elusive that Wood's descriptive summary is actually William Livingstone's account of Aaron Burr, *Senior,* published earlier that year in James Hardie's *New Universal Biographical Dictionary and American Remembrancer.* Thus, Wood's remark that "it is impossible to draw a character of Colonel Burr in more applicable and expressive terms than Governor Livingston has done of his father" (463) is less a rhetorical gesture than an admission of the difficulties of the task. So ends the account of Burr—associative yet imprecise, open yet secret. Even the brief image of teenaged Burr—"display[ing] that quickness of comprehension, blended with an ease of expression and gentleness of manners, though closed with a prudent reserve" (457)—evokes less clarity and precision than a paradoxical self-negation.

Thus, the Democratic-Republicans but also the Federalists struggled to define Burr. In a January 1801 editorial about the electoral tie, the *Washington Federalist* observed, "What is the language the people of America express in this vote? Why certainly that in their opinion Mr. Jefferson is equal to Colonel Burr, and Colonel Burr equal to Mr. Jefferson!"[9] We may appreciate here the unusual but perceptive wording of the question—what *language* do Americans express in voting?—as well as the wishfully formulaic answer. No doubt this editorial was a desperate attempt to prevent Jefferson's presidency with various convolutions (if Burr says he *does not* want to be president, he therefore *should* be, etc.), but it here unwittingly reveals the mathematical dimensions of the struggle. Like all mathematical formulas, this one can be read in two ways: quantitatively or formally. It is precisely in the divergence of these two readings that we can locate the two ways of treating the electoral controversy: either with a naive empiricism (*Jefferson and Burr were tied! The outcome could go either way! Let's see what happened behind the scenes*) or extimately (*Burr was so far from being equal to Jefferson that the electoral tie prompted a scramble to create and fill the Burr figure*). The "Epaminondas" pieces published in the *New-York Gazette* during the election crisis were similarly lopsided.[10] Jefferson was drawn in great detail as the cowardly, philosophizing, leveling Francophile. In a passage anticipating the eventual drama of Burr, Epaminondas speculated about Jefferson's response to racial violence inspired by "the massacres and desolation of St. Domingo":

> I tremble when I think of the consequences in which an organized revolt might terminate, when fomented by daring and desperate chiefs, and nourished by ill-disposed foreign powers. On such an occasion, a President ought not to be slumbering in an Epicurean chair: dissecting the wings of a butterfly; indulging ingenious dreams concerning the various hues of his species; or estimating the cubic contents of a volume of water, necessary to the production of an universal Deluge. (9)

A Jeffersonian government, overwhelmed by race war, could only be prevented by looking for "*a Deliverer*" in "*the camp of the Enemy*"—Aaron Burr. He was an enemy, yes, but an imprecise one, as the portrait went on to suggest. "The slave of no party; in pursuit of no office," Burr was "unbiassed by personal affections," characterized by "the most bland and conciliating manners"—"his unprejudiced mind will readily assimilate to those plans of policy, which the experience of years has proved to be conformable to the genius and dispositions of his countrymen" (10, 12). In sum, Burr was like "a changeable silk": "there is a variety of colors; but it is difficult to say where the one ends or the other begins" (12).

These Federalist assertions of Burr's obscurity eventually gave way to the first major Federalist delineation, which revealingly had to draw on the semiotically rich resource of the best-selling novel in the United States. In May 1801, a single-page Federalist handbill titled "Aaron Burr!" began circulating.[11] It opened with references to Burr's conspiratorial tendencies, his hatred of the Constitution, and his greed and deceptiveness but focused primarily on his *"abandoned profligacy."* The tale it unfolded was that Burr, in Washington to take the oath of office, had *"seduced* the daughter of a respectable tradesman there, and had the cruelty to persuade her to forsake her native town, her friends and family, and to follow him to New York," where she was "now *in keeping."* The father had journeyed to New York to find his daughter, and *"vengeance* will soon light on the guilty head." If anyone did not read here the plot of *Charlotte Temple,* the handbill made the allusion extremely clear:

> It is time to tear away the veil that hides this monster, and lay open a scene of misery, at which every heart must shudder. Fellow Citizens, read a tale of truth, which must harrow up your sensibility, and excite your keenest resentment. It is, indeed, a tale of truth! And, but for wounding, too deeply, the already lacerated feelings of a parental heart, *it* could be authenticated by all the formalities of an oath.

The narrative address, the insistence on possible authentication, the sentimental reference to the monstrous rake, the appeal to "sensibility," and especially the iteration of the subtitle of Rowson's novel—"a tale of truth"—show the desperation with which Federalists sought to fill up the capaciously empty (w)hole of the vice president. Nancy Isenberg has noted that from this point forward, Burr was understood as the sexual deviant, but we note that this is more than simply a sexual characterization. Recall the sexual components of the primary figures of the Founders Square: celibate Washington, father of us all; randy Franklin, of an epicurean sexual appetite; Jefferson, drawn to the improper dalliance with his friend's wife or Sally Hemings; Hamilton, bastard child and blackmail victim in the Reynolds affair. The "empty" and "full" positions of Washington and Franklin give way to specific violations of marital sex in Hamilton and Jefferson. Burr, by contrast, emerges as a *"debauchee,"* seducing innocent daughters, working his way through the "wretched haunts of female pros-titution," and consuming such "celebrated courtezan[s]" as "N—," "U—," and "S—"; the Federalist handbill adds details, as well, of "half a dozen more whom first his intrigues have *ruined,* and his *satiated brutality* has afterwards thrown on the town, the prey of disease, of infamy, and wretchedness." This is less an additional sexual position than a qualita-tively expanded attempt to fill the empty Burr with sexual voracity—he is a "monster" brutally fucking his way through the United States. One imagines that, after each conquest, such a monster can only declare its fullness: "Aaron Burr!"

The Burr Pamphlets

Even this extreme language, however, did not help the figure of Burr coalesce. We can sense his unimportance in the battle over government appointments, which unfolded in late 1801. Prominent among the pam-phlets was the fifty-four-page polemic by "Lucius Junius Brutus," which bitterly attacked Jefferson's decision to remove some Federalist appointees. While the pamphlet extensively referenced the deceased Washington and Franklin as paragons of impartiality and genius, and while it referenced numerous officials in the administration, Burr is mentioned only once, and that in a footnote.[12] In fact, it was only between mid-1802 and mid-1804—with Burr's unsuccessful run for the New York governorship—that something like Aaron Burr is formed. We turn here to that construction, which we trace through another flurry of characterological texts includ-ing John Wood's *History of the Administration of John Adams*; a series of pamphlets and newspaper pieces by James Cheetham, who edited New York's *American Citizen*; William P. Van Ness's "An Examination of the Various Charges Exhibited against Aaron Burr" (December 1803); and a series of pro-Burr texts published in Peter Irving's New York newspaper, the *Chronicle-Express*.

The characterological work of Cheetham—one of the transatlantic political refugees-turned-journalists, who settled in New York, where he worked for the Clintonians—is most illuminating, as it shows the chal-lenges posed even in the most dogged attempt to create the Burr fig-ure.[13] In December 1801, Cheetham informed Jefferson and Madison of an attempt by Burr to prevent publication of a two-volume *History of the Administration of John Adams* by Burr's acquaintance John Wood.[14] Later that month, writing to Jefferson, Cheetham conceded the uncertain significance of this act:

> [The Burr circle's] motives for suppressing it are not yet *completely* Developed; but they are sufficiently understood to convince us that they are not the most honorable. The work is Republican; and why *Republicans* should be solicitous to suppress it, is enigmatical. One of the avowed reasons is that it contains remarks Calculated to offend many of the federalists, from which and many other Circumstances it is inferred that to form a *Coalition* with them at a suitable time is in Contemplation.[15]

A few pages later, Cheetham notes that Wood's history, so clearly "Republican" in the preceding reference, "is a *mere Compilation* totally uninteresting, and Cannot possibly be any service to [their] Cause."[16] One might read such passages as documentation of a political intrigue—Clintonite and Jeffersonian forces beginning to unite to eliminate a rival, with the émigré journalist so cynically pitching his case that he contradicts himself. The suppression is "enigmatical," or rather "not yet *completely* Developed," but here is the reason: the history is clearly "Republican" but is also uninteresting and politically worthless. We prefer, however, to see here a cultural dynamic at work, in which the political journalist emerged as a sort of conduit for broader signifying forces. In this view, Cheetham's uncertainties and contradictions are less markers of his cynical calculations than indices of extimacy at work. Cheetham is less the person who, "almost single-handedly, orchestrated Burr's fall from political grace"[17] than an idiot-savant displaying the semiotic struggle.

In the first pamphlet, for example, Cheetham proposes the theory that Burr, wishing to "supplant Mr. Jefferson,"[18] set out to court the Federalists in the hopes of achieving a second vice presidency under Charles Cotesworth Pinckney (18). But such arguments are marginal—sometimes literally in footnotes—and we might better read the dynamics sloppily mapped in the larger argument. At the most basic level, in fact, Cheetham proposes a theory of history. Because history is inextricably linked to freedom, "precious" would be any narrative that documented the evil years of the Adams administration's police state (5). This is not an argument, however, praising a "secret history" of original research and never-before-compiled facts. Rather, it is analogous to that history read ceremoniously every year—the Declaration of Independence—which "reminds us of those covert and open acts by which attempts were made to enslave the colonies, . . . instructs us in our rights, and cordially invites us to guard against similar attempts within the union" (6). Thus, "history" here is not new information but rather the symbolic encoding of the loose imaginary details and experiences through which we live. It is in this sense that history is "a compass, which safely guides us through the devious paths of adverse vicissitudes" (6).

But shortly after these reflections, in one of the pamphlet's most stunning passages, Cheetham turns the screw a bit, describing George Logan's private diplomatic mission to France in an attempt to end growing US-French hostilities:

> After the result of those amicable offices performed by Dr. Logan, was known, the mantle of delusion which had been artfully thrown over the country, rapidly disappeared.
>
> Our citizens began to cast their eyes about them like men awakening from a disorderly dream; and they plainly perceived that our government was the principal, if not the sole obstacle to a reconciliation of the two nations. Thus the charm was broken, and the "pleasing hope, the fond desire, the longing after" a government dissimilar to our own, which was expected to arise from, and which was suspended on the event of war, instantly vanished. The foundation gave way, & the fancied edifice fell. (8)

Here the lived experience of history is recoded as that of "the mantle of delusion," a "fancied edifice," a "charm," suddenly shattered by a changed state of affairs. More precisely, the "disorderly dream" of life is (quoting Addison's "Cato") the "pleasing hope, the fond desire, the longing after" something different than what is. Perhaps the most telling detail of this description is its self-negating syntax, whereby the imagined fantasy government, "dissimilar to our own," seems like a Möbius strip: it was supposed to emerge at the moment of war *and* was suspended on the event of it (*sic*) *and* "instantly vanished" when war was finally averted. Thus, the lived experience of history is cast as the search for the unattainable object of desire (Lacan's *objet petit a*), never there, never reachable, collapsing and vanishing no matter what happens. Thus, "history"—specifically John Wood's history of the Adams administration—is the symbolic ex post facto corrective to the uncertainties of imaginary experience and the delusions of unattainable desires.

It is all the more ironic, then, that Cheetham is unable to provide the clear history of "the Suppression by *Col. Burr*" of Wood's book—in fact,

Cheetham's narrative ends up delineating and proliferating the very disorders that a solid historical narrative is supposed to remedy. There are certainly pages that describe the ostensible suppression of John Wood's book—Burr complained about libelous content, tried to negotiate with the publishers to stop production, intercepted a lone copy bound for an English printer, and so on. But more generally, the narrative produces fundamentally self-negating contradictions. Burr forcefully directed the writing of Wood's narrative, including the insertion of a ridiculously positive sketch of himself—but then he tried to suppress it. Burr wanted to manage and control an improved replacement text, to harm Jefferson and boost his own reputation—but then he failed to write it. Burr was excessively secretive about his involvement—and then took center stage in the suppression efforts. Burr's efforts to suppress the narrative show he is incredibly powerful in his machinations—but he has not an "atom" of influence outside New York (38). The paradox, throughout the narrative of Wood's book, is therefore fundamental—the very history Burr purportedly, spectacularly, undemocratically suppresses is a history he directs, manipulates, orchestrates, and, given every chance, refuses to reproduce. Rather than a "Narrative of the Suppression," what Cheetham presents is a suppression of the narrative.

Recall Cheetham's opening comments on "history": we cannot discern it clearly as we live it; indeed we typically fixate on some unattainable fantasy object, which stands in for reality; so we need written histories to give it a stable symbolic meaning. But in his own telling of the story of Burr's suppression of Wood's narrative, he unwittingly chronicles a different landscape. Burr sets out to produce a (self-serving, pro-Burr) symbolic narrative, but his attempts to do so devolve into confusing, self-contradictory details, such that Cheetham's pamphlet concludes by elevating Burr to the status of the unattainable object of desire. Where the symbolic order of history was supposed to negate, decisively, the object of desire, the reverse is actually the case: the attempt to craft an orderly symbolic history (whether by Wood or by Cheetham) produces an overwhelming object of desire: Burr. Cheetham says as much in his preface, in which he describes the Jeffersonian ascendancy as the restoration of order: "universal placidness reigns over the nation" (4). This is all the more reason, however, for Cheetham to declare "that something 'is rotten in Denmark'; that under an exterior, which, though not altogether pleasing, is calculated to make false impressions on unsuspicious minds, SOMETHING EXCEEDINGLY UNPROPITIOUS TO THE FREEDOM OF THE UNION, IS AT THIS MOMENT CONTEMPLATED BY THE VICE-PRESIDENT" (3).

What Cheetham unwittingly describes, then, is an integral instability in the symbolic order of Jeffersonian America, such that an elusive object of desire is called forth. In the *Narrative of the Suppression*, this object is variously described as an "invisible spirit" "versed in the art of hocus-pocus," "habituated to secret movements and dark consultations," a figure whose "*legerdemain*, . . . while it defies conclusive proof, eludes the most acute research" (Wood 9–11). There was no more precision in the pamphlets that followed, *View of the Political Conduct of Aaron Burr, Esq.*, and *Nine Letters on the Subject of Aaron Burr's Political Defection*, despite their hundreds of pages documenting Burr's evil machinations. How could these pamphlets say so much and yet say so little? We identify here four tendencies in the pamphlets that speak to this process.[19]

The first of these is a structural equation of Burr with the Republicans' bête noir, Alexander Hamilton. Cheetham's narrative of Burr briefly returns to the post-Revolutionary moment when Burr aspired to lead the New York Federalists: "You were a coadjutor of General Hamilton," Cheetham writes in *Nine Letters*, "and united with him in federal committees to oppose the election of governor Clinton. This was your first stand" (13). But finding Hamilton a figure of "superior lustre," Burr recedes, bides his time, and eventually moves up the ranks of the Republicans. This is obviously an attempt to insinuate that Burr was actually a Federalist at heart, though even this point is nebulous—Burr is here an opponent of Clinton, not an advocate of Federalist views—and, in the aftermath of the 1800 electoral tie, serves to shift the equation of Burr with Jefferson to an equation of Burr with Hamilton. Thus is Burr situated as a disruption between the semiotic pairing of Jefferson and Hamilton: TJ (=(AB)=) AH. Of course, the power of this equation still resonates today in almost biblical fashion, as the mythical early years of the republic are read as the setting for a series of crypto-twins locked in lifelong, fraternal, even mortal rivalry, best exemplified in Joseph Ellis's *Founding Brothers*.[20]

This equation of Burr with Hamilton, as with Jefferson, is at once so ephemeral and insubstantial because it lacks semiotic substance—it speaks only to a formal symbolic logic. But although Cheetham produced over five massive pamphlets and endless newspaper columns on Burr, the semiotic details are remarkably minimal. Much of the 120 pages of *A View of the Political Conduct of Aaron Burr* and the 139 pages of the *Nine Letters* is a detailed, ex post facto narrative of Burr's political career—from his absence from the political struggles of the post-Revolutionary era to his various attempts, successful or not, to obtain state or national positions and finally to his response to the electoral tie of 1800. Perhaps these narratives could be summarized with this phrase: "You aspired to fill the vacant seat" (*View* 13). Often Burr did not fill the vacancy, but when he did, he avoided taking political positions by lukewarm support, disappearance, or the avoidance of voting.[21] This was the partisan recoding of the formula TJ (=(AB)=) AH; as Cheetham elsewhere put it, Burr "appeared to oscillate between the two parties."[22] This narrative of Burr—at once desperately seeking a position but simultaneously avoiding taking any position—should be read symptomatically. It is not simply that Burr aspires to fill a vacant seat but more profoundly that he does not exist except in the pursuit of these essentially formal positions. We might say that the positions sought and achieved by Burr are thus not semiotically substantive but are rather symbolically *formal*. Hence, the achievement of any (political) position is immediately neutralized by the avoidance of any (policy) position. So frustratingly self-negating are Cheetham's pamphlets—hundreds of pages of details, with almost no characterization of Burr—that the last two pamphlets are devoted not to Burr but to two relatively minor supporters. *A Letter to a Friend on the Conduct of the Adherents to Mr. Burr* (1803) examines Peter Irving (Washington Irving's brother), editor of the pro-Burr *Morning Chronicle*, while *A Reply to Aristides* (1804) sketches the career and writing of Burr confidant William Van Ness. These pamphlets, too, are devoted to baroque details of this letter or that meeting, but Irving, the social-climbing druggist with literary pretensions, and Van Ness, the blustering, immigrant-hating sidekick, emerge much more clearly as characters than does Burr, who remains obscure throughout. As Cheetham put it at one point, "The character faithfully drawn of Mr. Burr in the following pages is so complex, so stript of precise and indelible marks; so mutable, capricious, versatile, unsteady and unfixt, one to which no determinate name can be given, and on which no reliance can be placed, that serious questions may arise from it" (*View* 5).

Very much related here is a third trope: Burr's avoidance of writing or speaking before two or more people. "I do not believe," writes Cheetham, "that Mr. Burr, who is indebted to the abilities of others, for the most splendid speeches he has delivered at the bar, has a talent for composition" (*Reply* 4). Again and again, we are told that Burr will not speak, or if he does, his remarks are rhetorically ineffective and brief; his writing, likewise, is criticized for its ambiguities, alternately a sign of evasiveness or ineptitude. This notorious silence has long been a trope of Burrologies—as for instance in Gordon Wood's recent sketch, which notes, "Writing out his thoughts was not Burr's way. As he once warned his law clerks, 'Things written remain.'"[23] But the issue here is less the quantitative than the qualitative dimensions of Burr's communication. Consider one of Burr's most famous utterances: his February 1802 toast, "To the Union of All Honest Men." We could explore the context of Burr's statement—the toast was given at a Federalist celebration of Washington's birthday; Burr supposedly came to the dinner late and gave a perfunctory toast; Federalists may have seen it as a commentary on the debates of the Judiciary Act repeal; and so on. Such details attempt to locate the meaning of the toast, which in fact remained obscure until, apparently, James Cheetham made it an anti-Burrite catchphrase months later—thereafter the phrase is linked with Burr through 1803 and 1804.[24] This innocuous phrase (sometimes abridged to "The Union of Honest Men") is evocative not because of its historical context but, conversely, because of its intratextual potential—the echoes in Cicero's *Philippics* ("homines honesti") or the speech in Shakespeare's *Julius Caesar*, for example. But the favored intratextual reference, promoted by Cheetham, was Paul's statement, "I am made all things to all men" (1 Cor. 9:22). Here the issue is not context but a broader interpretive maneuver, whereby a bland phrase becomes an ironic heuristic for any accusation against Burr. He becomes all things to all men, at least to those who are obsessed with him.

The three elements of Burr's construction that we have just identified—the uneasy insertion of Burr into an oscillating symbolic logic, the insistence on Burr's formal position absent semiotic content, and the assertion of a radically capacious hermeneutic—could each be identified with any number of political (or otherwise) characters of the moment. What is remarkable is the coincidence of these three components around the figure of Burr, such that he comes to loom large in a formal position of tremendous significance yet with almost no content. When Gordon Wood begins his sketch of Burr, noting that he "is not normally considered one of the founders of the nation. Yet he was an important revolutionary. . . . His relation to the founders, however, is really one of contrast,"[25] he is offering less an insight into the historical figure than registering, from a distance, these dimensions of Burr's formation from 1800 to 1804. Perhaps the most succinct assessment of what Burr is comes in this February 14, 1804, squib in the *American Citizen*, titled "Multitudes Crying Out for Aaron Burr as Their Next Governor":

Doctor! Doctor! help, help!—the people want your *bolusses*, your *panacea's* and your remedies—The Multitude want your skill—they are sorely afflicted, with an itching for Col. Burr—and you have a sovereign remedy that will cure half a million a minute—I will vouch for your pills being genuine, and that one box will cure all the infected—Your skill is more famous than the man, who advertises that secrecy and honor may be depended on, on moderate *terms!*—And as this famous empiric is famous for curing the —, I think you may fairly be put in competition with him as the curer of the *Burr-itch*.

The physician referenced here ran regular advertisements in the paper under the heading "Secret Diseases and Seminal Debilities," which promised "the management, and speedy cure of every symptom of Venereal infection, whether recent or of long standing, together, with those deranged affections which so frequently torment the patient with extreme anxiety, and are generally the consequence of specifics or other medicines improperly administered by ignorant pretenders."[26] The author of the first piece was likely inspired in this interpretive play by the doctor's name—"Burrel"—but in any event offered an incisive reading of Burr as a venereal itch in both senses of the word: as the metaphor quickly falls apart, Burr emerges as both the itch caused by venereal disease and also the itch of desire leading to the disease. Surely the sense of Burr that emerges here, in part because of the "seminal debilities" involved in defining the itch, is that of the object of "deranged affections" that "torment[ed]" contemporaries with "extreme anxiety" fostered by inadequate medicines—such as Cheetham's pages, which in seeking to scratch the itch made it tingle ever more sharply.

We have said that a fourth tendency began to appear in the coalescence of Burr, which might be located in the initially tentative reference to the "sable cloud" in which Burr had "been so long and so conveniently enveloped" (*Nine Letters* 8). But before exploring this facet of the Burr-itch, we return for a moment to the other important characterological drama of the era: the constitution of Toussaint L'Ouverture in late 1801.

Toussaint's Constitution

We turn, then, to what in our view was the most disruptive and challenging of the characterological portraits that appeared at this moment—that of Toussaint L'Ouverture, intimately linked with a narrative of Saint-Domingue's 1801 constitution. In the summer of 1801, Toussaint had promulgated a constitution signaling the quasi-independence of the island. A series of texts describing that constitution in relation to Toussaint proliferated through US newspapers in the second half of 1801, beginning with the first reports that appeared in the *Baltimore American* on August 3. About a week later, this report was reprinted in the national Democratic-Republican standard-bearer, the *National Intelligencer*, as well as the chief Federalist organ, the *Gazette of the United States*. Months thereafter, variants of this report appeared in at least twenty-four newspapers from Virginia, Maryland, and the District of Columbia, northward to Philadelphia, New Jersey, New York, Connecticut, Massachusetts, and New Hampshire, even into Vermont and the district of Maine. At least seven papers in Connecticut reported the 1801 constitution, with at least fourteen in Massachusetts, four in New Hampshire, two in Maine, one in Rhode Island, four in Vermont, two in New Jersey, nine in New York, and five in Pennsylvania. In the South, the reports appeared in at least three papers in the District, two in Maryland, one in Virginia, and three in South Carolina.[27]

What were the texts in question? We do not isolate just the text of the 1801 constitution itself, as it typically appeared as one component within a textual constellation of as many as four texts. The first of these reports was on events of April 6, 1801 (17th Germinal in the French Revolutionary calendar), when Toussaint ordered the preparation of a new form of government. In this text, of just under 800 words, Toussaint appoints a committee of eight deputies—two each from the four departments—and orders it to prepare "a constitution suited to [the] climate, soil, culture, trade, and to the manners" of the inhabitants of the "Island of St. Domingo."[28] The second text, just under 4,000 words, is a full translation of the constitution itself.[29] The third text, just over 3,500 words and sometimes appearing in two installments, describes the formal acceptance and promulgation of the constitution on July 7, 1801 (19th Messidor). This textual sequence begins with Toussaint's arrival at Cape-François and his formal reception; a speech (of about 1,100 words) by the president of the central assembly, Citizen Borgella; an answer from Toussaint (of about 650 words) accepting the constitution and calling on the citizens of the island to honor the new system; a concluding speech again by Borgella (just over 1,000 words); and a quick summary of the closing ceremonies. Finally, a fourth text (of slightly more than 800 words) sometimes appeared proximately to these other texts: the "Character of the Celebrated Black General, *Toussaint L'Ouverture*." These components, taken together, produce a fascinating and multifaceted cluster.

Let us begin with the constitution itself. One should first note that it contains some of the organizational features of the US Constitution and would therefore have been readily identifiable as belonging to the same "family" of texts. Titles 7 through 9 outline Saint-Domingue's legislative, executive, and judicial branches, albeit with important distinctions. Most notably, power is concentrated in the executive branch—here forcefully equated with the "Government" itself—and, at the moment of the constitution's enactment, the supreme executive, "the Governor," is Toussaint. Indeed, not only is Toussaint named in the constitution six times, but his "firmness, activity, indefatigable zeal, and . . . rare virtues" earn him the office until "the melancholy event of his decease," at which point his successor will have been named by Toussaint himself.[30] As for the governor's powers, he oversees the military (§ 34); "proposes laws," even those that change the constitution (§ 36); "promulgates" them (§ 34); and "exacts the observation" of all laws, contracts, and obligations (§ 35). In these points, the constitution codifies its own creation: it exists because it has been called forth and then promulgated by Toussaint. Toussaint is furthermore granted the duties and powers of overseeing finances (§ 38), monitoring and censoring "all writings designed for the press" (§ 39), and suppressing any "conspiracy" against the state (§ 40). With this tremendous, individual concentration of power, the responsibilities of the legislature and the tribunals are definitively subordinated to the governor. The assembly, for instance, "votes the adoption or the rejection of laws which are proposed by the Governor" (§ 24). They are further granted the power of providing opinions on existing laws (§ 24) and of managing the details of the national budget (§ 26). Tribunals shall exist in three tiers (§§ 44–45), but "special tribunals" organized by the governor shall oversee all military infractions, as well as "all robberies and thefts," and also "house-breaking," "assassinations, murders, incendiaries, rapes, conspiracies and rebellions" (§ 47). Furthermore, Titles 10 through 12 extend the power of the governor over local or "municipal" government, the armed forces, and the basic financial matters of the island. Toussaint is granted the authority to nominate all "members of the municipal administration" (§ 49), to control with total authority the armed forces (§ 52), and to appoint a commission of three to "regulate and examine accounts of the receipts and expences of the colony" (§ 62).

The hegemonic hermeneutic of the US Constitution leads many modern readers to interpret Toussaint's constitution cynically. The US text implied a series of beliefs about politics and human nature, laboriously expounded in accounts of Florentine political thought, early modern British history, and the principles of the Scottish Enlightenment, as per the usual exercises of modern intellectual history. Whereas the US Constitution, therefore, enacted theories of collective power and private property, the 1801 Saint-Domingue text concentrates power in the hands of an autocrat, and, read through this same US hermeneutic, seems a power grab of the highest order. It would be more productive, though, to see Toussaint's governmental apparatus enacting a different hermeneutic, one based not on political principles inflected by theories of human nature and commerce but on a particular local history and a state of society that might be called slave-ethnographic. Indeed, this latter foundation becomes clear when we consider the stunning departures of the 1801 text from that of 1787. For Toussaint's constitution's opening segments detail Saint-Domingue's territorial extent (Title 1), its "Inhabitants" (Title 2), its religion and morals (Titles 3 and 4), "Men in Society" (Title 5), and its "Agriculture and Commerce" (Title 6). As even these headings indicate, it would have been difficult not to see the parallels between the 1801 constitution and the older colonial genre of the ethnographic "true relation," which structured its analyses of the indigenous other within a similar progression from region and demographics to morality and religion and then to economy. The insertion of these elements—associated in the turn-of-the-century US with nonwhite peoples—demonstrated a competing hermeneutic with an unusually radical defamiliarizing potential: constitution = ethnography.

More importantly, this ethnographic strand was aggressively accentuated by its association with the slave code. The latter, from the memorable moment of the Barbados Code of 1661, demonstrated a transmutation of ethnographic genres, taking a descriptive analytic frequently tooled to penetration and mastery (the "true report" of Native Americans) and rendering it a supervisory code for better management and domination. This may be the most remarkable aspect of the 1801 constitution, which can be read as a revolutionary, emancipatory answer to the French *Code Noir*, accepting its strictures and structures to emphasize its repudiation. Article 2 of Louis XIV's well-known 1685 code enjoined, "All slaves that shall be in our islands shall be baptized and instructed in the Roman, Catholic, and Apostolic Faith," while subsequent articles outlined the rules for marriage, bastardy, and ownership. Article 6 of the 1801 text echoes its predecessor—"The Catholic, Apostolic, and Roman religion, is the only one publicly professed"—while subsequent articles elevate marriage, ban divorce, and declare the need to address illegitimate children. This is nothing less than the slave code rewritten for ex-slaves—an antislavery code in which abolition is emphatically announced at the outset. Section 3 declares, "Slaves are not permitted in this territory; servitude is forever abolished—All men born here, live and die freemen and Frenchmen." As abstract as this principle is, the overall context of the document shows that this revolutionary assertion must be understood as a moral and practical resistance to a specific counterpart to the North, so uneasy with historical and sociological details as to veil these realities with such euphemisms as "Persons as any of the States now existing shall think proper to admit" through "Importation" (Article 1, § 9) or the "Person held to Service or Labour in one State . . . escaping into another" (Article 4, § 2). From this perspective, the details of Title 8, "General dispositions," display not odd particularities inappropriate to (Anglo-American) political theory but a particular historical consciousness that wants to reward innovations in agricultural technology (§ 70), punish the arbitrary seizure of persons (§ 65), and monitor local "associations inimical to public order" (§ 67). When Section 76 proclaims that "every citizen owes his services to the country that has given him birth, and to the soil that nourishes him, to the maintenance of liberty, and the equal divisions of property, whenever the law calls him to defend them," it is also insisting that allegiance and service to the state have a very particular meaning at a crucial point in the Revolution. This is a constitution assuming crisis, not stasis. We will return later to the jarring revelation that the 1801 constitution offers in its combination of constitution and slave-ethnography but must turn now to the element with which we introduced this remarkable textual cluster: the characterological romance in the portrait of Toussaint himself.

The simplest narrative of "Toussaint's Constitution" is that of the constitutional ceremonies, summarized earlier and quoted here from the *Commercial Advertiser*: Toussaint greets the eight members of the assembly (seven of whom were white, one "mulatto," and all former slave owners); he demands that they draft a constitution, "consult[ing] past events to avoid their repetition"; he warns them against "publish[ing] any of the legislative acts [they] may think proper to make" before receiving Toussaint's approval. After the constitution has been drafted, Citizen Bernard Borgella, head of the assembly, greets Toussaint in a public ceremony of tremendous pomp and circumstance. Borgella delivers two long speeches, Toussaint one, somewhat shorter. These declamations offer a situational explanation of the new constitution, summarizing details of colonial history, the revolution in France (including Bonaparte's return to France

from Egypt), the difficult relations between the two realms, and the struggle for order in the island. It is clear that the concern, in these speeches,
is the legitimation of the constitutional enterprise itself, since, despite
all assertions of fidelity to France, the "unfortunate colony" has suffered
from the "perverse influence" of "the Metropolis." This more broadly
colonial narrative confirms and reinforces the ethnographic elements
of the constitution summarized earlier. For a major problem of governance heretofore was the old French constitution, in which a "multiplicity
of wheelworks" had "run afoul of each other, . . . giv[ing] rise to popular cabals, diversity of opinion, and public Calamities." In short, it was
the mechanical differentiation of structures that had provoked first "the
Spirit of Party," as devious politicians had known how to "interpret [laws]
according to their interests"; conflict, anarchy, and disorder had followed.
These catastrophes had been averted by the actions of Toussaint, who,
at every moment of seemingly terminal chaos, had risen "like a phoe-
nix from the ashes." He had "take[n] charge of the rein of an abandoned
colony," suppressing unrest, unifying the regions, and even "conquer[ing]
inveterate prejudices," replacing them with "the most tender fraternity."
The new constitution would enact, in writing, the heroic achievements of
Toussaint himself, specifically addressing the demands of the immediate
colonial situation:

> [Toussaint] announces to you that the time of convulsions is past; he dem-
> onstrates the necessity of giving you laws of convenience; and adopting this
> constant maxim, that laws are conventions established by men, to conform
> themselves to, for the regulation of the order of society. He makes you con-
> ceive that it is with them as it is with the production of the earth, that every
> country has its manners, its statutes, as well as its appropriate fruits.

Inspired by and modeled on Toussaint, this new text thus answered those
"circumstances which present themselves but once during a long series of
ages, to fix the destiny of mankind"—*not* to embody timeless principles,
as the US Constitution might have it. Finally, the Messidor speeches made
clear the pressing demands of the near future: the need for new planters,
unification of the island, property regulation, and reestablishment of the
plantation system.

Thus, the texts of convocation and promulgation had both told the
story of the constitution as a kind of textual analogue or extension of
Toussaint: he had requested, assessed, endorsed, and proclaimed it and

was now beginning to enact, perform, and embody it; his actions were demanded and affirmed within it; its internal logic and propositions reflected those of his behavior in resisting French interference. He was even cast as the local counterpart to the "re-edifying genius" of Bonaparte, who had restored order and unity to France. It is not surprising, then, that these texts were at times accompanied by the "Character of the Celebrated Black General *Toussaint L'Ouverture*," which described the "extraordinary man" in terms of his intelligence, achievements, gratitude, and humanity, but above all his practicality. It mentions his (apocryphal) education in France, his rise to military leadership, and his attempts to restore economic order. The culminating anecdote, however, concerns the appeal of the British general Thomas Maitland, who requested the favor of the restoration of twelve planters to their estates. Upon their return, Toussaint "clapped them in prison" but within days had them brought to a church in which he preached a sermon of reconciliation:

> "We were for a while Spaniards, (the blacks fled to the Spanish protection, in the beginning of their troubles), but we were missed. We were born Frenchmen, and now we are Frenchmen again. These twelve men have also been missed. They were born Frenchmen. For a time they have been British; but now they have returned, and are Frenchmen again. Let us embrace." Here Toussaint embraced them, and reconciled his followers—He restored them to their estates, and gave them negroes as servants.

At one level, the episode exemplifies a pragmatism consistent with the ethnographic formulation of the other texts and in contrast to which patriotic affiliations are fickle and relatively meaningless. Even as the sketch affirms Toussaint's service to the French republic, it likewise stresses that same republic's incompetence and antagonism toward Toussaint. Insisting that Toussaint is *not* concerned with amassing power for its own sake—he "did not treat as an independent prince as some of the papers have said"—the sketch presents him as the most practical of figures, ultimately concerned with restoring "commerce and prosperity." Thus, the character sketch simultaneously emphasizes Toussaint's self-effacing qualities and his heroic actions, such that he becomes the paradigmatic republican.[31]

What did the Toussaint texts mean in the US context? Here we want to depart from the usual literary practice of reading discursive strands and how they relate to dominant epistemes—for example, reading the concentration of Toussaint's power as a confirmation of racist US discourses about the power-hungry and violent nature of black slaves, who simply want to reverse the master-slave relationship. Undoubtedly this kind of reading is true in some way, but we want to insist that the cluster of texts surrounding Toussaint's constitution had a deeper and more traumatic impact—one that the drama of Aaron Burr was to play out.

We may begin with the remarkable conjunction and collapse of discrete discourses, the melding of political-constitutional and ethnographic discourses. That these two discourses are related is indisputable. The influential 1688 Barbados Slave Code, for instance, opens with a clause admitting that it is a constitution for slaves:

> And forasmuch as the said Negroes and other Slaves brought unto the People of this Island for that Purpose, are of Barbarous, Wild, and Savage Natures, and such as renders them wholly unqualified to be governed by the Laws, Customs, and Practices of our Nations: It therefore becoming absolutely necessary, that such *other Constitutions, Laws, and Orders* should be in this Island framed and enacted for the good Regulating and Ordering of them, as may both restrain the Disorders, Rapines, and Inhumanities to which they are naturally prone and inclined, with such Encouragements and Allowances as are fit and needful to their Support . . . (emphasis added)[32]

In US culture, however, the insistence on the distinction and separation of these genres has obviously been central. The euphemistic veiling of constitutional references to slavery must be understood as more than a dishonest or hypocritical gesture, but as rather a prophylactic barrier between two different legal discourses: the constitution (or charter), written to delineate the parameters of white subjectivity and the mechanical workings of white institutions, and the ethnography, written to describe the depths and complexities of nonwhite cultures. The separation of these discourses becomes clear with a few thought experiments. Imagine an ethnography beginning with an abstract assertion of identity ("All Shawnees are created equal, and endowed by their creators with certain inalienable rights, among these . . .") or a colonial charter venturing into cultural details ("The wanderings and meetings of the people of Connecticut, more especially on Saturday nights, and their using and carrying of rifles, or using and keeping of fiddles or other loud instruments . . ."). As we have said, the most radical formal gesture of Toussaint's Constitution was to collapse the symbolic divide between these two modes of thinking.

What is more, both of these genres, in the US context, were essentially analytic in tendency. The Constitution assumed and reasserted clear and distinct functions—most famously the "three branches of government" held in perpetual balance—such that the Constitution was treated as a work of art.[33] The ethnography, likewise, was a genre of the clear mapping of cultural traits and classes, its divisions formally anticipating already nascent disciplines of aesthetics, economics, political science, and the like. The conflation of these two discourses, however, had the effect of rendering the 1801 Constitution less analytic than synthetic. It did this in two ways. First, the narrative of a state of emergency, of degenerate French political meddling, but more importantly of the constant social war that slavery entailed, revealed the constitution to be situational, rather than timeless like a work of great art. As important, however, was the centrality of the figure of Toussaint. As the protagonist of the constitution's situational-military narrative—he is the "General-in-chief," a title used no less than ten times—Toussaint must constantly act to integrate ethnographic details within a political framework in the very creation of Saint-Domingue—hence the profound integration of Toussaint into the constitution, as the political-theoretical mode suddenly shifts to include a proper name: the six references to Toussaint; the story of the constitution being demanded, assessed, and promulgated by Toussaint; the packaging of the constitution with the character sketch. One more thought experiment might clarify this effect: imagine the first clause of Article II of the US Constitution reading, "The executive Power shall be vested in a President of the United States of America, commencing with General Washington, whose firmness, activity, indefatigable zeal, and rare virtues will continue to guarantee our tranquility until the melancholy event of his decease." We must be clear here: we are not arguing that the 1801 Constitution was so generically divergent as to defy comprehension. Such an argument belongs to a trend in considerations of the Haitian Revolution, in which the event is viewed as "incomprehensible," beyond the ability of people in the US to grasp. But the 1801 Constitution was *not* a text that was unreadable—rather, it was because it was so readable that it fundamentally destabilized the political understanding of US whites. The United States was fundamentally a "slave nation," a point not only increasingly understood by contemporary historians but one made with increasing explicitness and eventually urgency in the literature of abolition.[34] This realization was increasingly admitted in the aftermath of 1800, for example, in the Federalist designation of Jefferson as the "Negro

President," in the dawning sense of the impact of the Louisiana Purchase, in the 1806–7 consideration of the constitutionally mandated abolition of the slave trade, in William Jenks's 1808 counterfactual dystopia of the United States broken into northern and southern kingdoms. Consequently, Toussaint's Constitution offered what was essentially an alternative history of the United States, a momentary collapse of the parallactic separation of the slavery system and the political apparatus, as if two analytics that were not supposed to touch each other briefly made contact. A similar short-circuiting occurred within the semiotics of the Founding Fathers. As we have suggested, the Founders constellation functioned both orthopedically (to guide and structure perception) and prophylactically (to prevent certain insights). If the racial dimensions of the Founders were always implicit, by the late 1790s they were increasingly explicit. The attempt to symbolically register Toussaint proved another moment of short-circuiting, not simply because Toussaint disrupted the Founders' codification—for example, revising Washington's passive doing as active revolution—but simply by virtue of inserting a black man, a former slave, an antislavery revolutionary, into that system.

Certainly the US newspapers aggressively attempted to process Toussaint, and it was not at all uncommon to find the "Character of the Celebrated Black General" alongside Federalist attacks on Jefferson and Paine or hagiographic celebrations of Washington.[35] The August 4, 1801, *Independent Gazetteer* of Worcester, Massachusetts, included the Toussaint portrait with a defense of Washington and Adams (singling out the Alien and Sedition Acts for special praise) and attacks on the hypocrisy of "Jacobins, democrats, whigs, and other mock republicans."[36] William Duane's *Aurora General Advertiser*, the leading Republican paper, went as far as offering an editorial response to the Toussaint texts, beginning with a seemingly principled objection to its antirepublican articles but ending with a race-conscious warning to southern compatriots. "We are among those who deny the competency and question the legality of the authorities assumed by the extravagant organization which has lately been set up in St. Domingo," argued Duane. "In the new system of what is called a constitution, we see nothing to respect, nothing to admire, and much to excite abhorrence and disgust." The constitution was "a spurious mimicry" of its French antecedent, "a new made monster, . . . a despotism of the worst kind, formed in the worst manner, conceived in treachery and masked by hypocrisy." Furthermore, the constitution stands as "a bitter and malignant satire on free government."[37] This revealing insight—that the constitution functioned as a satirical critique of the US text—found an odd complement in the opposition's paper, specifically the August 13 *Gazette of the United States* (Philadelphia). Alongside the promulgation text from Saint-Domingue, the following piece was presented, complete with editorial introduction:

{The following outlines of a Constitution, framed after the model of modern systems of government, are extracted from a work lately published and entitled, *"My Uncle Thomas": a Romance. From the French of Pegault Lebrun.* It will be observed that *My Uncle Thomas* is to *make* the Constitution, and then the people are to *obey* it. This is doubtless the natural and necessary result of persuading the people at large that they are able to govern themselves, and of flattering them with titles of sovereignty till they have wearied themselves out with their own commotions and are glad to gain tranquility by a quiet submission to the constitution of an *Uncle Thomas*, an Uncle *Buonaparte*, an Uncle *Gallatin*, or any body else who will be at the trouble of taking the burthen off their own shoulders. The basis of this excellent Constitution is: *"We are all free and equal*—but you shall obey me; because—I will have it so"*}
   * That is, "all Republicans, all Federalists."[38]

EXTRACT

"You Uncle! You make a Constitution!

"S'death, why not as well as another?

"I fear it will not answer.

"Well, then, I will make a second.

"Which will be no better.

"Then I will try a third.

"Which will not last longer than the other.

After meditating *two hours* he produced the following:

Rights of Man—"Every man has a right to live in plenty, and without doing any thing for his livelihood.

Of the Government—"General *Thomas* having been proclaimed Grand Regulator, shall regulate and misregulate just as he pleases.

Civil and Criminal Code—"As the only difference among men consists in one wanting what another possesses, no man shall have any exclusive possessions of his own.

"As Magistrates are useless where there are no disputes, there shall be no Magistrates among us.

"As there can be no occasion for prisoners, or gaolers, or attornies, or hangmen, where there are no Magistrates, there shall be neither hangmen, attornies, gaoler or prisoner.

"We have thus got rid, in a moment, of what has embarrassed the whole world from the earliest period.

The same humorous writer observes,

"Vanity and self-love transform us into strange creatures. There is no man, however low his condition, but thinks himself superior to every one else. I have no doubt but my shoe-black would accept the office of first Consul. All I hope is that it will not be offered to him."

Can Americans *rationally* hope so of their shoe-blacks?

The source for this satire was Pigault-Lebrun's 1795 comic romance *Mon Oncle Thomas* (which incidentally included a long segment about the expansion of slavery), but we see the text here retooled in such a way that the critique of Jefferson gains force from the racially charged Toussaint texts, even to the ambiguous reference to the "shoe-blacks"—a seeming commentary on the ex-slave-turned-general. The power of this juxtaposition is all the more apparent when we consider the odd politics of the satire. For if the Federalist newspaper presented the Toussaint texts in essentially positive terms, its attack on "Uncle Thomas" Jefferson activated their dangerous elements as well as their racially charged language. That is, when the allusion to Jefferson inspired another layer of satire, the latent dangers of the Saint-Domingue pieces became explicit.

We are not suggesting that Toussaint somehow defied symbolic registration—the contemporary pairing, in Caribbean studies, of Toussaint and Jean-Jacques Dessalines as generative complements shows the ease with which he has been encoded. Rather, for white readers in the US, he could not be assimilated into a clear position, and he emerged in late 1801 as a disruption—in the sphere of racial politics—of the semiotic field that simmered in the background. Most disturbing in these short-circuits was the emergence of a variant of the already popular story of the origin of politics. Thomas Paine presented several versions of this tale, the best known of these in *Common Sense*, where he cast off "the dark covering of antiquity"

to imagine that primal moment in which the first king, "the principal ruffian of some restless gang," concentrated his power and "overawed the quiet
and defenceless."[39] The tales of the US founding were specifically inoculated
from this narrative through stories either of reluctant defensive action (the
Founders, the Declaration) or of mechanical destiny (the Constitution). But
the Toussaint story recast the temporal and historical referents of Paine's
story to imagine a revolution in which slavery was thrown off and a new
power and morality proclaimed. Thus, the Toussaint texts presented nothing less than an alternative account of politics in which supreme power—
Toussaint's dominance of Saint-Domingue—inaugurated a new morality
that solved the constitutive sin of the United States. Such a gesture is beautifully captured in the tale of Toussaint's arrest and then pardon of the
twelve planters—because of his power, he represented the capacity for evil
(the murder of whites) but then demonstrated the supreme ethical gesture,
embodying morality within the church itself. Transposed into the US context, we hear echoes of Jefferson's inevitable race war (in *Notes on the State
of Virginia*) assuaged with a fantasy of a restrained and restraining black
leader, one who offers absolution through familiar Christological remedies.

Thus, the rise of Dessalines after Toussaint's expatriation catalyzed, for
white US observers, an apocalyptic vocabulary, the sword replacing the
martyred son. After Napoleon disgraces himself by violating the promise
of pardon, having Toussaint arrested for conspiracy and sent to prison in
the Jura Mountains, rumors circulate *"that he was murdered in his prison."*[40]
Blacks then celebrate the (yellow fever) plague that hits the French army and
rekindles their insurrection. The end of the world seems nigh:

> A long war succeeded, marked by more atrocities than any which has
> occurred in modern times. The French, bent on the extermination of the
> blacks, invented new methods for their destruction. Thousands of them
> were thrown into the sea, or many were suffocated with the fumes of burn-
> ing brimstone, and the most ingenious tortures were practised upon them.
> The blacks, in retaliation, put to death all the whites who fell into their
> hands, but it does not appear that they tortured their prisoners as their
> enemies had done.

Though this anonymous chronicler has clearly chosen sides, he could
not yet foretell the end; the "fate of that island was quite doubtful in
the end of the year 1802." Even Haiti's declaration of independence in
January 1804, and Dessalines's crowning himself emperor at the end

of the summer, left a gap once occupied by Toussaint. When the press covered Dessalines, it was solely to reprint his vengeful proclamations. As if turning the clock back to 1798, prior to the stabilizing reign of L'Ouverture, Dessalines gave the Jefferson administration the excuse to revisit the trade policy that had been friendly to quasi-independent Saint-Domingue. The tenor of the debate the ensuing winter was almost unanimously negative. Senator James Jackson took the floor to call for "the self created emperor of Haiti [to be] subdued," and his colleague William Eppes was ready "to *pledge the Treasure of the United States,* that the Negro government should be destroyed."[41] All trade with the new black republic was halted indefinitely in December 1805. The Toussaint Moment, then, was distinctive not because Toussaint was inassimilable, alien, or hostile but because he was always *also* the opposite—readable, familiar, a peacemaker. His alternating current is what proved too much for the semiotic network.

Burr in the Breach

As Reconstruction came to an end, Henry Adams immersed himself in the state papers of the Jefferson and Madison administrations as he prepared a series of histories: *Documents Relating to New England Federalism* (1877), *The Life of Albert Gallatin* and *The Writings of Albert Gallatin* (1879), a biography of John Randolph (1882), and the massive histories of the Jefferson and Madison administrations (1889–91). In 1880, he wrote to Henry Cabot Lodge (who was at work on a biography of Alexander Hamilton and who later compiled an edition of Hamilton's papers), "My material is enormous, and I now fear that the task of compression will be painful. Burr alone is good for a volume."[42] By 1882, he had written a biography of Burr, but, as he wrote to John Hay, "[Henry] Houghton [of Houghton Mifflin] declines to print Aaron because Aaron wasn't a 'Statesman.' Not bad, that, for a damned bookseller! He should live awhile at Washington and know our *real* statesmen."[43] But within a few years, Adams had destroyed his sketch of Burr, and it is unclear what that sketch might have looked like. But there is an intriguing hint in a letter to John T. Morse, the editor of Scribner's American Statesmen series: "If I find Randolph easy," he writes, referring to his sketch of the Virginia congressman, "I don't know but what I will volunteer for Burr. Randolph is the type of a political charlatan who had something in him. Burr is the type of a political charlatan pure and simple, a very Jim Crow of melodramatic wind-bags. I have something to say of both varieties."[44]

Two things are noteworthy here: first, Adams offers something like a parallactic assessment of his own historiographic work (separating works of substance—"*real*" statesmen with "something" in them—from the more phantasmatic "wind-bags"); but second, Adams finds in Burr a fundamentally racialized figure. The Jim Crow figure did not coalesce until the 1830s,[45] and it is not clear if Adams was familiar with the details of the antebellum reference, but the first sheet version of the "Jim Crow" song included these verses:

> I'm a full blooded niggar,
> Ob de real ole stock,
> And wid my head and shoulder
> I can split a horse block.
>
> De great Nullification,
> And fuss in de South,
> Is now before Congress,
> To be tried by word ob mouth.
>
> Dey hab had no blows yet,
> And I hope dey nebber will,
> For its berry cruel in bredren,
> One anoders blood to spill.
>
> Should dey get to fighting,
> Perhaps de blacks will rise,
> For deir wish for freedom,
> Is shining in deir eyes.
>
> An if de blacks should get free,
> I guess dey'll fee some bigger,
> An I shall consider it,
> A bold stroke for de nigger.
>
> An I caution all white dandies,
> Not to come in my way,
> For if dey insult me,
> Dey'll in de gutter lay.[46]

This narrative—of white politics catalyzing black insurrection, of the disintegration of the Union through nullification, of the comic black man suddenly, seriously, laying out his white counterparts—is, we believe, the heart of the Burr story. For while the radically disruptive figure of Toussaint seemed to recede in the years after the Constitution (he was arrested and taken to France in 1802, dying in 1803), the traumatic significance of Toussaint migrated and metastasized in the figure of Aaron Burr.

We mentioned earlier the first hint of this phenomenon in Cheetham's assault on Burr—the reference to the "sable cloud" surrounding Burr. But the racialization became clearer only in 1804, as Burr, excommunicated from the Democratic-Republicans, attempted a run for the New York governorship against Morgan Lewis. The *American Citizen* and other Republican newspapers ran multiple anti-Burr pieces daily, many rehearsing old charges in the strangely empty fashion we have outlined earlier. But as Burr's political career came to an end, the semiotic construction of Burr began to mutate as he shifted decisively into the realm of fantasy. In one poem titled "Another Meeting!!" published April 11, 1804, Burr fortifies his political campaign with the help of black slaves. The poem is in the form of a dialogue. Two slaves, Pompey and Sambo, debate who to support in the upcoming election. Pompey will support the Clintons' candidate Morgan Lewis, but Sambo has other plans. He will "vote for Burr." Why? Because Burr and his "little band" will empower the blacks and topple the white establishment: he "to crush dem wakes de 'little band.'" Sambo does not mind that Burr has accepted the Federalists' support, because he is of the "Old School" or, like Burr, a revolutionary.[47] With Burr, the blacks will rise up in rebellion.

Prior to the election, Burr's critics blackened him by association. An active campaigner with a host of supporters canvassing neighborhoods, Burr had demeaned his honor, even stooping to court blacks. But it is after the campaign and his political defeat that Burr *becomes* black. The starkest example of this is a brief story that appeared in the April 28, 1804, *American Citizen*, immediately after the election:

On Monday evening last, the day preceding the commencement of the election, Mr. Burr had assembled at this house, by special invitation, a considerable number of *gentlemen of colour* —upwards of twenty. These gentlemen were headed by a celebrated perfumer in Broadway. They were invited by Mr. Burr to a ball and supper, *in his own house*, and the federal candidate, the *rejected* Vice-President, did himself the honor of superintending their *elegant amusements*. This, as the reader will perceive, was to court the favour of the people of colour in aid of his election.

This explanation itself followed a poem that deserves to be quoted in full:

> *Alba Ligustra cadunt dum nigra varcinia stent,*[48]
> OR, AARON'S LAST SHIFT.

> When Marshal John return'd to town,
> And Lanky from Long-Island came,
> On Aaron's brow a rueful frown,
> Portending he had lost the game
>   In sad despondence sat.

> Quoth he my valiant Marshal John,
> And thou my Lanky wily wight,
> Unless we rouse each mother's son
> Of visage dark as sable night,
>   Lewis will lay us flat.

> Alexis swarthy pander true,
> Tho' late discharg'd and in disgrace,
> To save his sinking master flew,
> And thus with sympathetic face,
>   Bespoke the chap-fall'n Chief.

> Have I not ever faithful been,
> Your pimp expert for many years?
> Have I not very often seen
> Your bosom wreck'd with doubts and fears,
>   And brought you sure relief?

> I pledge myself ere morrow's dawn,
> Each sombre son of Afric's plain,
> From cellar dark and kitchen drawn,
> An host shall form to swell thy train,
>   And make thine 'lection sure.

> But mark me sir, for well I ween,
> Blacks ne'er refuse a little prog,

A supper then in parlour clean,
With plentiful supply of grog,
  Must be the certain lure.

At this advice most ghastly stared
Lanky and John with visage pale,
For if pursued, 'tis said, they feared
Lexy's preponderance in the scale
  Would make their's kick the beam.

They therefore urged it would not do,
And offered many a reason,
That blacks were faithless, never true,
Fond of deceit, of basest treason,
  Of gliding with the stream.

The little Chief mused for a while,
When thus elate he silence broke;
I love the blacks, they know no guile,
Lexy, my boy, you well have spoke,
  You've counseled wise I ken.

The motley crew this night shall meet,
We'll triumph with such aid I think;
Call them from every lane and street,
I'll take the chair, and we will drink,
  Union of honest men.

Alexis was Burr's personal servant, here depicted as a swarthy pimp. He counsels his chief to throw a party to gather the city's blacks and appeal for their aid on election day. Despite his white companion's misgivings, Burr agrees. Lanky and John, for their part, worry whether they will be outmanned by Alexis and his compatriots, while Burr embraces the blacks. He will organize them with sex and booze to create a "motley crew" and in "triumph . . . take the chair." The famous toast to a "union of honest men" is redirected from the Federalists, to whom it was originally offered, to the blacks, who "know no guile." One can read this conclusion in two ways: either Burr is the gull of the blacks' duplicity, or he is a sinister conspirator whose manliness cannot be questioned. This split persona—the drunken clown with his band of fools *and* the evil manipulator—takes us back, once more, to *Ormond* and Brown's insight that the black servant could shuffle his feet as the ignorant fool while also witnessing everything, planning his next move, and waiting for the moment to strike. Thus, the plantation slave may one moment have been docile and tractable but the next join with maroon rebels to destroy the plantation both from without and within.

To this conspiratorial image of Burr and the blacks, other allusions to Haiti were added. In September 1804, Boston's *Repertory* published a short piece titled "THE MODERN CAIN" reporting rumors that Burr was on the lam in "Spanish America." The overdetermined reference to Cain— the figure of agriculture killing the urban, Hamiltonian Abel but also the marked figure of servitude—was juxtaposed to an analysis, on the same page, of Jefferson's 1800 victory over Adams: "Mr Adams was excluded from the chair and Mr. Jefferson placed in it, by the weight of the *Constitutional black votes.*"[49] Explicit reference to Burr and plantation slavery appeared a year later in a series called "The Commoners" published in the *American Citizen.*[50] In this analogic history of New York, George (Clinton) is chosen to be the first overseer of the plantation following the American Revolution. Though a successful overseer, Old George experiences trials. He finds that the seed for his fields has been corrupted with *"Living-tares"* (the Livingstons), which he fights with moderate success by lopping off their heads and "burning them over." Here we see a conflation of New York political culture, the Jacobin terror, and the American South, but new challenges arise once Old George is chosen by the "chief of the great household," Thomas (Jefferson), to be Second Captain. Then "another pestiferous weed, of the *Burr* kind, had by some means made its way into the plantation." This Burr weed is "sweet to the taste, though it was very poisonous to the constitution." It was intoxicating "when drank in form of a *decoction.*" The drinkers are described in their "mad fits" demanding a new overseer, who would "cherish and cultivate the growth of their favorite weed." Producing a frenzied and delirious mass, the Burr weed spreads as a "sort of contagion, creating great thirst, and a hunger which could not be satiated, but by devouring large quantities of the good grain, which was stored away and reserved for the common stock." To interdict the Burr weed, there is talk of burning all the crops and retreating into the woods. The Burr weed is like sugar cane converted to rum; the commoners' appetitive desire and revelry is a cancer to be eradicated. Moreover, the plant sows dissention, dividing the commoners from their overseer, further endangering everyone. The drinkers "were hollowing and spouting, riding on broom stick, throwing dirt in the air, and, frightening the children." They threaten all order, "digging, rooting up, and laying waste to the whole plantation." Paganism, witchcraft, vodou—all reference to the mysterious origins and inspirations of slave rebellion:

> [These Burrites/blacks] grew madder than ever, and began to contrive seriously how to carry their point. They would often meet together at sun-down in the woods and caves, and hold *kintikoys*,[51] where they drank largely of the Burr decoction; stripped themselves star[k] naked, and sung, and fiddled, and capered, and danced, and played the fool all night long. They would mark themselves too in the day time, and dress themselves up like mountebanks, jugglers, and rope dancers. Then they would run along upon the tops of the fences, tumble in the dirt, act pantomimes and make speeches, with many other diverting tricks, to the amusement of the bye-standers. At such times too they had a remarkable fondness for filth, and would lie down in the drains and ditches, and smear and daub themselves all, and throw nasty matter at the travelers.

All these signs are racially coded, but they are also metaphors for semiotic gathering and dispensing, of collecting the shit of culture and throwing it back. We are here no longer in the Toussaint Moment, where the Saint-Dominguen example might be cautiously praised and its leader courted as an ally against Napoleonic France. Instead, this is the Burr of Dessalines, whose famous proclamation was published widely in the US: "Yes, we have rendered to these true cannibals war for war, crime for crime, outrage for outrage; yes, I have saved my country; I have avenged America." As Burr's blackness comes to the fore, so too looms the conspiracy against America.

5

Burr's Deployment, 1804–1807

The debate on the bill to prohibit the importation of slaves was resumed, but seemed to have lost all its interest.
     —Memoirs of John Quincy Adams, January 26, 1807

Mr. Burr and his conspiracy have begun to occupy our attention.
     —John Quincy Adams to John Adams, January 27, 1807

Quid Memoranda

Between 1800 and mid-1804, the symbolic system of the Founders worked to process Aaron Burr, and in its failure to do so, suddenly, overtly racialized Burr, who thereafter became a displacement of the phantasmatic challenges posed by Toussaint L'Ouverture. The ultimate expression of this was the so-called Burr Conspiracy, which occupied the US press from 1805 through its anticlimactic conclusion in 1807. The chaotic components of this conspiracy have been assessed and evaluated by a host of Burrologists determined to find out whether a conspiracy existed and what Burr was actually doing. But, as with the Founders more generally, it is important here not to hastily debunk the fantasy with the facts, for the fantasy is the more illuminating. Biographers and historians have generally concluded that Aaron Burr was interested in political office in the western states or Louisiana and was involved as well in the fairly common enterprise of filibustering—launching a paramilitary invasion of foreign territory for the eventual incorporation of that land into the United States. To this end, his various tours through the West in 1805–6 were networking ventures. The reality thus pales in comparison with the fantasies which, in Burr's case, exhibited the semiotic frenzy, the manic aggregation of anxieties, that Brockden Brown had earlier depicted around the figure of Ormond. For Burr was purportedly leading a conspiracy to separate the western states from the Union; to launch an invasion of and/or seize power within Louisiana; to invade Mexico and become its emperor; to move into the Floridas and work his way into the Caribbean; to march on Washington, DC, and kill the current administration. One of the most acute literary readings of the conspiracy was that of Luther Martin, Burr's defense counsel during his 1807 treason trial: "If I were to name this, I would call it the *Will o' wisp* treason. For though it is said to be here and there and everywhere, *yet it is nowhere*."[1] We may read this assessment as an allusion, and an attempt to return, to the empty formal Burr of 1800–1804, while also acknowledging the intensive layering of semiotic details that had occurred between 1804 and 1806, when Burr emerged as the "Quid Emperor."

On the face of it, the label "Quid" seems to refer to the alliance with, and involvement of, Federalist and Democratic-Republican political figures in the Burr Conspiracy at a moment when party alignments were shifting, when the Federalists began to implode and the Democratic-Republicans fractured.[2] The standard narrative of the era notes the emergence of Quid factions in the various states—the "Old Republicans" led by John Randolph in Virginia, the modern Democratic-Republicans led by McKean in Pennsylvania, the Burrites (later the followers of Lewis Morgan) in New York—as "moderate" Republicans formed alliances with "moderate" Federalists against the Democratic Left. What this narrative obscures is the prominence of Burr in the very concept of the "Tertium Quid," a term of largely eighteenth-century provenance referring to the chemical (or alchemical) "Result of the Mixture of some two Things which form something very different from both."[3] As political epithet, the term was first used by William Duane in reference to partisan splits in New York. In a short piece titled "Tertium Quid!," the *Aurora* referenced Alexander Hamilton's diagnosis of New York politics, in which Burr could obtain "a very respectable majority."[4] By the summer of 1804, Duane was using the term predominantly with reference to the split among Pennsylvania Democrats but often with explicit reference to Burr or tacit reference to the toast made famous by Cheetham, "the union of honest men." Describing the Pennsylvanian "Quid" attack on Michael Lieb, Duane observed the appearance of a third-party newspaper, its editor lured "as Mr. Burr had before *seduced* Mr. Irving to a like purpose."[5] In October, the *Aurora* published an address that essentially provided a genealogy of the Quids, extending back to the Burr faction in New York.[6] In the theory of the *Aurora*, the Quid phenomenon originated with Burr and was mysteriously spreading across state lines. If the term later became a generic label for partisan splits in different states, it nonetheless originated around

Burr, who by 1806 was frequently referred to as "the Quid Emperor"—the anything emperor, the something emperor, the alchemical emperor of the interrogative "why?" "what?" "how?" The term powerfully expresses the uncertain symbolic investment in Burr, who by 1805 emerged as the figure in which the contradictory fantasies of slave agency, resistance, and justice gathered. It was at this point that Burr fully, decisively became the traumatic colonel, the quid or Thing beyond signification, around which so many people uneasily circulated as they played out their fantasies.

Our goal in this final chapter is to make sense of this transformation of the Burr, the Quid, not through a chronological account of this and that event but by moving through the constituent layerings of Burr—the duel, the Chase impeachment trial, the Senate farewell, the Louisiana Purchase, and so on. The sheer complexity of this narrative sequence— which has led many scholars to highlight the most dramatic of moments, the duel—seems at first to demand a carefully linear plot of Burr's rise, tragic error, decline, and resurfacing again as a criminal. Such gestures reveal the deeply literary imperative of historians, who diligently labor to impose order on chaos—what Michel-Rolph Trouillot describes as the selective making of the archive.[7] Such narrativization aims to contain the play of the signifier, its coherence coming at the cost of selectivity. As much as a narrative makes a case for causal relationships, it must exclude details which seem irrelevant to the story being framed; the professional historian aims to reduce productive misprisions in the service of narrative communicability. Yet as a contemporary of the Haitian Revolution understood matters, deploying a literary metaphor, the history of an independent Haiti could someday stand as "a curious chapter in the book of contingency."[8] We see here a paradoxical reversal of terms, with the historiographic striving for the purported clarity of the literary, while the phantasmatic or imaginative mode more comfortably explores contingency and divergence.

Accordingly, our guide to this fluid and contingent period will be William Plumer, Federalist senator from New Hampshire, whose remarkable *Memorandum of Proceedings of the United States Senate, 1803–1807* appears at first glance to be the kind of crude archival raw material that awaits sifting and sorting.[9] Yet we would note, immediately, the recurrent conjunction of Burr and Haiti that runs through his pages. When the Senate came to order on November 7, 1804, Plumer, who the previous March had praised Burr for managing the Senate "with great ease, dignity & propriety" (74–75), wrote of his shame at finding a "murderer . . . preside over the first branch of the National Legislature" (185). The next day, he took up the philosophical distinction between rebellion and revolution, a topic prompted by the debate over arming American merchant ships as they traded between the States and Saint-Domingue. The following January found Plumer chronicling the impeachment trial of Justice Samuel Chase, over which Burr presided as judge. On January 2, 1805, Plumer called Burr's "violent measures" against Chase "very rude and highly reprehensible," meriting "contempt & indignation" (239). But days later, he was writing about the House's consideration of the Saint-Domingue trade, recording on January 5, 1805, that Representative Eppes had said "he would venture to *pledge the Treasury of the United States*, that the Negro government [of Haiti] should be destroyed" (243).[10] Weeks later, in a fundamentally different take on the Chase trial, Plumer noted, "Mr. Burr has certainly, on the whole, done himself, the Senate & the nation honor by the dignified manner in which he has presided over this high & numerous court" (310). He joined a unanimous resolution praising Burr for "the ability talent & impartiality with which he had discharged his official duties," noting that "several [senators] shed tears very plentifully" at the conclusion of Burr's farewell address (313).

We find similar imbrications over a year later, in the winter of 1806–7. In November 1806, Plumer reflected on the New England secession movement, born in the winter of 1803–4 but temporarily suspended after Hamilton's death. He confirmed his previous support for separation of the northern states from the Union and related the details of a dinner with Burr to court his support. Burr equivocated, but a month later, Plumer was noting that an arrest warrant had been issued to detain "persons suspected to be carrying on an expedition unfriendly to the United States" (540). What was Burr doing? Still uncertain about Burr's motives, Plumer wrote that "Burr's lawful business always appears enveloped in mystery" (540). The very next day, Plumer recollected the passage of the law banning commercial intercourse with Saint-Domingue. A dinner on the twenty-seventh with Jefferson sealed the connection. Jefferson wanted to discuss the evidence against Burr but also the failure of his embargo: "He believed supplies were, under English colours, sent from the United States to [Haiti]—& if the law should be continued the supplies would be still furnished in that way" (545). On January 17, 1807, Plumer sifted more evidence of Burr's guilt, including the purported plan to seize New Orleans. Four days later, he revised his record of January 18, having neglected to mention that he had reviewed secret papers from the Virginia legislature "upon the subject of procuring some place to which they could send such negroes as should become dangerous" (580–81). The Virginians, alarmed by Saint-Domingue, had suggested an answer: Louisiana.

Plumer had begun his *Memorandum* on October 17, 1803, the first day of the new congressional session, and over the next years, he recounted the major episodes of Burr's drama: the departure to New York and the gubernatorial run; the duel and its aftermath; the return to the Senate to preside over Chase's impeachment trial; the Farewell Address; and the first reports of the western conspiracy. His notes conclude with an account of a conversation with Jefferson (March 4, 1807) in which the president speculated that Burr would ultimately be acquitted of treason and weighed whether the trial ought to be held in John Marshall's court in Virginia. But the *Memorandum* was not a history of Burr but rather a chronicle of political complexity, valuable for its wild juxtapositions, emendations, vacillating judgments, and self-reflections. To quote Walter Benjamin, this is less a document of unified "remembrance, . . . the muse-derived element of the novel" or epic, but of "recollection, the muse-derived element of the story."[11] The twists and turns of the text may accordingly be read not as disjunctures to be corrected or ironed but as a record of an imaginative, parallactic assessment of the moment, oscillating between Burr and Haiti, with a host of supercharged switch points (New England secession, Louisiana, the embargo, etc.).

In all the perambulations of Plumer's *Memorandum*, it exceeds its titular promise. There is a digressive, even dilatory, movement in the text that is in turns personal and, like a scrapbook, selectively archival. Thus, the seeming seriality of the *Memorandum* as "proceedings," its procession through chronological time, must accommodate a different textual unfolding. What some readers might describe as its cross-purposes, we view as its signal relevance. With neither the pretension to professional objectivity nor a self-conscious construction as with a piece of art, Plumer's *Memorandum* is Shandean. Formally, it shares an affinity with Laurence Sterne's experiment in what Christina Lupton calls "epistemological fiction": Plumer, like Tristram, "engages . . . with the explicit and often comically paradoxical fact that while reading and writing are by nature secondary to the lives they refer to, . . . they are, at the same time, activities which take up time and space in these lives." We are reminded, writes Lupton, that the "secondary" world of writing "both lag[s] behind the world and partak[es] in the life which it ostensibly represents."[12] To mine the text for eyewitness details or opinions of this or that thus effaces the text's provocative movement between recording and reflection, as well as its juxtapositional insights.

We thus take Plumer as our heuristic touchstone in this final chapter precisely because of the ways in which he entangles and layers his memories. While we could present a sorted narrative of the person called Burr (*he lost the election, he fought a duel, he returned to Washington, etc.*), we believe it more useful to explore these various facets of the thing called Burr in a series of layerings attentive to their narrative construction, yes, but with greater focus on their relational or formal position within the traumatic colonel that took shape by 1806–7. In this final chapter, then, our goal is less to provide a clear, sequential narrative or even an exhaustive symbolic reading than to outline a literary-cultural alternative to the usual reading practices. We begin with the nonevent of the duel, which we read alongside the much less spectacular but nonetheless important final months of Burr's Senate career. And after a few regional forays, we turn to that massive semiotic cluster, that panicked fantasy, of the Burr conspiracy, embracing the historiographic frustration that its precise events and significance cannot be clarified—such is precisely the point of the conspiracy and of the thing called Burr, which increasingly functions as an aggregator of the racially charged conflicts and crises of the moment.

The Duel

Let us begin with the July 11, 1804, "interview at Weehawken," the episode that has most captured the popular imagination about Burr. The event need not be rehearsed here and in any case is unimportant—a meaningless, violent accident. And yet the duel has generated a flurry of historiographic responses and reactions that may be usefully summarized. We may begin with the most obvious—*mythologization*—whereby two fraternal figures play out their deadly agonistic rivalry. This is the encoding exploited by Joseph Ellis as he begins his *Founding Brothers*, calling the duel a "fascinating tale designed to catch your attention" or a clash that should "assume its rightful place of primacy among such touted competitors as *Gunfight at the O.K. Corral* or the classic film *High Noon*."[13] Then there is the related formulation of the duel as a *paradigmatic* episode—typically a clash between premodern codes of chivalry and honor and some variant of capitalist modernity. Here the lesson is clear: modernity loses the battle but wins the war, time marches on, the Founders are transcended. These broader framings are often complemented by a range of historiographic inflections, including the spectacular enjoyment of *scandal*—the vice president shooting a man!—which we have recently seen reactivated when Dick Cheney shot his hunting partner in 2006. This encoding revels in reading Burr as the Bad Boy of Early America, an idea beautifully parodied by the line from the *Saturday Night Live* skit "Lazy Sunday": "You can call us Aaron Burr from the way we're dropping Hamiltons!"[14] Yet another strain dissects the event like a scientific experiment to weigh and assess this or that detail—this is the historical mode that we have come to associate with the history of military battles and that in consideration of the duel takes up such matters as sunlight and pistol triggers.[15] Such an approach might conclude with the inevitability or *predetermination* of the conflict (as in the story of the lifelong rivalry of Burr and Hamilton, destined from youth to clash) or, conversely, the *counterfactual* fantasy (if Hamilton had lived, what might have happened?).[16]

These various interpretive dances reveal that the duel remains, two centuries later, a highly charged contact point with the Founders' system and certainly the most irritable *Burr-itch* for contemporary readings of Burr. Even the historians writing of the event frequently concede, directly or indirectly, its political vacuity. "By the summer of 1804," writes one, "history had pretty much passed [Burr and Hamilton] by. . . . Neither man had much of a political future."[17] "By 1804," writes another, "both men had been cast off the national stage."[18] This strange emptiness is only confirmed all the more if we invert the conclusion—either survivor had any number of career options had he survived the duel. Nancy Isenberg, for instance, stresses the "several possibilities" open to Burr, from land speculation to filibustering to a political career in the western states.[19] Plumer in *Memorandum* expresses a variant of this contradiction, noting, after the duel, "[Burr] can never I think rise again," and then immediately adding, "But surely he is a very extraordinary man & is an exception to all rules. . . . Considering how little restraint laws human or divine have on his mind [it] is impossible to say what he will attempt—or what he may obtain" (213).

Perhaps the best contemporary reader of the duel was Aaron Burr himself, who, through the New York gubernatorial campaign, seems to have perceived the growing disconnect between his actions and his empty/full construction. In January 1805, he wrote his daughter, Theodosia, that she "treat[ed] with too much gravity the New-Jersey affair," which instead "should be considered as a farce."[20] It would be easy to shrug off this comment as itself a casual dismissal, but we prefer to read it as a literary-critical insight: the duel is farcical because it draws together improbable characters and events in empty fashion, intended only to excite laughter. Burr continued his letter:

> You better suspend history till you have gone through B. You do wrong to read so slow the first reading of B. I had rather you went through it like a novel, to get fixed in your mind a kind of map of the whole; after which, when you come to read *scientifically*, you would better see the relations and bearings of one part to another. In all journeys, whether on foot or on horseback, it is a relief to know not only where you start from, but where you are going to, and all the intermediate stages.[21]

The reference here was to the recently published *History of Virginia* by John Burk, but we might productively suggest this as a strategy for reading a different "B"—not a history to read slowly but more quickly, like a novel, fixing a "map of the whole" to "see the relations and bearings of one part to another."[22]

Louisiana

Such a map of the whole would of course have to register Louisiana, soon to become one of the purported sites of Burr's treason. As the reports of Burr's defeat in the New York gubernatorial election were being assessed in the spring of 1804, Republicans in Connecticut announced their plan to make the annual commemoration of Jefferson's election into a celebration of the president *and* his greatest achievement. "We will Rejoice," Connecticut papers announced on May 1, "in the election of President Jefferson, and in the course of his administration, especially in that most distinguished act, which crowns all his other measures, the ACQUISITION OF LOUISIANA, . . . a treasure, which, while it opens a new world to industry and enterprize, is giving occasion of festivity throughout the continent."[23] Similar celebrations, repeating this toast, followed throughout the country. If we recall the celebrations of Burr in the election season of 1800–1801, we may conclude that Louisiana increasingly functioned somewhat like the former vice president had—as an uncharted "new world"—a not unreasonable assumption given the similarly imaginary circulations around the Purchase. It is no coincidence, either, that at this moment of substitution—Louisiana for Burr—we also see the transfer of the heavily racial encoding of Louisiana onto Burr or that Burr's conspiracy would activate many of the Louisiana fantasies crafted before, during, and after the Purchase. Thus, we might say of the Louisiana Purchase what we have already said about the Founding Fathers—that the behind-the-scenes historical narratives that give us the straight facts do a real disservice by veiling the remarkable fantasy work evoked by Louisiana. We therefore turn here to a brief review of the discourse surrounding Louisiana.

Louisiana figured prominently in US discourse during the spring of 1801, when first reports began to circulate of the cession of the territory from Spain to France—reports that coincided with news that the Spanish governor "has forbid the introduction of slaves into that country from the United States, and has ordered all slaves that have been taken there within the last twelve months, to be removed from the territories of his Catholic Majesty without delay."[24] If this subtext was not immediately clear to all, Louisiana reentered the news in late 1801 with the first reports of a massive French expedition being fitted for Saint-Domingue and Louisiana. At the time of the bicentennial of the Purchase, historians reminded us of the connection between the two territories—Napoleon had planned to suppress the slave revolution under Toussaint, then send his armies to fortify the Louisiana territory; Jefferson understood this and awaited the outcome of events in Saint-Domingue, knowing that in Toussaint's success lay US prospects on the Mississippi. The success of Charles Leclerc's expedition was unclear through 1802—Henri Christophe and Jean-Jacques Dessalines joined Leclerc's army in the spring, and Toussaint was taken prisoner in June, but the major Revolutionary generals deserted the French forces in the fall, and Leclerc was dead in November. The French did not evacuate Le Cap until a year later, when the eight thousand survivors of the original army of forty-three thousand surrendered to the British; Dessalines took Le Cap, renaming it Cap Haïtien, in November 1803, declaring an independent black republic in January 1804. Such was the backdrop for the first Louisiana flashpoint, when the Spanish intendant of New Orleans, in October 1802, revoked the right of deposit statutorily granted US merchants in a 1795 treaty with Spain. In November, the Spanish minister to Washington officially informed the State Department that the intendant had acted on his own, and the administration continued negotiating with France for the cession. Federalists, however, agitated for war—a military seizure of Louisiana—while complaining of Jefferson's effeminate inactivity.

Prominent among the Federalist polemics was Charles Brockden Brown's 1803 pamphlet *An Address to the Government of the United States, on the Cession of Louisiana to the French, and on the Late Breach of Treaty by the Spaniards.*[25] Brown's rhetorical strategy was to frame the pamphlet around a "memorial" (some three-fourths of the full text) prepared for Napoleon by a sycophantic "counsellor of state," in which the latter advised a policy of renewed imperial expansion in North America. France must of course reclaim "St. Domingo" from the "quondam slaves and furious banditti" of "a servile and barbarous race" (5–6), but it must also reflect that, "under a provident and valiant leader"—Toussaint—the people of Saint-Domingue had been transformed from "helpless and timorous slaves . . . into men, and citizens, and soldiers" (10). The danger for the French forces was that they might be "inspired with contemptuous notions of the blacks whom they are going to subdue" and become "brutes" in turn—a disturbing reversal of racial positions (7). France should therefore pursue "a *different path*" (7), "not to an island, indeed, but a *world*" (14). In Louisiana, the French would also have to learn from their foils, in this case the United States, "which in all respects will bear an honourable comparison with any nation of Europe" (10). Nonetheless, the US was a deeply flawed society: the result of the English practice of fragmented colonization, the current nation amounted to "a score of independent and unequal states" (17), "dissimilar," "motley," and "dispersed" (62), incapable of "coalescing into one symmetrical and useful body" (63). Well-laid schemes might "set this heterogeneous mass into commotion," for not only were the whites "an undisciplined and faithless rabble," but the enslaved fifth of the population meant that the US "harbours in its bosom" a potentially vengeful "nation" that might be aroused with a local "L'Ouverture" (69–70, 73). The "INDIANS" likewise constituted a potential "terrible militia" of some thirty thousand troops, adding to the "train of powder" that might exploit US weaknesses (76, 74, 80).

Scholars of Brown have made much of his rhetorical strategy—one called the pamphlet his "most ambitious piece of fiction"[26]—and the mass of racial positions has been mined by many readers, to different conclusions. Our interest in this piece, however, is in how Brown, much as he had anticipated the construction of Burr in *Ormond*, announced the construction of Louisiana. Four features of this construction seem particularly important. First, the pamphlet presented a counterfactual fantasy—a diplomatic garden of forking paths—that opened Louisiana to intensive semiotic investment. What was actually happening in Louisiana was overshadowed by a range of possible presents and futures. Second, the pamphlet rehearsed a theory of revolutionary transformation that equated the transformed blacks of Saint-Domingue with the "undisciplined and faithless rabble" of the US, to the obvious advantage of the former: blacks had been fused into a disciplined national force, unlike their Anglo counterparts to the north. Relatedly, through a serial chain of geospatial associations (France → Saint-Domingue → Louisiana → United States), the pamphlet essentially rendered the US a variant of Haiti, much as Toussaint's constitution had done a year earlier. Whereas France had set out to retake the island, it now could impose on the United States, which, under the feeble rule of Jefferson, might "*admit into their vitals a formidable and active people, whose interests are incompatible in every point with their own; whose enterprises will inevitably interfere and jar with theirs; whose neighbourhood will cramp all their movements; circumscribe their future progress to narrow and ignominious bounds; and make incessant inroads on their harmony and independence*" (53). Finally, and perhaps most significantly, Brown articulated a fantasy position through which US citizens could imagine themselves the object of fantasy—the content of enunciation rather than the obfuscating enunciators. We would stress that this point of enunciation was not so much French as Louisianan—the view of the US as riven by faction and regionalism, open to Indian attacks, and nurturing a resentful nation (not to mention a potential Toussaint) was precisely a view from the hitherto unimagined "*world*" west of the Mississippi.

By February, Brown's pamphlet was exposed in the *Aurora* as the work of a "romancer," but that kind of distinction is largely meaningless in the discourse surrounding Louisiana. In fact, it is difficult to keep track of the racialized counterfactual fantasies of Louisiana that proliferated between 1802 and 1805. In June 1802, the Federalist *Gazette of the United States*, commenting on Republican hostility to Saint-Domingue, asked, "Why do the Jacobins so anxiously take part with LECLERC against TOUSSAINT? Are they afraid the French will not come soon enough with a fraternal army to *Louisiana*? Do they really wish to see TOUSSAINT himself and all his negroes reinforce that army, & come to rouse the southern Blacks to liberty."[27] The *Aurora*, among other papers, fantasized that Louisiana would finally render the abolition of slavery possible: "Instead of establishing slavery in Louisiana, we look upon the acquisition of that country as a blessing, since from its possession we are in a fair way of dispersing our present coloured population over such a vast surface, and of finally eradicating slavery altogether."[28] As importantly, the Purchase has "secured our country from the importation of French negro officers into the Mississippi country."[29] The 1803 pamphlet by St. George Tucker (writing as Sylvestris), *Reflections, on the Cession of Louisiana to the United States*, embellished this position: not only might the US "colonize those unhappy people, whom our ancestors have brought in chains from their native country," but "it may be adviseable to entice those to remove who have already, or may hereafter obtain their freedom, through the benevolence of their masters," and "thither, also, delinquents, whose lives may be forfeited to the considerations of self-preservation, may be banished for attempts to regain their native freedom." Tucker also had an addendum: Louisiana could be "a place of exile, also for other criminals."[30] Another piece widely reprinted proclaimed the "SUPPLY OF SUGAR" that might come from Louisiana, directly playing on the association with slave plantations: "The white American farmers and planters will have an opportunity to prove, that sugar can be produced on many plantations without slaves," it noted, adding, "Three or four hundred white farmers, with their families, will produce more sugar than a negro estate with two thousand slaves."[31]

Another prominent text here was US minister Robert Livingston's essay to the French government, titled "On This Question—Whether It Is Advantageous for France to Take Possession of Louisiana?" Slavery figures prominently throughout, with Livingston first noting, "slavery alone can fertilize those colonies"; hence, "it will be necessary to lay out immense capitals in slaves," in fact to divert the capital that "would have been carried to the islands, if this new channel had not been opened." Livingston expands on the problems of setting up plantations—"Who then will cultivate Louisiana with slaves?" he asks—before concluding with the grim picture of "new settlements in a marshy country, and a burning climate; the invasion of Indians; the insurrection of slaves; the insubordination of the troops; the abuses committed by officers, remote from the sovereign's vigilant eye." As for a French Louisiana's neighbor, "the Government of the United States will not be able, in a thousand instances, to restrain the petulance of the near inhabitants bordering on the limits of the Mississippi" or "to confine their vengeance wholly" as they wait for remote justice. "Hatred will take place between the two people; the bonds of friendship will be destroyed," and the US government "will be forced, by its situation, to alter its political relations." Livingston's arguments and threats are straightforward enough—the Federalist maneuver, here, was to turn these negative arguments into revelations about a US Louisiana,

here imagined as a land absorbing capital to build a threatening slave society so remote from "the sovereign's vigilant eye" as to cleave the country
into at least "two people."[32]

Perhaps the most explicit version, predicting the fracture of the United
States, came in the much-reprinted, two-part "Reflections on the Treaties
with France," which first appeared in *Poulson's American Daily Advertiser.*[33] The piece moved through a series of objections to the Purchase:
first, "*It will haste the dissolution of our union*"; second, "*It will weaken
and obstruct our population*"; third, "*The cession will be injurious to the
interest and prosperity of the Atlantic States in a variety of aspects*"; and
fourth, "*It is calculated to produce a most unfortunate change in the system
of our policy, if not in the form of our government.*" These are essentially
the same argument, ultimately focused on the definition of the United
States as a slave nation, a land "covered with a corrupt and rotten population of Negroes." The essay concludes with a listing of alternatives: "You
must either authorize the most infamous and detestable commerce that
ever existed, and have a black population utterly useless as to all the purposes of national vigor and defence; or you must neglect the interests and
opinion of those whom if you adopt you are bound to protect, cherish
and defend." What is fascinating about the formulation of the problem
is the phantom status of the New England Federalist. In arguing that the
Jefferson administration must promote slavery or disappoint the white
Louisianans, the option that cannot be named is the disappointment of
the white New Englander, a sign that the real dilemma here is the disappointment of "us" (white New Englanders) or "them" (white Louisianans).
What the Purchase means, and what this essay cannot finally say overtly,
is the fracture of the Union.

A Northern Empire

The sectional split was easy to imagine given northern fantasies of secession, which also circulate around the figure of Burr. To appreciate the
contemporary vacuity of the duel and to understand how and why "Burr"
was not simply or clearly demonized (or lauded) after it, we may return to
Plumer's *Memorandum.* In early December 1804, Plumer noted with disgust the return of the "murderer" to the Senate: he found Burr's presence
"odious" and noted that his Federalist peers "appear to despise neglect
& abhor him," whereas Burr was but a shell of his former self, "uneasy,

discontented, & hurried" (213). Within months, the departure of Hamilton's killer was described in the Federalist press as an event moving Federalists to tears—a powerful illustration of Burr's oscillating status. The complex position of Burr can be explained in part by his odd involvement in the New England secession movement, which percolated subterraneously—as a kind of elite discursive buzz—through to the 1814 Hartford Convention. Plumer later recalled a conspiratorial meeting with Timothy Pickering (Federalist senator from Massachusetts), James Hillhouse (Federalist senator from Connecticut), and Aaron Burr:

> Mr. Hillhouse unequivocally declared that it was his opinion that the United States would soon form two distinct and separate governments. On this subject, Mr. Burr conversed very freely; and the impression made on my mind was, that he not only thought such an event would take place, but that it was necessary that it should. To that opinion I was myself then a convert. Yet, on returning to my lodgings, after critically analysing his words, there was nothing in them that necessarily implied his approbation of Mr. Hillhouse's observations. Perhaps no man's language was ever so apparently explicit, and, at the same time, so covert and indefinite. (517)

This report confirms Burr's odd status—warily courted by the Federalists in the summer of 1804—and his tenuous association with secession more broadly.[34]

If explicit secessionist discussions were confined to regional elites, the discourse of regional distinction was nonetheless significant as Burr took shape. Plumer himself had written a pamphlet—*An Address to the Electors of the State of New Hampshire*—under the pseudonym "Impartialis," in which he warned readers of "the danger to which you are exposed from the overbearing influence of Virginia." The Virginia plantocracy, empowered by slave representation, would "destroy the independence and the sovereignty of the States," he wrote. "The voice of New England is not *now heard* in Congress," and the expansion of slavery into the Louisiana Territory would seal the deal: New England's interests could not be entrusted to the slaveholders.[35] Plumer's critics rushed to paint Impartialis as a betrayer of Washington's legacy, a point captured by a list of contrasts, setting Washington's Farewell Address against Impartialis's views. The contrast here usefully, if indirectly, illuminates the stresses on the symbolic system of the Founders, in which the unifying registration of Washington increasingly yielded to the regional tensions of the early nineteenth

TABLE 5.1

WASHINGTON.	IMPARTIALIS.
"It is of infinite moment that you should properly estimate the immense value of your NATIONAL UNION, to your collective and individual happiness; that you should cherish a cordial, habitual and immovable attachment to it; accustoming yourselves to think and speak of it as the palladium of your political safety; watching for its preservation with jealous anxiety...	"The manners, habit and *interests* of the *southern* and *northern* people are very *different.*—Can you believe that the *former* are the real friends of liberty and equality? "A few facts will demonstrate, that the *southern* states have not only a *different interest* from the *northern*, but that the *former* have *privileges* that are denied to *us.*"

century. Federalist newspaper pieces reiterated this point: a widely reprinted piece from the *Boston Repertory* declaimed against "disorganizers and anti-federalists; who are labouring for a DISSOLUTION OF THE UNION" and who have left "the influence of New-England humbled in the dust" as "new territories"—Louisiana, above all—"are purchased, which distort the body politic as well as the boundaries of the American empire."[36]

Federalist overtures to Burr to lead a secession were hinted at, as well, in Republican newspapers. An April 16, 1804, *Ontario Freeman* address was also widely reprinted during the New York gubernatorial race. Noting that Federalist newspapers had "for years past teemed with arguments enforcing the propriety and even necessity of a division of the union," it claimed "the nomination of Col. Burr" for the governorship of New York "as the first leading attempt to effect a separation of the United States." Burr, it concluded, was "cheerfully consenting to be the center of an union, the primary of a system, which shall blend the heterogeneous wishes of the motley group [of Federalist conspirators], into one great northern whole which shall do away the political distinctions, and establish on their ruins a party which shall be distinguished only by geographical demarcations." Four years later, William Jenks alluded to this moment in his anonymously published novella *Memoir of the Northern Kingdom*, a dystopian retrospective on the breakup of the United States from the vantage point of 1901. Its narrator told of the merging of the northern states with British Canada in a "northern kingdom," while the southern states, relying on French troops to control their slaves, had become a French-speaking, Napoleonic southern kingdom; only a small group of republicans in Illinois held to the original promise of the United States. Germane to our discussion of Burr is the moment in this fantasy when New Englanders believed that the Union could not succeed without New York support, earned by granting a "Presidency for life" to an unnamed, prominent New Yorker.[37]

The semiotic entanglements with Saint-Domingue may not be immediately evident, but they were nonetheless powerful and are perhaps best broached through Plumer's *Memorandum*. In late 1804—the day after the murderer of Hamilton opened the new Senate session—Plumer took up the question of Saint-Domingue, prompted by Jefferson's fourth annual message to Congress, in which the president complained of privateering efforts to trade with the revolutionary island. "That individuals should undertake to wage private war, independent of the authority of their country, cannot be permitted in a well ordered society," he wrote, anticipating the eventual characterization of Burr.[38] Plumer, however, took the address as a prompt to assess events in Saint-Domingue. How could one characterize events there? "It is difficult to draw the distinction," he wrote, "between a revolution & a rebellion" (187). The blacks had risen up against their white masters and, after a struggle, had won freedom and become "part of the community"—that is, French. This, of course, echoed Toussaint's position of 1801—"all men are born, live and die there free and French."[39] But then the rebels had separated from France—the French and the blacks becoming "two independent parties." By this logic, Saint-Domingue "must be treated under the law of nations" (188). Accordingly, the United States should not interfere with its (northern) citizens' pursuit of a profitable trade. Within a few months, this "Virginian Influence" on trade with Saint-Domingue was put to the test, with a bill that prohibited *armed* US vessels from trade with the West Indies. Senator George Logan of Pennsylvania sought to amend this bill with a provision banning *all* trade with the newly formed black republic of Saint-Domingue. A vote on the amendment resulted in a tie, only broken by the last vote Burr was to cast in the Senate.[40] Against the wishes of both Jefferson and the French ambassador, Louis Marie Turreau, the Congress voted to allow northern merchants to continue to conduct business with Saint-Domingue.[41]

But let us return here to Plumer's larger intellectual puzzle—revolution versus rebellion. The answer to such a question is normally determined by the "issue" of events: "Success stamps it a revolution, subjugation marks it rebellion" (187). Plumer's detailed reflections on Saint-Domingue concluded that it was a revolution, though the lack of clarity on the question harked back to the puzzle of the Toussaint sketch, in which the condemnation of the twelve planters (rebellion) was paired with their pardon (revolution). But in late 1804, the question was surely not limited to the Caribbean and posed questions for New England separatism. Were the Federalists scheming rebels or legitimate revolutionaries? Perhaps they were legitimate rebels against the scheming revolutionaries of the 1800 election? The definitional conundrum, which in this context had to assess the legitimacy of treasonous acts, could only be determined by the outcome. In 1804, this meant that the secessionists' definitional status was profoundly linked to Aaron Burr, whose involvement might break the tie of the regional split. In the event, the secession movement was to become more of a scandalous memory for later historians, but in 1804, it was bound up conceptually, symbolically, with Saint-Domingue, with Aaron Burr as the quilting point. Indeed, in his farewell address of March 2, 1804, Burr addressed the state of the Union, insisting that he hoped "that the constitution of the US would never be destroyed but he would venture to predict that if such an unfortunate event should ever take place, on this floor it would meet with its last & most noble defence—Here it would draw its last gasp" (312). Plumer noted that Burr's address was "very correct & elegant & the sentiments very just" and that "many shed tears plentifully" (312–13). Thus, the "odious" "murderer" could coincide with the paragon of virtue, the scheming ambitious separatist with the voice of patriotic integrity. It was not that Burr was the one and then became the other; for he was assuming the oscillating, short-circuiting position of Toussaint *as both at the same time.*

The Chase Trial

We must, finally, assess one more drama from early 1805, which further clarifies Burr's emergence as an American Toussaint: his management of the impeachment trial of Supreme Court Justice Samuel Chase, which occupied much of the Senate's time in the early months of 1805. Chase followed John Pickering, a federal circuit judge in New Hampshire, becoming the second justice to be impeached after the repeal of the Judiciary Act of 1801. Chase had been targeted for removal on seven articles of impeachment. Among these, two stood out. He was accused of presiding in a "manner highly arbitrary, oppressive, and unjust" in the capital trial of John Fries for rebellion against the United States. Another article claimed that in 1803 Chase delivered "an intemperate and inflammatory political harangue, with the intent to excite the fears and resentment" of the jury and the people of Maryland against the government.[42] Chase had excoriated the Jefferson administration's effort to purge the courts of John Adams's midnight appointments, calling it an attack on liberty and the balance of powers. Jefferson considered Chase's comments to be seditious.

Chase was impeached in the House in March 1804. The Articles of Impeachment were then forwarded to the Senate, where the trial was scheduled to begin in January. The trial was to be the first and still as of today the only impeachment of a Supreme Court justice. It was political theater of the highest order. Burr had had the Senate renovated for the trial. He placed himself in a central chair raised above the prosecutors and defendant's counsel, while the senators, who were to sit as jury, occupied benches covered in crimson. A gallery designed for women was ultimately opened to the public, special boxes being set aside on the wings for the "ladies."[43] One commentator called the arrangements "elegant,"[44] and another thought it "beyond anything which has ever appeared in the Country" a "great, interesting and super spectacle."[45] And for the main event? Jefferson and the Democratic-Republicans against the remnants of Federalism and, depending on partisan orientation, a battle between the rights of the people against an overreaching, unelected judiciary or one that pit the constitutional republican experiment against mob rule. It featured an aggressively contrarian Federalist judge, who had precipitously sentenced a Pennsylvanian tax rebel to death, and Aaron Burr, presiding as judge of the court, still under indictment for murdering Hamilton, first among Federalists. The murderer stood in judgment of the hanging judge. This point was not lost on Federalist newspapers. A writer in the *United States Gazette* opined with disgust that "the man who has been pronounced by the voice of the people (which according to the true doctrine, is the voice of God) to be the second man in the nation for virtue and all the republican accomplishments, but whom the voice of a grand jury of his country has pronounced a *Murderer*, this man, I say is at the present moment presiding in the most august tribunal in the nation." Could Chase possibly get a fair trial? The gazetteer noted even broader ironies in Burr's conduct toward Chase at the beginning of the trial. Burr's "detestation of forms and etiquette is well known to all who know him or who have noticed the proceedings of the court during the present trial," he wrote. When Chase first entered the court, "the seat which had been prepared for him was ordered to be removed"; by contrast, when "[John] Fries was tried before Judge Chase, a seat was provided for him."[46] Consider the algebra: Fries had plotted against the government. None other than the recently promoted general Alexander Hamilton had deployed the federal militia to quash the rebellion. Chase then had his turn to discipline and punish Fries. A chair may have been the only decency the judge had shown to him before sentencing Fries to be executed; but now Burr, having dispensed with the first of Fries's persecutors, appeared to have Chase in his sights—and would not even allow him a chair! Another Federalist paper referred to the "*bull baiting*" of Judge Chase.[47] There was even a rumor that, once Chase had been removed from his seat on the High Court, Jefferson meant for Burr to once again take away his chair. As long as Burr performed his role, Jefferson, who had maneuvered to have Burr's murder indictment rescinded, would return the favor and appoint him to the court, quid quo pro.[48] These Federalist fantasies, for no one *knew* Burr's mind, *proved* that Burr had returned to complete what he had begun in Weehawken, to put the final nail in the Federalist coffin. Each detail seemed to confirm a broad, apocalyptic fantasy in which the rabble overran the federal republic and Aaron Burr seemed positioned to deliver the fatal blow. We can already see hints of the satanic Burr that was fully to appear in the 1807 conspiracy trial in Richmond.[49] What we must note is how a formal juxtaposition lent itself to narrative elaboration. Burr versus Hamilton had become Burr versus Chase under the signifying motif of Burr versus Federalism. Since Federalist power had dissolved Fries's insurrection, it seemed clear that Burr was another Fries to challenge Federalist authority.

Republicans, too, compared Fries and Burr, though they were more likely to trip awkwardly over the abounding ironies at the trial. In his opening address as manager of the Articles of Impeachment, Representative John Randolph of Virginia made a "peculiarly *unfortunate*" remark addressing Burr. Referring to the prejudicial instructions that Chase had given the jury in Fries's treason trial, Randolph transposed treason into murder, supposedly to clarify his point. "Suppose Mr. President, a man was indicted for *murder*, that the fact of the killing *was admitted* and that the judge who tried the cause, before any argument by counsel, declared, that murder was a killing with *malice prepense* would it not be irregular and a prejudication of the cause??"[50] A writer reporting on the trial was amused: "This absurd idea he dwelt upon for a considerable period. Its folly, as you may well imagine, was much less attended to, than the countenance of Mr. Burr, who however betrayed less emotion than might have been expected, or than if I was his friend, I would have WISHED on the occasion; but how disgraceful it is to the character of the nation, that in

the highest court of judicature known to our constitution, the word MUR-
DER cannot be pronounced before the *presiding judge* without exciting
universal surprise and observation."[51] The world seemed turned upside
down. So powerful was the resonation of Burr with Fries that it resurfaced in 1807. Only now Burr was no longer the Federalist bugbear but the
agent of Jefferson's discontent. An opinion piece in the *Aurora* anticipating Burr's trial claimed the Federalists would "be as ready to exult in the
escape of Burr as they were ready to triumph in the expected execution
of *Fries*."[52] Another Republican paper reveled in what appeared an ironic
peripety, that, as it had been reported, the acquitted Samuel Chase would
preside at Burr's trial for treason and have his just dessert.[53] No matter
that the appeal to Fries as referent led to incompatible narrative conclusions. The formal juxtaposition is what proved irresistible.

We turn again to Plumer to see how Burr both seemed to fit and also to
evade consistent coding. Plumer took note of Burr's demeanor throughout Chase's trial. He began by articulating the standard Federalist fantasy
that Burr was a tyrant set on destroying Federalism at Jefferson's bidding.
But this wholly negative coding shifted as the trial continued. Once more,
we see that any attempt to fill in the position that Burr occupied was to
prove futile. At first, Plumer's Burr is impatient, "fretful & peevish." Days
later, he is "remarkably testy—he acts more of the tyrant—is impatient &
passionate—scolds—he is in a rage because we do not sit longer" (278).
Far from turning the court upside down, making a carnival of the affair,
the murderer becoming king, Burr instead is officious, demanding, and
determined to enforce the rules. Plumer notes that Burr chastised some
Federalist senators for rude behavior (eating in court, walking around
while a witness was testifying, leaving the chambers before testimony
had concluded). "The conduct of Mr. Burr is really extraordinary!" wrote
Plumer. "What, cannot a judge of a Court retire from the Court peaceably
& quietly without being censured by him—especially when those retiring
still leaves a large majority!" (283). But, indeed, Burr seemed determined
to force everyone to act his part with thoroughness and decorum. What
meant this fixation on the rules? Confused, Plumer wondered what could
possibly inspire the man, motivate him to enforce strict discipline when
he "can neither intimidate his enemies, or flatter his friends, to any purpose." The best Plumer can come up with is that Burr fancies himself a
schoolmaster: "Mr. Burr has for this few weeks assumed the airs of a *pedagogue*—& rather considered the senators as his scholars than otherwise. I
am unable to divine his motive.—It may be he acts according to his nature

having nothing to hope by disguise" (283). Accused by another Federalist of having no concern for etiquette, Burr serves a precisely contrary function for Plumer. "Really *Master Burr*," he marveled, "you need a ferule, or birch, to enforce your lectures on polite behavior!" (285). We ought to take this rich comment less as an attempt to ridicule the presiding officer than as one nervous attempt to deflect the discomfort of not knowing who or what Burr was becoming. The vice president had once again become an enigma. He was a pedagogue without a lesson plan, a master with no discernible mission. Partisan orthopedics were ultimately powerless to set the fracture that was Burr.

As the final vote on Chase's guilt loomed, it suddenly occurred to Plumer that what was at stake in defending Chase was not the future of Federalism but the regional sovereignty of the northern states—in other words, slave power. How to convince his New England compatriots was now the concern. Plumer was once himself an enthusiastic celebrant of Washington's birthday, and this February 22 he was concerned with setting the proper tone for regional camaraderie. He lobbied his Federalist peers to dispense with the usual festivities (the music and balls, the cannonade, the fancy meals and accompanying toasts) lest it "have an ill effect upon the pending trial of Judge Chase." In private, he reiterated his secessionist views, urging the northern senators to consider that their "interest was one—& the *slave states* had interests & views inimical" to theirs. He congratulated himself for his "prudent firm & decided conduct" that had "prevented a festival" that would do them "no good" (299). Was Plumer now a Burr-like disciplinarian? Was the semblance of unity and orderliness enough to draw attention to a substance that could not otherwise be articulated?

There was one last effort to fix Burr to a violently partisan function, but it played out not as drama but as farce, so great were the charges and so small the stakes. Just days before the Senate voted on the Articles of Impeachment, a "long and extraordinary debate" took place over whether to grant Burr the franking privilege after he had concluded his service as vice president. Federalists tried out a fiduciary argument against the bill but then trotted out the killing of Hamilton as if on cue. Republicans played the foil. Senator Robert Wright of Maryland was most direct. "The secret is now out," he railed. "The reason why gentlemen oppose this bill is because Mr. Burr has fought a duel & killed a man." Arguing that dueling was not only necessary but lawful, Wright celebrated Burr's actions: "Our *little* David of the Republicans has killed the Goliath of Federalism—&

for this I am willing to reward him" (305). It was, however, but a tempest in a teapot. The Senate approved the honor by a wide margin. Though Plumer voted against the bill, his assessment of Burr's conduct had radically shifted. Upon the acquittal of Judge Chase for all charges brought by the House against him, Plumer did not merely *concede* that Burr had done justice to his post but *praised* him for his management skill. "[He has] certainly, on the whole, done himself, the Senate & the nation honor by the dignified manner in which he has presided over this high & numerous Court" (310). The members as a whole seemed to mirror Plumer's appraisal. Despite these last interparty pyrotechnics, Burr returned to give a farewell speech for the ages, drawing plentiful tears from several of the assembled senators. The murderer in chief was now the champion of the Senate's legacy.

How are we to understand the transformation of the criminal into the embodiment of the law itself? As we have already noted, Thomas Paine regarded the legal authority of King George as nothing more than the legacy of a brutal ruffian who had subdued his challengers and asserted his will. In the contemporary language of Slavoj Žižek, this is the obscene underside of the law. At base, it always begins with a criminal act that retroactively is coded as justice. Each time we follow the law, we must also repress the "hard resistant kernel" (colonel?) of this truth. Today, writes Žižek, we prefer a virtual reality wherein we have the semblance of the truth without the trouble of its substance (coffee without caffeine, beer without alcohol, chocolate without calories, etc.).[54] This is how we have proposed to read Burr. He is a form without substance. The sublimation of Burr's crime repeats the veiling of the most foundational injustice: the compromises over slavery that made the republic possible. As a formal realization of the justness of the law, but purged of its obscene content, Burr's conduct *seemed* patriotic, *seemed* to legitimate the Union even as Plumer *knew* of its manifest injustice. The tears Burr provoked had nothing to do with Burr but with the semblance that his orthopedic conduct had sustained: a nation founded on freedom from tyranny and injustice via the law. The acquittal of Chase indicated that the Founding had not collapsed (in the abstract, a positive good), even as the Founding compromises had been acknowledged to be unjust (in practice, secession would be better). The senators cried not because Burr turned out to be a good guy in the end but because he marked something that could only be recovered through its fleeting semblance.[55] What was overlooked was the really significant act of Burr's last days as vice president, his tie-breaking vote to sustain trade with Saint-Domingue, linking him once again with Tous-saint L'Ouverture, under whose reign the original trade pact had been established. But this hard resistant kernel of the Real was the traumatic colonel and not the empty signifier filled in with sentimental nostalgia.

The Conspiracy: The Rebellion Was to Have Taken Place Soon

Because most of the evidence of Burr's conspiracy was conjecture or hear-say, there is no definitive account of what Burr was doing or getting ready to do or had decided no longer to do. We can best engage the conspiracy through a different question: what did the public think he was doing or had done or had abandoned? Soon after his farewell address, Burr began to travel west. His itinerary was followed in the press as each local paper reported the vice president's arrival. These notices gradually appeared throughout the country. We pause here to remark on the formal structure of breaking news at the turn of the century. By the time the announce-ment of Burr's arrival in Marietta, Ohio, reached Washington papers, Burr had almost certainly moved on. This future past juxtaposed reports of Burr's often cordial and welcoming reception with suspicion about his itinerary as a whole or expressions of anxiety from the place where he was next expected to descend. The nefarious Burr was not to be found where he was but where he would soon have been—not by any one stop but by the totality taken together. Burr returned east briefly before heading west once again. This inspired a new round of speculation, conjecture, rumor, and insinuation in both the press and private correspondence.

Some sense of the confusion that this structural belatedness occasioned may be captured with the circulation of an accusation against Burr by General William Eaton, who became a star witness in the Richmond trial. Eaton had returned to Boston after receiving commendation for his defeat of Tunisian troops at Derne and for securing the release of Americans held captive in Tripoli. In October 1806, an extract of a letter began to cir-culate, first in New Hampshire, of Burr's plans to equip an expedition and endeavor to create a separate government west of the Alleghenies. Eaton had seen a letter, he reported, testifying that Burr was recruiting young men in Ohio to accomplish this end. Eaton amplified his account at Bos-ton, where he regaled his hosts with a story about having been offered sec-ond command in Burr's expedition the previous January, an offer he had refused. Jefferson was moved to act. He issued a proclamation declaring that a plot was under way to draw the States into war with Mexico and authorizing western governors to arrest any conspirators. At this point, he did not mention Burr by name. But it was not until early December that the president's message and Eaton's comments appeared in newspapers in Kentucky, where a district court judge had already overruled the federal district attorney's request to subpoena Burr to account for his activities in Ohio. Hearsay evidence was not sufficient to demand Burr's appearance. A request for a warrant for Burr's arrest was then made to a grand jury, which refused the petition on December 5. Burr was exonerated locally of all suspicion of conspiring against the interests of the United States at the very same time that in Washington, Jefferson was becoming convinced that he was up to no good.

This pattern was repeated in New Orleans and Mississippi at the turn of the new year. Having revealed the infamous cipher letter to Jefferson in November, General James Wilkinson, who like Eaton claimed inside knowledge of Burr's plans, now declared that Burr would attempt to take the city with seven thousand men. He used Jefferson's proclamation of November 22 to justify fortifying the town, censoring the press, and placing an embargo on trade. Burr learned that Wilkinson had arrested five of his associates at New Orleans and hastened from the scene to avoid a similar fate. He headed south but no longer aimed to reach New Orleans. His new plan was to get to the Mississippi Territory as quickly as possible. Back in Washington and under the influence of Wilkinson's accusations, Jefferson issued a second proclamation on January 22, 1807, that left little to the imagination. He now named Burr as the master conspirator. "It appeared that he contemplated two distinct objects," wrote Jefferson to Congress, "which might be carried on either jointly or separately. . . . One of these was the severance of the Union of these States by the Alleghany Mountains; the other an attack on Mexico."[56]

Here was an inversion of the Louisiana Territory debate of 1803, but in place of a French invasion, now what had been unveiled was a revolution from within. This is exactly what Federalist opponents of Jefferson's Purchase had predicted, though the absence or weakness of the foreign power replaced the omnipotent Napoleon. The effect of this power vacuum was to condense in Burr the already explicit racial fears triggered by the Purchase and the Quid Emperor. We recall that in the Louisiana debate, Saint-Domingue, domestic slave revolts, and Indian aggression were to be the result of federal inaction. "The tomahawk of the savage and the knife of the negro would confederate in the league (with France), and there would be no interval of peace," wrote Representative Samuel Purvi-ance of North Carolina.[57] Now here was Burr filling the space left in the wake of the Haitian Revolution, waging war against Spain, and drawing together his forces to claim the West for a new empire that he would gov-ern from New Orleans no less. In the fantasy doubling of the Louisiana debate, Burr was to "wield the tomahawk of the savage and the knife of the negro." Burr and his associates had become the structural equivalent of the nonwhite population. Consider the outrageous claim that Jeffer-son had suppressed in his January proclamation but that surfaced in the coming days as General Eaton gave his formal deposition in court. Eaton repeated a claim he had made privately with several senators (includ-ing William Plumer), telling the court that Burr had been determined to "turn Congress neck and heels out of doors; assassinate the President; seize on the treasury and the navy, and declare himself the protector of an energetic government."[58] Here is Burr revealed as the American Toussaint, "whose guilt," according to Jefferson, "is placed beyond question." Jeffer-son authorized the governor of New Orleans and Mississippi "to hold the militia of their Territories in readiness to cooperate for their defense with the regular troops and armed vessels."[59] Burr was now on the lam, the full force of the federal government bent to capture and bring him to justice. In the meantime, Burr made it to Mississippi in late January before Jef-ferson's order had been received, and a grand jury once again refused to indict Burr since he had arrived with but forty men and a couple of house boats. Not waiting around for the deputized Wilkinson to drag him back to New Orleans, Burr then disappeared into the Mississippi wilderness.

Burr was now on the run. The papers were quick to pick up on another condensation of Burr: a parallax of Toussaint and the fugitive slave, the rebel conspirator (having already carried out the conspiracy) and the run-away (pregnant with revolutionary potential unless caught). Under the title "Burr—Acquitted and Eloped," an excerpt of a letter from Natchez to a correspondent in Trenton, New Jersey, marveled at the "singular fact that the late Vice President of the United States, is now advertised in all the public places in this Territory, as well as in the Newspapers, as a run-away."[60] The cotermination of the rebel slave and the fugitive slave in Burr is key to codification of the Burr Conspiracy and reveals its underlying racial economy. To illustrate this further, we need to recognize the spe-cial grammar of the Burr Conspiracy: the future anterior, or what we have referred to earlier as the future past. A simple example of this tense is the statement, "By the time you get back, I will already have left." My leaving is posited as past to an event that has yet to occur but is also something that itself has not happened yet. The figure of the revolutionary/runaway slave capitalizes on this structure: by the time you surmise my plans, I will have either abandoned them or run away; by the time I run away, I will already have executed my plans; by the time you want to catch me for running away, I will already have done something else that will make you want to catch me. As with the chimney sweep in *Ormond* and with Scipio in *Female Quixotism*, Burr (and the black characters) are always one step ahead. Looking back from 1808 (after Burr's acquittal), the New Orleans merchant Edward Livingston captured this tangled web of the future anterior and gives us a real sense of the ineffable quality of any resolution: "The rebellion had been crushed, it was said, in the womb of speculation; the armies of Colonel Burr were defeated before they were raised."[61] One cannot miss the fantasy structure of this statement. It contains both the self-congratulatory claim that because we did something, we prevented something else from happening, but also the same claim in inverted form: something may still happen because we have not done anything yet. This is what had led Burr's defense counsel, Luther Martin, to argue that the so-called conspiracy was nothing but a "Will o' the wisp treason"—or, in other words, a phantasm.

In the conventional portrait of early American conspiracy thought, the focus is on the conspiratorial logic of Revolutionary rhetoric or post-Revolutionary alarms about Jesuits, Freemasons, and Illuminati. This tradition has focused almost exclusively on what Bernard Bailyn concisely calls "ministerial conspiracy"—plots within or against the state.[62] But the Burr Conspiracy suggests a broader and longer tradition of conspiracy thought in which non-European adversaries take center stage early in the seventeenth century. This earlier moment of conspiracy rhetoric has been recently intimated by Peter Charles Hoffer, who notes a critical change in the legal definition of conspiracy in the 1661 revision of the Barbados Slave Code. If English common law had defined conspiracy as "a combination or discussion among men whose purpose was to bring a false prosecution in law," he writes, the New World colonies "entirely transformed the older conception of conspiracy in order to apply it to slaves." "A conspiracy of slaves was an entirely different offense," Hoffer writes, and the resultant slave code, "unparalleled in scope, coherence, and completeness," took as its premise "that slaves would commit crimes and plot rebellion," while mapping out the avenues by which owners would "ferret out slave crimes and uncover slave plots." This obsessive concern with conspiracy "would find its way into the law of almost all the colonies."[63] The Haitian Revolution was a shocking reminder that slave conspiracy was both phantasmatic and real. The mania over the Burr Conspiracy is the traumatic kernel that both hides and reveals this truth.

The Trial

The high point of the conspiracy was of course its construction, as version after version piled on more signs, added more details, in an effort of definitive registration. The "conclusion" of the conspiracy had potential rewards as well. After the pattern of past and future insurrections, Burr could have been captured, tried, and executed or (like Fries) neutralized and pardoned in court—the former was the pattern with rebel slaves, the latter with white agrarian rebels and filibusterers. Indeed there were momentary attempts to reduce Burr to a byword, as in the Democratic-Republican toast reported from Virginia: "May the conduct of a Bacon of the 17th century, a Shays of the last, and a Burr of the present, be lasting mementoes for the public to beware of the sophistry of popular office-hunters, possessed of inordinate ambition."[64] Ultimately, however, the trial failed to achieve resolution and catharsis for several reasons: it failed to produce either a coherent narrative of events *or* a clear verdict, shifted attention to the conspiracy's partisan inflections and constructedness, and diverted attention to legal abstractions. Burr's departure for Europe, the Democratic-Republican return to the battle with the judiciary, and the fortuitous occurrence of the *Chesapeake-Leopard* Affair (late June 1807), which announced the British-American conflict that was to play out over the next decade, also dissipated the imaginative processing of the conspiracy. "The United States vs. Aaron Burr" resulted in a draw; the Burr Conspiracy was to survive as a fantasy for later generations to ponder.

The trial, as we noted before, has been treated at length by historians, biographers, and legal scholars. We do not want to rehearse that narrative here—our task, rather, is to locate its distinct interpretive modes and moments, of which we identify two.[65] The first of these encompasses the period from January to August 1807. The holding of two of Burr's alleged coconspirators, Swartwout and Bollman, led to a lengthy battle over habeas corpus, with the Senate voting to suspend it, the House refusing, and the Supreme Court upholding habeas. In late March, Burr was turned over to civilian authorities, and Chief Justice John Marshall soon thereafter made his second famous ruling on the constitutional definition of treason. The early weeks of the legal proceedings—late May to late June—were devoted to the empanelment of the grand jury, the initial hearing, indictments, questions of bail, and the matter of the subpoena duces tecum (ordering Jefferson to provide state papers about the conspiracy), with the trial proper deferred to August. During this time, virtually no new details about the conspiracy entered the press, and the discourse surrounding the trial turned increasingly to legal matters (the treason definition, habeas, the subpoena) with a concomitant partisan encoding of the battle: Marshall and the Federalists obstructing the Jefferson administration. With the empanelment of the grand jury in May, the defense strategy was made clear: it would defend "the only man in the nation whose rights are not secure from violation" and "convert this judicial inquiry into a political question."[66] General Eaton's testimony about Burr's plan to march on Washington gave way, for instance, to discussions of partisan attacks on Eaton.[67] The *Aurora*, in pieces widely reprinted, predicted the alliance of "*federalists* and *quids*" to "impeach the veracity" of state witnesses, while lamenting the "extreme corruption in what is called the *middle* or *upper* class of society, from which grand juries are selected."[68]

Perhaps the best account of the trial comes from an anonymous letter, seemingly from a Richmond socialite, published in that city's *Enquirer,* one of the crucial source papers for coverage. Asked to provide some sense of the city during the trial, the author opened with a complaint about the "*tedium* of repetition," for the "subject has been presented to the public in such a variety of attitudes, and every incident so fully and minutely scanned," that an original assessment would be almost impossible. So much information filled the papers "that ingenuity is foiled in extracting the truth, and credulity is put to the test in its belief." Burr's arrival in Richmond had created a "state of anxiety and agitation," but Burr remained imprecise: "as yet we have but a confused view of the outward form, without being acquainted with the native hue and figure of the design." The author went on to condemn the politicized response of both Federalists and Republicans alike. At one point, discussing Federalist Supreme Court Chief Justice John Marshall, and his seemingly improper meal with Burr, the author speculates, "He was unapprised of the invitation of B. but this I presume could not have deprived him of his faculty of locomotion, unless he had been touched by the transforming wand of Circe." Elsewhere, the author condemns the *Aurora* for its fabrications, noting that, for the right kind of reader, such libels only "bleach the more and whiter to the view."[69]

During this period, however, Burr's formal position, stripped of conspiratorial content, was reaffirmed. A lengthy piece, titled "Look at THIS Picture—and Then at THAT," appeared in the *Richmond Enquirer*, structured around the contrasting Greek and Roman portraits of Plutarch's *Lives*: "between the same being cast into the pursuits of very different careers; between what *he might have been* and what he *is*; between the destiny of A. Burr such as it would have been at this very moment, if he had but pursued the path of honorable ambition; and such as it actually is." This contrast included a chart (excerpted below). The article explained Burr's fall as the result of his unbridled ambition, leaving him "a *Traitor!!*" serving now as a "melancholy example."[70] Another favorite piece commented on the potential (and never realized) irony that Samuel Chase, recently on trial under Burr, might now sit "as chief justice on the case of Burr, who is arraigned as the most unprincipled traitor—as the vilest conspirator, that ever existed!"[71] The wax exhibit at Third and Market Streets, Philadelphia, included a statue of Burr alongside one of Napoleon and a figure of "Hamilton, in the attitude of bleeding, and gasping for life."[72]

He might have been	*He is*
President of the U. States.	*A prisoner.*
Decked with a wreath of glory.	Covered with a crown of thorns.
Elevated by new plans of beneficence.	Degraded by plots of treason.
Trusted by all.	Suspected by all.

Again and again, Burr appears as he did in Cheetham's pamphlets, a capacious formal position of uncertain designation. He is variously defined in relation to other figures in almost mathematical fashion—a juxtaposition, an inversion, a bifurcation—but with surprisingly little semiotic substance. A comical, Federalist parallax of these formulas put it well:

A gentleman, the other day, remarked to another, as a singular fact, that the initials of the name of A. Burr, were those of the two greatest conquerors that had ever spread ruin and devastation over the face of the earth, to wit, Alexander and Buonaparte. It is by no means singular, retorted his facetious friend; they will stand for the vilest traitor that ever disgraced humanity, Benedict Arnold, but in fact they will stand for ANY BODY.[73]

Absent substantive consideration of the conspiracy, enmeshed in legal formulations, surrounded by the partisan inflections on the trial procedures themselves, Burr was again evacuated into an empty abstraction. This formation, with the layered pleasures it generated, is beautifully captured in the visual fantasy described in another newspaper piece, one reminiscent of the Baxter episode in *Ormond*. "Shall we pause over the enormity" of the Burr Conspiracy and "wait until its miscreated visage has turned to appal its inventors? Or shall we instantly strip off the mask, beneath which the horrours of its effects are concealed." The answer to this question was, of course, to act immediately, lest "our country be defiled with the slaughter of her children."[74] But the oddity of the formulation speaks volumes and outstrips the seemingly simple rhetorical questions, which should not be read too quickly. The first question asks not "Should we expose Burr?" but rather "Should we wait until the horrors of Burr are visible *to its own inventors*?" And the second asks not "Should we strip off the mask to find the *source* of horror?" but rather "Should we not strip off the mask to *end the effects produced by the mask*?" Together, these rhetorical questions implicitly concede the construction of the Burr Conspiracy by Burr's enemies (the "inventors") *and* aver the importance of the mask—Burr as a traumatic colonel—to the very horror of the conspiracy. The mask must be at once ignored *and* removed as the source of horrors—essentially an admission that the elaboration of Burr through the semiotic aggregation of 1806 had gone too far.

The second moment of the trial then extends from the actual trials of August and September into the fall of 1807. Here the crucial procedural factor was the defense's move to block corroborative testimony on the grounds that an overt act of treason had not been proven—in short, without the evidence conforming to legal standards, much of the integrative semiotic material accumulated around Burr was compartmentalized. The prosecution then presented testimony from a range of witnesses that accentuated the stark contradictions of different narrative strands about the conspiracy. In September, the jury, which included partisan Jeffersonians, returned a verdict that Burr himself protested as "unusual, informal, and irregular": "Aaron Burr is not proved to be guilty under this indictment by any evidence submitted to us. We therefore find him not guilty."[75] This convolution was understood by newspaper readers. Because Marshall had restricted corroborative testimony until treason had been proven, the jury's verdict was not on Burr but on the trial—*within the parameters of the court, Burr was "not proved to be guilty," but this was not the usual "not guilty" verdict.* The conclusion of the trial confirmed its inconclusiveness: Burr was committed for trial in the venue of the conspiracy—Ohio—and forced again to give bail. That Ohio declined to prosecute confirmed the open-endedness of the case and its ambiguous verdict. And though the most sensational trial testimony—rehearsing and embellishing some of the conspiratorial details—trickled through the press into late October, the details were not processed in any kind of unified theory. Instead, the ambiguity of the verdict—upholding Burr's position as the traumatic kernel—was maintained. As we have implied, this was the ideal result, better than Burr's execution, and the *Aurora* was predicting this outcome, repeated in other papers, as early as June, two months before the actual trial.[76] By the announcement of the quasi-verdict, Duane could editorialize, "I presume there's scarce an intelligent man in society, but is satisfied of the guilt of Burr. . . . We therefore assume the ground that he is guilty."[77] The acquittal itself was increasingly cast as a relaunching of the conspiracy—"Burr has again escaped," noted the *Aurora*.[78] Another piece, titled "Burr's Acquittal," began, "Now may the ensign of rebellion be once more unfurled, and *all* may hurry to its standard fearless of punishment. . . . [Burr] may promote discord, and dismember union, trample laws, and mock the power of man."[79] Burr's defense council, Luther Martin, predicted that Burr would divide the Union within six months, and in Baltimore effigies of Burr, Marshall, Harman Blennerhassett, and Martin were burned.[80]

The conclusion of the trial thus reestablished Burr in his most useful formulation, as an imprecise formal position that signaled but also shielded the horror of the Real, the extensive and necessary violence and justice of a slave revolution. The traumatic colonel could retain its tenuous position as "Burr within the bosom of the union," as the *Aurora* put it.[81]

We cannot conclude our discussion of the treason trial, however, without discussing the one text that survived it: William Wirt's famous closing argument for the prosecution, focusing on Burr's satanic domination of his codefendant and Eve, Harman Blennerhassett:

> In the midst of all this peace, this innocence, and this tranquillity,—this feast of the mind, this pure banquet of the heart,—the destroyer comes. He comes to turn this paradise into a hell. Yet the flowers do not wither at his approach, and no monitory shuddering through the bosom of their unfortunate possessor warns him of the ruin that is coming upon him. A

stranger presents himself. It is Aaron Burr. Introduced to their civilities by the high rank which he had lately held in his country, he soon finds his way to their hearts, by the dignity and elegance of his demeanor, the light and beauty of his conversation, and the seductive and fascinating power of his address. . . . Such was the state of Eden, when the serpent entered its bowers![82]

This was the speech that was to survive the trial, excerpted in rhetoric textbooks for a century, but in the context of the trial, it was a simplistic reversion to biblical binaries reminiscent of the crude Federalist attack on Burr in the 1801 handbill. Burr was again cast as the "author," "projector," and "active executor" of the plot, but the metaphorical avoidance of both racial *and* legal content was telling. Benjamin Botts, speaking for the defense, noted as much:

I cannot promise you, sir, a speech manufactured out of tropes and figures. Instead of the magnificent image of Bonaparte ascending to quench the stars, so fitted for the dry law question in debate, my humble efforts will be altogether below the clouds. Instead of the introduction of a sleeping Venus with all the luxury of voluptuous and wanton nakedness to charm the reason through the refined medium of sensuality, and to convince us that the law of treason is with the prosecution by leading our imaginations to the fascinating richness and symmetry of a heaving bosom and luscious waist, I am compelled to plod heavily and meekly on through the dull doctrines of Hale and Foster.[83]

Just as the prosecution had turned from evidence to "tropes and figures," the defense turned to legal details. Wirt's speech was widely reprinted but no more than any other transcript from the trial; in 1807, its ridiculous simplicity and ineffectiveness warranted no special attention, while its rhetorical excesses signaled the analytical failures of the prosecution. But once the Burr Conspiracy was entered into the ledger of the United States' political imaginary, it could be trotted out to schoolchildren as the essential text of the moment, an exercise of cheap frisson. In April 1807, Burr had written his daughter another insightful piece of literary criticism—a kind of metacommentary on how to withstand the trial. "You have read to very little purpose if you have not remarked that such things happen in all democratic governments," he wrote. "I pray you to amuse yourself by collecting and collating all the instances to be found in ancient history, which you may connect together, if you please, in an essay, with reflections, comments, and applications." Giving her four weeks to submit her assignment, he concluded that he expected "great pleasure in the perusal," but he rightly concluded by turning back to Theodosia, who could herself expect "great satisfaction and consolation in the composition."[84] Thus, he predicted the satisfying exercise of nineteenth-century students, who might memorize Wirt's feeble cartoon and make it their own.

Conclusion

Apart from our reading of Burr's symptomatic significance at this time as one of the most important displacements of the Haitian Revolution already coded through Toussaint L'Ouverture, we have been concerned to explore and foreground alternative phantasmatic experiences of history. In other words, rather than examine the relationship between some kind of historical reality and a secondary literary reflection, we have wanted to trouble that relationship, to look at the distortions of history as imaginative and the tensions of literary expression as diagnostically illuminating. If scholarship has traditionally assumed a real-life Burr distorted by secondary imaginative adornments, it has missed the potential insights of taking the Burr fantasy not as distortion but as truth, with historical details often scandalously emerging to flesh out the story. If Burr continues to have vestigial significance for some people today—as the slightly charged punchline of milk-commercial trivia, for instance—it is not because of his historical importance but because of the erstwhile power of the imaginative (and often literary) creations of 1800–1807. What we respond to is the cultural, historical charge of the referent, less the semiotic data than the structure, however much degraded by the passage of time. The passages we quote in our opening pages speak to just that literary-characterological appeal, the leakage of an old isotope.

What the Burr case evokes, we hope, is a reconstituted project of literary history, one of a much greater purview. The anticipatory moments of the writing and reading of Burr came with the characterological work of the Revolution: the formulations of Washington and Franklin, the anecdotal processing of war atrocities around the figures of Arnold and André, and finally the partisan emergence of Hamilton and Jefferson. At this point, some of the moment's novels demonstrated diagnostic and predictive insights, exploring the disruptions-to-come (*Ormond*) and the emergent geopolitical permutations of the drama of US slavery (*Female Quixotism*).

And then, with spectacular force, the drama of Burr was constructed in fits and starts, in serial fragments, twists and turns, before its remarkable denouement in Richmond's flashy revue. Here the Burr phenomenon is best calibrated alongside the rise in biographical writings, political pamphleteering, newspaper sketches, the larger imaginative experiments we term novels—in short a much wider range of writing with which scholars have barely begun to grapple. We conclude with a few speculations about the aftermath of the Burr moment, evoked by a few texts of the end of Burr's decade.

The first of these is John Davis's *Walter Kennedy: An Interesting American Tale*, published in London in 1805 and then again in 1808, right after the Burr trial. Davis had arrived in the United States from Britain in 1798, taking a quick stab at the novel with *The Original Letters of Ferdinand and Elisabeth*, based on a recently scandalous murder-suicide in New York; thereafter he wrote several other fictions set in the United States or featuring US characters, including a series of variations on the John Smith and Pocahontas story, which he did much to popularize. As a novel written by a recent migrant, unconstrained by the literary conventions, traditions, or expectations of the major US population centers, *Walter Kennedy* aggregates the most basic semiotic material in wide circulation at the moment, though often not in fiction. The protagonist is raised in Ireland, where, after a failed marriage proposal within the local nobility, he resolves to move to the Indian societies of Louisiana. He journeys up the Mississippi after an initial embarkation at New Orleans, and much of the novel comprises a backwoodsman's adventures with nature, Native Americans, and finally a princess whom he courts and marries. The wilderness travels that occupy the latter half of the book are culled from descriptions of wildlife and Native Americans that appeared in other narratives, giving Davis's novel a magazine-like quality. Even in this context, the initial voyage to Louisiana is particularly fraught, with an almost ludicrously overdetermining sequence of events occurring in the Atlantic crossing. Kennedy's ship encounters Algerine/Turkish pirates seeking to take the ship for slaves. What follows, then, is an encounter with a New York ship bringing word of "a deep plot laid among the blacks of North Carolina to recover their liberty, massacre their white masters, seize the women, and establish a system of equality."[1] The leader of the conspiracy—"only detected a few hours before it was to have been executed"—was hanged, but not until he was revealed to be "a sort of wild poet."[2] Then, safely in the middle of the Atlantic Ocean, we are given the full song:

QUASHEE'S SEDITIOUS ODE.

Our massa Jeffeson he say,
    Dat all mans free alike are born;
Den tell me, why should Quashee stay,
    To tend de cow and hoe de corn?
    Huzza for massa Jeffeson!

And if all mans alike be free,
    Why should de one, more dan his broder,
Hab house and corn? For poor Quashee
    No had de one, no hab de oder.
    Huzza for massa Jeffeson!

And why should one hab be white wife,
    And me hab only Quangeroo?
Me see no reason for me life!
    No! Quashee hab de white wife too!
    Huzza for massa Jeffeson!

For make all like, let blackee nab
    De white womans. . . . dat be de track!
Den Quashee de white wife will hab,
    And massa Jef. shall hab de black.
    Huzza for massa Jeffeson!

Why should a judge (him always white)
    'Pon pickaninny put him paw,
Cause he steal little? Dat no rite!
    No! Quashee say he'll hab no law.
    Huzza for massa Jeffeson!

Who care, me wonder, for de judge?
    Quashee no care. . . . no not a feder;
Our party soon we make him trudge,
    We all be democrat togeder.
    Huzza for massa Jeffeson!

For where de harm to cut de troat
    Of him no like? Or rob a little?

> *To take him hat, or shoe, or coat,*
> *Or wife, or horse, or drink, or vittle?*
> *Huzza for massa Jeffeson!*
>
> *Huzza for us den! we de boys*
> *To rob and steal, and burn and kill;*
> *Huzza! me say! and make de noise!*
> *Huzza for Quashee! Quashee will*
> *Huzza for massa Jeffeson!*[3]

The song was not created by Davis and had appeared in print before, originally in the *Port Folio* in 1802,[4] after which it was reprinted in several Federalist newspapers in the summer of 1802. It appears to have referenced a planned uprising in North Carolina: Winton is mentioned in all the accounts, including Davis's, and there was an insurrection apparently discovered in that region at that time.[5] The original *Port Folio* version was clearly a partisan attack and included the conceit that Quashee hoped his poetry "would be collected and published by the democratic society, of which he (poor fellow!) had been a member." Two other details served to delimit the scope of the poem: first, a Latin epigraph preceded the song, while Quashee is characterized as knowing only the languages of "the Gold Coast, and a little English." Davis's reworking of the poem, several years later,[6] recontextualized it significantly: gone were the Latin phrase, the Africanization, and the explicit link with the Democrats. In the context of the transit to Louisiana, the anecdote now seemed more generally societal—it appeared, after all, in an "American Tale"—and where the paratext of the first version casts the song as plucked from the slave rebel and inserted in the newspaper, Walter Kennedy tells us that Quashee's "songs are still sung in Carolina to the artless music of the banger [banjo]."[7] Granted, the critique of Jefferson is still clear. In 1803, Davis had dedicated *Travels of Four Years and a Half,* his memoir of building a career in the United States, to Thomas Jefferson, though he had also pointedly referenced Burr as a patron figure in New York. Indeed, Davis narrated how Burr had gotten him a position under Albert Gallatin at the Treasury Department, but after traveling to Washington to accept the post in person, Gallatin informed Davis that Burr had misunderstood: the detailed recounting of this disappointment may indict the Jefferson administration and signal awareness of the Jefferson-Burr rift. But *Travels* had also concluded with the somewhat unique literary innovation of an interpolated slave narrative, "Story of Dick the Negro."[8] Though a mere ten pages, the narrative conveyed a strong sense of the evils of slavery, the realistic possibility of abolitionism (one heir of a plantation frees his slaves and gives them land), and a clear sense of interracial sexuality (Dick's first young master has many black mistresses and is finally killed by a slave for approaching his wife). And Dick plays the banger/banjo—learned at the instigation of his sexually active young master, who was a gifted dancer of the "Congo Minuet"—a dance that may have had its origins in white Haitian fantasies.[9]

From our perspective, then, the tremendous semiotic accretion in Davis's writings of the moment—the journey to Louisiana overdetermined by potential Algerine enslavement *and* the North Carolina eruption with its Haitian echoes—shifts qualitatively from partisan slurs to a remarkable precursor of the minstrel tradition. The minstrel figure is typically located in the late 1820s or early 1830s,[10] though references to the banjo/banger tradition appear significantly earlier. What we see here is the aggregation of many components in a constellation that sensitively registers the Burr phenomenon about to unfold, from racialization to conspiracy. We have quoted Henry Adams's observation that Burr was a "Jim Crow of melodramatic windbags"—essentially a spouter of racialized political semes, as if in minstrel performance. What we see with *Walter Kennedy* is the same insight but from the other temporal direction: the Quashee scene seems to predict not only the Burr figure becoming the president's racially charged almost-double but the emergence of minstrelsy itself, clarified as a Haitian-inflected blend of love and theft.[11] Without being a text explicitly about the Burr event (it travels adjacently) *Walter Kennedy* suggests means of productively thinking about intertextuality and what an alternative sense of genre (perhaps a protominstrelsy) might be able to illuminate.

A different lesson is suggested by Leonora Sansay's *Secret History*, the subtitle of which—*or, the Horrors of St. Domingo, in a Series of Letters, Written by a Lady at Cape Francois. To Col. Burr, Late Vice-President of the United States*—would seem to confirm the basic premise of our work.[12] Here in 1808, at the denouement of the Burr Conspiracy, we are presented with the two pervasive and unstable signifiers that relationally define the semiotic dynamo whose motion we have aimed to capture: Saint-Domingue and Aaron Burr—two disruptive, even apocalyptic energies that together presage annihilation from both outside and within. In the preceding chapters, we have considered the frenetic oscillation of public attention between Burr and Haiti. But here, as in that optical illusion wherein images on two sides of a surface, when spun rapidly, appear to share the same plane, Burr and Haiti cease to displace each other. In the whirl of semiotic detail, two appear as one. Where is Burr? He is not proven to be guilty and is once again on the loose. What is Saint-Domingue to Burr? *There is a secret history of Saint-Domingue that involves Aaron Burr?* The trial had resolved nothing. A sense that an insidious new chapter of Burrite intrigue had just begun spread through the Democratic-Republican press. When Luther Martin supposedly predicted that Burr would divide the Union within six months of his acquittal, mobs burned effigies of the defense attorney, Burr himself, Blennerhassett, and John Marshall. The international tensions leading to what became the War of 1812 kept the fantasy international in scope. In 1808, President Jefferson wrote to an Ohio senator, "If we have war with Spain, he will become a Spanish General. If with England, he will go to Canada and be employed there. Internal convulsion may be attempted if no game more hopeful offer"[13]— an assessment that could have been written of Toussaint in 1801. In this context, *Secret History* promised new revelations. Sansay's publishers clearly wanted the public appetite for Burr-mania to drive sales of *Secret History*. The first bound volumes covering the treason trial appeared soon after Burr's acquittal in September 1807. In February 1808, the first advertisements for Sansay's *Secret History* appeared. Often, as in the February 4 issue of the *Democratic Press* (Philadelphia), notice of the publication of *Secret History* shared the page with an ad for the trial transcripts. The February 11 *New-York Evening Post* sandwiched an ad for the trial papers between two competing publishing houses' announcement of *Secret History*. A national market speedily opened as ads appeared in Boston and Alexandria, Virginia, throughout the spring. In content and context, then, *Secret History* presented a consistent message: Haiti and the Burr Conspiracy were linked. "How?" remained the question.

This question dominated our early conversations about this project. What had Burr *learned* from Sansay's field reports? What were the *lessons* of Saint-Domingue? Might Saint-Domingue have given Burr a strategic advantage in those chaotic western territories whose demographic diversity, speculative economic system, and political instability had more likeness to the Caribbean zone than to the partisanly binary politics of the littoral republic?[14] But we came to see these as the wrong questions— the very kinds of problems that literary recovery of novelness had set itself against. One might say that literary critics have reasonably evaded the problem of the Burr reference, seeing it as a trap of realist details of potentially little literary interest. Worrying about Burr (if not Haiti) was a problem for the historians. *Secret History* promised to be interesting because it was *not* patriarchal historiography but operated in a different register. Thus, much recent criticism productively turned to matters of genre, building on the Revolutionary history which an earlier wave of scholarship had treated.[15] Tamika Nadine Walker treated the novel as a counterromance; Sîan Silyn-Roberts, as engaging the captivity narrative; Elizabeth Dillon and Gretchen Woertendyke in relation to secret histories and romans à clef. What ties these readings together? Haiti in these accounts creates a rupture enabling women authors to reimagine the types of stories they could submit to the public. Thus, a racial and political rebellion creates the conditions in which different forms of solidarity are imaginable, especially among women. The result is a counterromantic lesson about the "dark nature of romance" and a desire for a potent, cosmopolitan alternative; or a narrative that overturns the cultural logic of captivity by inverting the association of the wilderness with barbarism and the patriarchal home with stability; or an Old World protonovelistic form (the secret history) developed into something different from the European novel that eventually superseded it on the continent.[16] When history as such returns, as it does in Michelle Burnham's recent essay, it seems to pour cold water on any new politics emerging from these generic experiments; the novel is ensnared in an expansive, messy tableau created by the expansion of capitalism from 1492 to the present that consistently makes practical modes of resistance impossible whether in the equally subordinated public or domestic sphere.[17] These attempts to read *Secret History* into an American literary history seem promising, though in these instances, Burr remains epiphenomenal.[18]

As we noted earlier, the Burr constellation emerged amid a wave of characterological writings from the 1780s into their most complete form in the first decade of the nineteenth century. In the terminology of literary history, then, what we have called Burr amounts to a significant episode in the US literary exploration of character. This, we believe, is a useful point of access to Sansay's novel, once we make the move from reading the proper name as either sensationalist marketing gimmick or extraneous private referent to seeing the name as a characterological marker, a structuring element. Of course, the most obvious rejoinder to this claim is that Burr, apart from the titular reference, is absent within the text, but this simplifies our task, by demonstrating that the odd framing signifier is so semiotically rich that it need *only* appear on the novel's title page to exert its force. So how does it work and what is it doing?

Burr's all-but-absent presence in the novel is best understood as marking a semiotic shift from character to setting. Burr's character was initially a formal space of cryptic emptiness *and* of excess; of stark logical necessity *and* tremendous hermeneutic capacity; of dangerous mutability and constancy at the same time. In this way, Burr revealed the importance, work, and outer limits of character as an organizing element in narrative—in this case the political narrative unfolding through the more stable dynamic of the Founders constellation. We might read Saint-Domingue as very much the formal counterpart, in setting, to Burr's characterness. We can see this manifest during the Revolutionary period with the multiple renamings of the island. Colonial, slaveholding Saint-Domingue is also St. Domingo, a Francophobic transcription; and the adoption of Haiti after the Revolution is itself a throwback to the original quasi-indigenous Arawak Indian name Ayiti, "mountainous region." In *Secret History*, this fragmented voraciousness is evident in the heavy inflections of space in the opening pages: the sea, site of slave trade and naval conflicts, becomes a site of utopian asylum; the town and its environs are seen as "a heap of ruins" and a "terrible picture of desolation," a fantasy of hedonism amid "silent slaves," a climate itself materially participating in the conflict, and dangerous sexually charged spaces of enclosure (61, 73). Doreen Massey writes of material space as a "sphere of multiple trajectories," calling for an "imaginative opening up of space . . . to refuse that flipping of the imaginative eye from modernist singular temporality to postmodern depthlessness; to retain at least some sense of the contemporaneous multiple becomings."[19] This conception stresses the semiotic and historical codings coexistent in a single space, some privileged and others overlooked, and suggests a way to understand Revolutionary space not as a product of a temporal break but as a multiply crossed topography of competing desires, practices, drives, and so on. Sansay's narrative experimentation aims at capturing precisely this phenomenon in space, offering a diagnosis of these competing spatial currents. The semiotic density, however, increasingly vies with a formal perspective of the imperial island, something readers first sense with the shift from Saint-Domingue to Cuba and even more so with the shift to Jamaica and the concluding flurry of letters between Jamaica *and* Cuba, even as Philadelphia remains in the background as another space in the series. The sense that one is reading a comparativist text of some sort emerges directly from this formal effect, confirming that setting is the text's dominant element.

The magnification of setting to almost intrusive dimensions—perhaps unique to the US novel at that point—seems directly linked with the collapse of character. In a revealing detail in *Secret History*'s first letter, Mary presents Madame LeClerc with "one of the beautiful silver medals of Washington, engraved by Reich" (65). The historical referent here was in fact a Jefferson medal, the detail likely changed to satisfy the partisan leanings of the publisher (65n. 2). Not long after, Clara visits the "Government house," where the dining room is adorned with panels naming distinguished military figures (Napoleon, Frederick the Great, Masséna): Clara observes "that Washington should also have found a place there!" and a few days later, his name is added (80). If the former instance suggests that Washington is but a formal position, the latter confirms that point explicitly. A similar point is made with a figure such as Don Carlos—of Irish birth, in Spanish service, a veteran of Peru, bound for Mexico, taken prisoner by the English, and encountering Mary through the French language—in a scene overdetermined by instances of linguistic misunderstanding (133–34). Here the brief and conventional sketch of the thwarted lover (Carlos, in loving Angelina, is opposed by both her father and the viceroy-as-rival-suitor) is recoded in spatial terms: the social-affective disorder of this old narrative is now an occasion to enact spatial instability: it is as if the traditional romantic formula is refit with a gazetteer. But the starkest example of the breakdown of character is the bifurcation of the protagonist into the Mary/Clara pair itself. What initially appears as a story with a sibling foil becomes dialectic as the sisters find themselves on parallel islands, and the interpretive puzzle of Clara's hyperbolic development—her characterological instability—has to be seen as a question of shifting literary conventions, not some protorealist assessment of personality.

Further study of this moment is needed to situate the shift we are describing, which at first glance enacts, in literary-historical terms, that famous anecdote about Toussaint: under arrest and boarding the ship for France, he reportedly declared, "In overthrowing me, you have cut down in San Domingo only the trunk of the tree of liberty. It will spring up again by the roots for they are numerous and deep."[20] This is the heroic version of a competing anecdote rehearsed in *Secret History*: "A short time before [Toussaint] was taken, he had his treasure buried in the woods, and at the return of the negroes he employed on the expedition, they were shot without being suffered to utter a word" (63). In each instance, Toussaint, removed from Saint-Domingue, is transubstantiated into the landscape, whether as the tree that will not be killed or as the treasure-absorbing earth. If the equation of Hero with Nation is unremarkable, *Secret History* perhaps demonstrates the difficulties of literary implementation.

Here we turn to one last text, Leonora Sansay's *Laura*, published a year after *Secret History* and perhaps a bit of an enigma for readers wondering how to relate the two works. The recent critical interest in *Secret History* coincided with the hemispheric turn in American literary studies, presenting a novel at once socially discerning and frenetically unfocused. It was the perfect conjunction for critics looking for a vantage point from which the cultural hybridity of the extranational Caribbean basin could be described.[21] *Secret History* was that odd mixture of the raw colonial travel narrative, cooked social critique, and boiled literary experimentation. In such a roiling text of generic confusion, Sansay as author-function almost seemed to disappear beneath a semic avalanche: hence an assessment such as Burnham's, that the novel's treatment of race and gender is "hopelessly entangled."[22] *Laura*, by contrast, seems a remarkably conventional text. Whereas *Secret History* decenters and disrupts character, showing it subject to rapidly shifting geographies and elective affinities, *Laura* seems invested in a certain melancholic type. The novel reaches an almost exhausted denouement as the narrator resigns herself to an abrupt ending. "To trace Laura through the many vicissitudes that awaited her, would be a task too painful," she concludes, leaving her readers with a pat and all-too-simplistic moral copestone: "Perpetual uneasiness, disquietude, and irreversible misery, are the certain consequences of fatal misconduct in a woman; however gifted, or however reclaimed."[23] If it is novel for Sansay to let Laura survive pregnancy, retain her beauty, and continue to enrich her mind, these achievements are surely compromised by the novelist's fatigue at the thought of engaging her character's continuing development. By contrast, *Secret History* had drawn to a close not with an anticipated elaboration of character but with the end of movement through a colonial geography and a return to what could seem a more stable setting. Anticipating a return to Philadelphia, Mary once again directs herself to Burr as Clara's future "protector and friend" and concludes with the hope that they "may still be happy" (154). We note that readers of *Secret History* in 1808 were certainly in a privileged position to see the irony in the novel's closing wish. After all, it appeared in print only months after Burr's trial concluded, and, in February, he was still under indictment in Ohio, his effigy had been sent up in flames at Baltimore, and he himself narrowly escaped imprisonment in Philadelphia for his debts. What longed-for stability could this BURR truly offer? This, however, only underscores the point that *Secret History* leaves its readers with not only the evacuated characterological position but also a setting that only the most naive could consider inoculated from the crises just described to the south.

In *Laura*, setting is trivial. The high-walled monastery in Lisbon, the markets of Dublin, and the pastoral banks of the Schuykill are conventionally drawn. Even the shockingly detailed eyewitness account of fever-stricken Philadelphia in chapter 12 is gothically imbued: the whole is like a "building which has remained long unopened," and grave diggers, navigating streets strewn with abandoned sickly dogs and dead cats, hasten the dead and dying in overloaded carts to burial "as if their contents could not be quickly enough committed to the earth" (178–79). The realist details of chapter 12 comment notably on the city's emptiness, its deserted streets and naked wharves. But there is an exception. Belfield, a medical student in the city, contracts yellow fever but is unable to reach Laura to tell her about his condition. He has seemingly disappeared, but in truth, he had been "abandoned" by his friends "to the care of a negro" at the start of the epidemic. In his feverish incoherence, Belfield's "ravings about Laura" are ignored. When Laura finally does locate him after traversing the desolated city, a "little negro boy" silently conveys her to Belfield's bedside (177, 179). Is it not revealing that these residual historical referents and the one possible link to Saint-Domingue in the novel must be an obstacle to communication or remain silent?[24] That is, what was explicit in *Secret History*, a spatial argument about intrahemispheric convergence and contradiction, is, in *Laura*, registered only obliquely by gesturing at defining features of character.

This silent "little negro boy" takes us back to our introduction, where the crooked-nose death mask of Aaron Burr stands in relation to that of a "Florida Negro Boy," included, writes the curator of these masks, as a point of comparison: "Whatever the head of a Bonaparte, a Washington, a Webster, or a Brougham is, his head is not." Serving as the negation of an apparently legible greatness in the masks of elite white men, the Florida Negro Boy's mask may be better appreciated by that other anecdote of Burr's life mask, attempted while he was in exile in London in 1809 and enthralled with his new friend Bentham's panoptical prison, allowing surreptitious surveillance from all angles. The Italian artist commissioned for the mask, we recall, had left a stain on the colonel's nose that could not be removed. As with an anamorphism that, when looked at awry, reveals an unacknowledgeable truth, this stain, which at least temporarily convinced Burr not to be seen in public, is a sign that the Burr function would continue to override his biographical self. That Florida Negro Boy is the supplement, the residue of what the biographical Burr "is not" and what the Burr function would continue to be. It is tempting to suggest that Burr had acknowledged the function he had become. He traveled home in 1812 under a new alias: Adolphus Arnot.

Notes

1. John Adams to Benjamin Rush, November 11, 1807, in *The Spur of Fame: Dialogues of John Adams and Benjamin Rush, 1805–1813*, ed. John A. Schutz and Douglass Adair (Indianapolis: Liberty Fund, 2001), 106–7. Correspondence from this volume hereafter cited parenthetically in the text by date and page number.

2. See also the later letter of April 22, 1812, citing Timothy Pickering's opinions on Washington. The same "Colonel Pickering who is now holding himself up as the Friend and Admirer and Lover of Washington" had earlier called Washington an illiterate clown who never wrote his own letters or read more than one book on military strategy (232–33).

3. The term appears to have entered recent discourse via a *Newsweek* article by Evan Thomas, "Founders Chic: Live from Philadelphia" (July 9, 2001, 48), and H. W. Brands's *Atlantic Magazine* essay "Founders Chic" (September 2003, 101–10), with notable reiterations in David Waldstreicher's review essay "Founders Chic as Culture War" (*Radical History Review* 84 [Fall 2002]: 185–94) and Francis D. Cogliano's review essay "Founders Chic" (*History* 90.299 [July 2005]: 411–19).

4. See Roland Barthes, *Mythologies*, trans. Annette Lavers (New York: Hill & Wang, 1972), 156–59; and Barthes, "Change the Object Itself: Mythology Today," in *Image-Music-Text*, ed. and trans. Stephen Heath, 165–69 (New York: Hill & Wang, 1977).

5. We here draw on Roland Barthes's sense of the semic, referring to the smallest connotative elements—semes—from which symbolic meaning is constructed. For Barthes they are unstable, dispersed "motes of dust, flickers of meaning." Barthes, *S/Z*, trans. Richard Miller (New York: Hill and Wang, 1974), 19.

6. One can see this in action in Robert Wuhl's popular HBO specials, *Assume the Position*, which feature the comedian in front of an NYU classroom.

7. We note here the obvious irony of John Adams schooling Benjamin Rush, analyst of manias, maniculas, and manalgias, on the Founders pathology.

8. Kojin Karatani, *Transcritique: On Kant and Marx*, trans. Sabu Kohso (Cambridge: MIT Press, 2005), 1; Slavoj Žižek, *The Parallax View* (Cambridge: MIT Press, 2006), 7.

9. Molly Anne Rothenberg, *The Excessive Subject: A New Theory of Social Change* (Malden, MA: Polity, 2010), 9.

10. Ibid.

11. Mladen Dolar, "Beyond Interpellation," *Qui Parle* 6.2 (Spring–Summer 1993): 78.

12. Slavoj Žižek, *The Plague of Fantasies* (New York: Verso, 1997), 3.

13. Garry Wills, *Negro President: Jefferson and the Slave Power* (Boston: Houghton Mifflin, 2003), 13.

14. Matthew Mason, *Slavery and Politics in the Early American Republic* (Chapel Hill: University of North Carolina Press, 2006), 35.

15. Michel-Rolph Trouillot, *Silencing the Past: Power and the Production of History* (Boston: Beacon, 1995), 70.

16. Joan Dayan, *Haiti, History, and the Gods* (Berkeley: University of California Press, 1995); Sybille Fischer, *Modernity Disavowed: Haiti and the Cultures of Slavery in the Age of Revolution* (Durham: Duke University Press, 2004).

17. See, for example, Laura Romero, *Home Fronts: Domesticity and Its Critics in the Antebellum United States* (Durham: Duke University Press, 1997); Jared Gardner, *Master Plots: Race and the Founding of an American Literature, 1787–1845* (Baltimore: Johns Hopkins University Press, 1998); and Carroll Smith-Rosenberg, "Black Gothic: The Shadowy Origins of the American Bourgeoisie," in *Possible Pasts: Becoming Colonial in Early America*, ed. Robert Blair St. George, 243–69 (Ithaca: Cornell University Press, 2000).

18. Mason, *Slavery and Politics*, 41.

19. "To examine the impact of notions of racial hierarchy, racial exclusion, and racial vulnerability and availability on nonblacks who held, resisted, explored, or altered these notions." Toni Morrison, *Playing in the Dark: Whiteness and the Literary Imagination* (Cambridge: Harvard University Press, 1992), 11.

20. Laurence Hutton, *Talks in a Library with Laurence Hutton, Recorded by Isabel Moore* (New York: G. P. Putnam's Sons, 1906), 168.

21. Laurence Hutton, *Portraits in Plaster* (New York: Harper & Brothers, 1894), 246.

22. Orson Squire Fowler, *Sexual Science; Including Manhood, Womanhood, and Their Mutual Interrelations . . . as Taught by Phrenology* (Philadelphia: National Publishing, 1870), 69–70.

23. Hutton, *Talks in a Library*, 169.

24. Ibid., 266.

NOTES TO CHAPTER 1

1. Quoted in Barry Schwartz, *George Washington: The Making of an American Symbol* (Ithaca: Cornell University Press, 1987), 22.

2. We cite here the 1793 Philadelphia edition: Richard Snowden, *The American Revolution: Written in the Style of Ancient History*, 2 vols. (Philadelphia: Jones, Hoff & Derrick, 1793), 1:101. Hereafter cited parenthetically in the text.

3. Brendan McConville, *The King's Three Faces: The Rise and Fall of Royal America, 1688–1776* (Chapel Hill: University of North Carolina Press, 2006), 254. Hereafter cited parenthetically in the text.

4. "These representations, along with the tiles, delftware, slipware, and glassware, allowed for an imperialized household" (ibid., 134).

5. Bernard Bailyn, *The Ideological Origins of the American Revolution* (Cambridge: Harvard University Press, 1967), 122, 148.

6. In two essays: "The Faces of Lord Bute: A Visual Contribution to Anglo-American Political Ideology," in *Perspectives in American History* 6 (1972): 95–116 (hereafter cited parenthetically in the text as *FLB*); and "The Misfortunes of Lord Bute: A Case-Study in Eighteenth-Century Political Argument and Public Opinion," in *Historical Journal* 16.1 (1973): 3–43 (hereafter cited parenthetically in the text as *MLB*).

7. "Such mob attacks as those on the favourite—either in person or in effigy—cannot be explained simply in terms of political hostility or personal antipathy to Lord Bute. Hatred of Bute, like the adulation of his political antonym Wilkes, provided a focal point, an outlet for many disparate grievances" (*MLB* 7).

8. On the ideological components, see *MLB* 23–40; on the "whig" critique as "tendentious" and unfair to "this scholarly and sensitive man," see 40–43 (quotes on 42 and 41).

9. See *FLB* 98.

10. John Leacock, *The First Book of the American Chronicles of the Times, 1774–1775*, ed. Carla Mulford (Newark: University of Delaware Press, 1987), 58. The Bernard here is Francis Bernard, Hutchinson's predecessor as Massachusetts governor.

11. John Leacock, *The Fall of British Tyranny; or, American Liberty Triumphant* (Philadelphia: Styner & Cist, 1776), viii.

12. John Trumbull, *M'Fingal: A Modern Epic Poem; Canto First, or the Town Meeting* (Philadelphia: William and Thomas Bradford, 1775), 2.

13. Hugh Henry Brackenridge, *The Battle of Bunkers-Hill* (Philadelphia: Robert Bell, 1776), 20.

14. *The Crisis* series has received little critical or historiographic attention, for reasons evident in Colin Bonwick's summary: "This scurrilous newspaper, published in 1775–76 and devoted to the American conflict, expressed many of the radicals' views but in a most extreme form and frequently in the most hysterical fashion; in particular, several issues contained savage personal attacks on George III and scarcely veiled threats of a domestic revolution. The authors probably included the pamphleteer William Moore and the historian Philip Thicknesse and did not represent any significant movement. Certainly they did not represent the radicals." Bonwick, *English Radicals and the American Revolution* (Chapel Hill: University of North Carolina Press, 1977), 83–84. Bonwick's suggestion that "scurrilous," "savage," and "hysterical" works have been beneath the measured attentions of intellectual historians betrays the artificially restricted generic field and the limited vocabulary for considering the affective and fantastic elements of political writing.

15. These passages are from *The Crisis, Number XVII* (New York: T. W. Shaw, 1775), 140; *The Crisis, Number XVIII* (New York: John Anderson, 1775), 153; and *The Crisis, Number XXI* (New York: John Anderson, 1775), 176.

16. *Reflections of a Few Friends of the Country, upon Several Circumstantial Points* (Philadelphia: [Henry Miller], 1776), 24.

17. Ibid., 25. Pady later complains, "I got my leg broke about fooletiks." "Politicks, you mean," answers a Parson (42).

18. Mercy Otis Warren, *History of the Rise, Progress and Termination of the American Revolution*, ed. Lester H. Cohen, vol. 1 (Indianapolis: Liberty Fund, 1989), 15.

19. Ibid., 150.

20. *The Crisis, Number XVIII*, 149.

21. The distinction is also implicit in *The Crisis, Number III* (Hartford, CT: Ebenezer Watson, 1775), which states, "It is now evident to the whole world, that there was a plan formed by Lord *Bute* and yourself, either before, or immediately after, you came to the crown, for subverting the British constitution in church and state" (20). Despite the conflation of Bute and king, the syntax nonetheless suggests Bute's intellectual scheming preceding George's physical ascension.

22. Greimas's work is best known in the US through the various explications of Fredric Jameson, who also wrote the introduction to the English-language translation of Greimas's *On Meaning*. Jameson's applications of the semiotic square tend to focus on specific cultural artifacts (novels or other artistic works, philosophical movements), to stress the strict logical constraints of the various terms, and to sketch out the various positions between terms. We adopt here a looser adaptation of Greimas, focused less on particular texts than on the aggregate effect within hegemonic political discourse.

23. Even the famous criticisms of Washington have an illuminating quality here—the common complaint that he was an American Fabius Cunctator, the overly cautious "Delayer" rather than bold military daredevil, nicely captures the relational distinction between Washington and the king.

24. Bruce Burgett offers a clear version of this view: "Like so many founding figures ('Jefferson,' 'Jay,' 'Franklin,' 'Hamilton,' 'Madison'), 'Washington' names not (only) a biographical and historical person, but (also) a public space where the abstraction of nationality becomes realizable through symbolic acts of political and cultural representation." Burgett, *Sentimental Bodies: Sex, Gender, and Citizenship in the Early Republic* (Princeton: Princeton University Press, 1998), 57.

25. Michel Guillaume Jean de Crèvecoeur, "Forty-Nine Anecdotes," trans. Ed White, *Early American Literature* 43.2 (2008): 425 (Anecdote 34). The reference to Ramsay's history confirms the symbolic distillation undertaken by Crèvecoeur's mélange.

26. See ibid., 415 (Anecdote 8), which deploys the Cincinnatus myth in reference to Lincoln and Heath, and 426 (Anecdote 37), which offers a variant for Putnam and Gates.

27. Gordon Wood, *The Americanization of Benjamin Franklin* (New York: Penguin, 2004), 140.

28. Ibid., 141.

29. Michael Warner, *The Letters of the Republic: Publication and the Public Sphere in Eighteenth-Century America* (Cambridge: Harvard University Press, 1992), 94.

30. We quote from Smith's edition, *American Poems, Selected and Original*, vol. 1 (Litchfield, CT: Collier and Buel, 1793), 3. Hereafter cited parenthetically in the text.

31. See Keith Arbour, "One Last Word: Benjamin Franklin and the Duplessis Portrait of 1778," *Pennsylvania Magazine of History and Biography* 118 (July 1994): 183–208.

32. Bailyn notes that Franklin's speech at the conclusion of the convention was published at least thirty-six times before mid-February 1788. Bailyn, *The Debate on the Constitution: Federalist and Antifederalist Speeches, Articles and Letters during the Struggle over Ratification*, part 1 (New York: Library of America, 1993), 1138.

33. Max Farrand, ed., *The Records of the Federal Convention of 1787*, vol. 3 (New Haven: Yale University Press, 1911), 154. In Martin's later version of the convention, published as "The Genuine Information," he is more explicit about the dynamic: "The honorable Mr. Washington was then on the floor, in the same situation with any other member of the convention at large, to oppose any system he thought injurious, or to propose any alterations or amendments he thought beneficial, to these propositions so reported by the committee, no opposition was given by that illustrious personage, or by the president of the State of Pennsylvania [Franklin]. They both appeared cordially to approve them, and to give them their hearty concurrence; yet this system, I am confident, Mr. Speaker, there is not a member in this house would advocate, or who would hesitate one moment in saying it ought to be rejected. I mention this circumstance in compliance with the duty I owe this honorable body, not with a view to lessen those exalted characters, but to shew how far the greatest and best of men may be led to adopt very improper measures, through error in judgment, State influence, or by other causes, and to shew that it is our duty not to suffer our eyes to be so far dazzled by the splendor of names, as to run blindfolded into what may be our destruction." Bailyn, *Debate on the Constitution*, 637–38.

34. Ibid., 162, 191.

35. Ibid., 412. Wilson here is James Wilson, whose widely printed pro-Constitution speech in early October 1787 may have been the most influential public statement on the Constitution.

36. Ibid., 54.

37. Ibid., 224.

38. See A. Owen Aldridge, "Charles Brockden Brown's Poem on Benjamin Franklin," *American Literature* 38.2 (1966): 230–35. See also Charles E. Bennett, "The Charles Brockden Brown Canon" (PhD dissertation, University of North Carolina, Chapel Hill, 1974), 8–9.

39. The General is typically read as Washington, but the presiding officer in André's trial was Nathanael Greene: Dunlap's choice of the generic term may therefore signal less modesty about naming Washington than an insight into the variable structural position of the hero-as-reluctant-agent.

40. *National Gazette*, July 7, 1792, 1.

41. The "Francis Oldys" (George Chalmers) biography of Paine appeared in England in 1791, though an American edition, published in Boston, did not appear until 1796. The basic elements of "Paine"—his arguments in the public sphere, his vernacular sensibilities, his sexual appetite and epicureanism, and his radicalism—ultimately accrued to the later version of Franklin.

42. William Laughton Smith, *The Politicks and Views of a Certain Party, Displayed* (Philadelphia, 1792), 2. Hereafter cited parenthetically in the text.

43. Madison would ever after be the diminutive offshoot and reiteration of Jefferson.

44. Seth Cotlar, "The Federalists' Transatlantic Cultural Offensive of 1798 and the Moderation of American Democratic Discourse," in *Beyond the Founders: New Approaches to the Political History of the Early American Republic*, ed. Jeffrey L. Pasley, Andrew W. Robertson, and David Waldstreicher (Chapel Hill: University of North Carolina Press, 2004), 277.

45. Alexander Hamilton to Edward Carrington, May 26, 1792, in *Alexander Hamilton: Writings*, ed. Joanne B. Freeman (New York: Library of America, 2001), 745.

46. The last paragraph of the last chapter of Mason Weems's *Life of Washington*, titled "Washington's Will," begins, "Having no children . . . " Weems, *The Life of Washington*, ed. Marcus Cunliffe (Cambridge: Harvard University Press, 1962), 226.

47. Again, the actual complexities of Washington's and Franklin's attitudes and practices regarding slavery—the focus of such recent works as Henry Wiencek's *An Imperfect God* (New York: Farrar, Straus and Giroux, 2003) and David Waldstreicher's *Runaway America* (New York: Hill & Wang, 2004)—are not the issue here.

48. Amélie Oksenberg Rorty, *Mind in Action: Essays in the Philosophy of Mind* (Boston: Beacon, 1988), 78–98.

49. Augustus Brevoort Woodward, *Epaminondas* (New York, 1801), 7.

50. See the discussion in Ed White, "Trends and Patterns in the US Novel, 1800–1820," in *The Oxford Handbook of the Novel in English*, vol. 5, *The American Novel to 1870*, ed. J. Gerald Kennedy and Leland S. Person (New York: Oxford University Press, 2014), 73–88.

NOTES TO CHAPTER 2

1. The reference here is to Herman Melville's *Moby-Dick*. Of Captain Ahab, Ishmael says, "All that most maddens and torments; all that stirs up the lees of things; all truth with malice in it; all that cracks the sinews and cakes the brain; all the subtle demonisms of life and thought; all evil, to crazy Ahab, were visibly personified, and made practically assailable in Moby Dick." Melville, *Moby-Dick*, in *Redburn, White Jacket, Moby-Dick* (New York: Library of America, 1983), 989.

2. Charles Brockden Brown, *Ormond; or, The Secret Witness*, in *The Novels and Related Works of Charles Brockden Brown*, ed. Sydney J. Krause, S. W. Reid, and Russel B. Nye, Bicentennial ed., vol. 2 (Kent, OH: Kent State University Press, 1977), 3; and Brown, *Ormond; or, The Secret Witness*, ed. Mary Chapman (Peterborough, ON: Broadview, 1999), 38. Hereafter cited parenthetically in the text, with page numbers in both the Kent State edition and the more available Broadview edition. Where discrepancies exist, we favor the former.

3. The 1798 publication of the collected *Gleaner* pieces revealed that the well-known essayists "Constantia" and "The Gleaner" were one and the same. We cannot do justice to this reference here but note that the conjunction of Murray's pseudonyms effectively overlaid a feminist Federalism on one of the most extensive articulations of republicanism from the period. *The Gleaner* remains an understudied work of uncanny insights, the

most germane of which, for Ormond, are probably found in the twenty-fifth essay, which not only suggests that republican citizenship may be read as a mythical formulation of a transcendent spiritual phenomenon but notes the significance of "encircling spectators": "These tenderly interested and sympathizing denizens of the celestial world, not unfrequently, with mildly sympathizing aspect, stand confessed to the patient sufferer, pointing him, with the finger of affiance, to that opening heaven, upon which he is so apparently verging." Judith Sargent Murray, *The Gleaner: A Miscellaneous Production in Three Volumes* (Boston: Thomas and Andrews, 1798), 247–48.

4. Slavoj Žižek, *Looking Awry: An Introduction to Jacques Lacan through Popular Culture* (Cambridge: MIT Press, 1991), 4.

5. S. W. Reid, "Textual Essay," in Brown, *Novels and Related Works*, 347–48. Russel B. Nye seemed to concur, believing the Baxter episode the synopsis of an abandoned novel; see "Historical Essay," in ibid., 303.

6. Charles Brockden Brown, "The Man at Home," *Weekly Magazine of Original Essays, Fugitive Pieces, and Interesting Intelligence*, no. 4 (February 24, 1798): 99–103, and no. 5 (March 3, 1798): 133–36.

7. Charles Brockden Brown, "The Man at Home," *Weekly Magazine of Original Essays, Fugitive Pieces, and Interesting Intelligence*, no. 1 (February 3, 1798): 3.

8. Charles Brockden Brown, "The Man at Home," *Weekly Magazine of Original Essays, Fugitive Pieces, and Interesting Intelligence*, no. 11 (April 14, 1798): 321.

9. Brown, "Man at Home," no. 4, 101.

10. Charles Brockden Brown, "The Man at Home," *Weekly Magazine of Original Essays, Fugitive Pieces, and Interesting Intelligence*, no. 6 (March 10, 1798): 167.

11. Brown, "Man at Home," no. 4, 101. The chest fantasy deserves more attention than we can give it here. We note, however, that when the Man at Home finally breaks it open—or rather has it broken open by "black Will"—he first finds it empty. He soon after discovers a secret compartment containing a manuscript of the American Revolution, written by its author in 1793 and completed just before his death from the fever. At that moment, the author's corpse is "thrown, without solemnity or reverence, into the common receptacle"—a final allusion to the chest (no. 8 [March 24, 1798]: 225).

12. Charles Brockden Brown, "The Man at Home," *Weekly Magazine of Original Essays, Fugitive Pieces, and Interesting Intelligence*, no. 12 (April 21, 1798): 352.

13. Ibid., 354.

14. These elements include the problem of financial indigence (which definitively afflicts Stephen Dudley), the mysterious chest (later linked to Craig), lovers' suicides (carried out by Helena), and political violence (here experienced by Miss De Moivre, later experienced by Martinette), as well as crucial references to the Haitian Revolution, which we address later.

15. The republican synthesis spearheaded by Bernard Bailyn, Gordon Wood, J. G. A. Pocock, and others defined itself against the Progressive view of republicanism as an insincere, sometimes propagandistic cover for underlying economic elitism. Central to the synthesis, then, was the insistence that republican beliefs were genuinely held and felt.

16. This detail perhaps suggests that in large families, male offspring may collectively meet the demands of economic servitude; the number of deceased children also seems to imply the desperation and frustration of Dudley, who is seemingly cursed with "only" a daughter.

17. See Julia Stern, *The Plight of Feeling: Sympathy and Dissent in the Early American Novel* (Chicago: University of Chicago Press, 1997), on "an abiding antipatriarchalism, a hostility to the regime of the fathers that carries revolutionary implications for the content as well as the form of the American novel he inaugurates" (182).

18. Whiston first abandons his dying sister, an act the narrative describes as a loss of "humanity" (48/74). When he collapses in the countryside, he is left to die by a nearby family which, in mirroring Whiston's asociality, also dies from the fever. The narrator comments, "The life of Whiston and their own lives [in the nearby house] might have been saved by affording the wanderer an asylum and suitable treatment, or, at least, their own deaths might have been avoided by interring his remains" (49/75).

19. If this argument strikes some readers as far-fetched, we note that Brown's later *Historical Sketches* features several strong aristocratic women who believe themselves to be incarnations of women saints: it is precisely because they are the incarnation of the women they worship that they believe themselves worthy of worship. This was clearly a fantasy dynamic that Brown found historically significant and misleadingly associated with Roman Catholicism.

20. In fact, Constantia interacts with two characters here: the waiter and, in the latter example, Craig's servant. Our analysis assumes a stylistic continuity between these two interactions, as the waiter hands off Constantia to the freshly arrived servant.

21. Charles Brockden Brown, "A Series of Original Letters," *Weekly Magazine of Original Essays, Fugitive Pieces, and Interesting Intelligence*, letter 2 (April 21, 1798): 391.

22. Charles Brockden Brown, "A Series of Original Letters," *Weekly Magazine of Original Essays, Fugitive Pieces, and Interesting Intelligence*, letter 3 (April 28, 1798): 391–92.

23. Charles Brockden Brown, "A Series of Original Letters," *Weekly Magazine of Original Essays, Fugitive Pieces, and Interesting Intelligence*, letter 4 (May 5, 1798): 8.

24. Ibid., 9.

25. The first substantial discussion of Ormond makes only a passing allusion to his "political projects," in chapter 12; the most cited discussion of Ormond's conspiratorial associations appears in chapter 26, close to the novel's end, though a brief discussion of his travels appears at the beginning of chapter 21.

26. Citation from 252/242, but see 205/204, 252–53/242–43.

27. Roland Barthes, *Mythologies* (New York: Hill & Wang, 1972), 112.

28. This is not the place to assess Brown's literary career, but we believe that the emphasis on Brown's "major" novels has distorted our reading of his work. This fixation has left the short fictions (works such as "The Man at Home" or the "Original Series of Letters") in the shadows, as raw material for the more accomplished novels. But the short fiction should rather foreground Brown's interest in stylized psychological puzzles, and the pieces read like an odd cross between fables and case studies. In this framework, a novel such as

Ormond is better read as a staged sequence of formal thought experiments rather than a unified novel or romance.

29. Clifford Geertz, *The Interpretation of Culture: Selected Essays* (New York: Basic, 1973), 29.

30. Ibid., 29–30.

31. We see this, for example, toward the end of the second volume of *Arthur Mervyn*, in which women proliferate as the plot turns to the question of marriage—a sharp departure from the novel's beginning. A similar interest seems to inform his final and critically neglected novels, *Jane Talbot* and *Clara Howard*.

32. This analysis conforms to Brown's reputed skepticism toward the New England ministers trumpeting the Bavarian Illuminati scare: see Bryan Waterman, *Republic of Intellect: The Friendly Club of New York City and the Making of American Literature* (Baltimore: Johns Hopkins University Press, 2007), 50–91. Yet, given Brown's later interest in the utopian potential of Roman Catholicism and cultic movements, in the *Historical Sketches*, we read Brown's analysis as more nuanced than any condemnation of political behavior.

NOTES TO CHAPTER 3

1. Although we come to different conclusions, we note Sharon Harris's similar focus on Scipio in chapter 5 of her provocative *Executing Race: Early American Women's Narratives of Race, Society, and the Law* (Columbus: Ohio State University Press, 2005).

2. In the course of our research, we came across a character profile of Samuel Tenney, Tabitha's husband, in the papers of William Plumer, a senator from the Tenney's home state of New Hampshire. Plumer and Tenney both served in the Eighth Congress. Plumer wrote over two thousand character sketches during his life, with the ambition of writing a history of the United States that he left incomplete. Plumer's sketch of Samuel Tenney was far from flattering. He described a man lacking in intellectual depth, overly concerned with dress and fashion, and a boring conversationalist. Plumer had kinder words for Tabitha Tenney, whom he regarded as a sharp mind, and he recalled her aspirations to be a novelist. One great surprise, however, was to find Plumer claim that Samuel Tenney coauthored *Female Quixotism* with his wife. We report this not to discredit Tabitha but because we have not seen this claim documented elsewhere. Plumer's acerbic account of Samuel Tenney as narrow-minded and lacking curiosity seems inconsistent with someone capable of writing this complex novel. See William Plumer Papers, Library of Congress, Box 5, Reel 2 (1816), 5–9.

3. Cathy Davidson, *Revolution and the Word: The Rise of the Novel in America*, 2nd ed. (Oxford: Oxford University Press, 2004), 278. This reading has been codified in the latest (seventh) edition of the *Norton Anthology*, in which Philip Gura's headnote describes Dorcasina as a character whose "judgment has been skewed by an overimmersion in contemporary novels that fill her with rosy, and unattainable, notions of true love." *Norton Anthology of American Literature*, ed. Nina Baym, 7th ed., vol. A (New York: Norton,

2008), 905. As we write this, the Oxford edition has more or less fallen out of print: we read the collapse of the novel's classroom status as a sign that this mode of reading has essentially rendered the novel unreadable.

4. See, for instance, Gillian Brown's assessment: "As the object of conversion—conversion into a model worthy of emulation—the Quixote commands both sympathy and respect." Brown, "The Quixotic Fallacy," *Novel: A Forum on Fiction* 32.2 (1999): 259–60.

5. Tabitha Tenney, *Female Quixotism*, ed. Jean Nienkamp and Andrea Collins (Oxford: Oxford University Press), 323. Hereafter cited parenthetically in the text.

6. These dates can be established by working backward from the beginning of book 2, where Tenney provides one of only two actual dates in the novel. The midpoint reference is 1791, noted by Tenney as the year "famous for the defeat of St. Clair by the Indians" (152). The other date explicitly mentioned is July 8, 1800, when Dorcas pens her final letter to Harriot Barry.

7. Judith Sargent Murray, *The Gleaner*, ed. Nina Baym (Syracuse: Syracuse University Press, 1993), 364.

8. Washington did not, however, exercise executive authority. The significance of the St. Clair expedition is confirmed by the anonymous 1793 novel *The Hapless Orphan*, in which the expedition plays a crucial role.

9. There is, of course, a third name—Dorcas*ina*—that seems to capture the element of romance so often the focus of critics; our argument here, however, is that the Dorcas-Tabitha parallax is more fundamental.

10. An exception is Stephen Carl Arch, "'Falling into Fiction': Reading Female Quixotism," *Eighteenth-Century Fiction* 14.2 (2002): 177–98; though he argues that The Compiler meant to contrast Cervantes and the story of Dorcasina.

11. "New Hampshire Convention," in *The Debates in the Several State Conventions on the Adoption of the Federal Constitution*, 5 vols., ed. Jonathan Elliot (Philadelphia: Lippincott, 1876), 2:204.

12. [Sally Sayward Barrell Keating Wood], *Julia, and the Illuminated Baron* (Portsmouth, NH: Oracle, 1800), 135.

13. Even before Scipio, the character, becomes significant to the plot, Tenney introduces the name with reference to the classical antecedent. She refers to O'Connor as a "Scipio in continence" (36).

14. "Detriments," *Online Etymology Dictionary*, Douglas Harper, historian, March 31, 2011, Dictionary.com, http://dictionary.reference.com/browse/detriments.

15. The phrase "Virginia influence" is from William Plumer's essays under the name Impartialis and written in the summer of 1804, when the political ramifications of the Louisiana Purchase were becoming clear. We take up these essays in greater detail in chapter 5.

16. "Virginia Dynasty" became a way to refer to the Virginian nativity of four of the first five presidents; however, the first usage of the term we could find comes from John Thierry Danvers's *A Picture of a Republican Magistrate of the New School, to Which Is Added a Short Criticism on the Characters and Pretensions of Mr. Madison, Mr. Clinton, and Mr. Pinckney* (New York: E. Sargeant, 1808), 33. In context, Danvers's epithet "Virginia

dynasty" attacks Jefferson as yet another Virginian willing to abuse federal power. The specific charge, indeed, concerns Jefferson's obsession with prosecuting Burr for treason.

17. Charles Brockden Brown's pamphlet *On the Cession of Louisiana to the French* draws this connection explicitly: "The only aliens and enemies within their borders, are not the blacks. They indeed are the most inveterate in their enmity; but the Indians are, in many respects, more dangerous inmates." Brown, "An Address to the Government of the United States on the Cession of Louisiana to the French" (Philadelphia, 1803), 45.

18. Once it is clear that Dorcasina will not marry James, he shows deference to her rather than disgust. Stranded at a farmer's house after their sleigh has overturned in the snow, James asks for no privilege and slips away in the night to avoid further humiliating Dorcasina. For her part, Dorcasina expects to be mortified at having to see James again in the morning; she descends the stairs to rejoin the farmer's family in the morning "with as much reluctance as a Frenchman to the guillotine" (198). But no Jacobin spectacle awaits her. She simply must treat her hosts with kindness and return home. And arriving at L—, she finds that news of her flight is not widely known.

19. The name bears another colonial referent as well. General Braddock (with the young George Washington) began his failed campaign during the Seven Years' War from Fort Cumberland.

20. The act did not prohibit ships equipped in foreign ports from continuing to disembark slaves in US ports. The slave trade was not thoroughly banned until 1808.

21. It is worth mentioning that in the novel that ostensibly catalyzes the John Brown reference, Roderick Random ultimately makes his fortune in the slave trade, treated fleetingly, almost with embarrassment, late in the novel.

NOTES TO CHAPTER 4

1. The election notice first appeared in the February 28, 1801, issue, on page 3, announced "BY THE LAST MAIL."

2. *Aurora*, February 12, 1801.

3. Ibid.

4. The first appearance is in the *Republican Watch-Tower*, October 25, 1800, 2.

5. This appeared around the second week in January—for instance, in the January 10, 1801, issue of the *Tree of Liberty*, 4, and in the *Mirror of the Times, and General Advertiser*, January 14, 1800, 4.

6. The text appears in the *Tree of Liberty*, March 21, 1801.

7. John Wood, *A Narrative of the Suppression by Col. Burr of the History of the Administration of John Adams, Late President of the United States* (New York: Denniston and Cheetham, 1802). Hereafter cited parenthetically in the text.

8. Newspaper publication of Senate records, open doors in the Senate and public chambers for visitors, a provision for newspapers to exchange information without postage fees, and requests for State Department correspondence.

9. Quoted in James Cheetham, *A View of the Political Conduct of Aaron Burr, Esq.* (New York: Denniston and Cheetham, 1802), 54.

10. Attributed to Augustus Brevoort Woodward, *Epaminondas* (New York, 1801). Hereafter cited parenthetically in the text.

11. Quoted in Nancy Isenberg, *Fallen Founder: The Life of Aaron Burr* (New York: Viking, 2007), 447n. 21.

12. "Lucius Junius Brutus," *An Examination of the President's Reply to the New-Haven Remonstrance* (New York: George F. Hopkins, 1801), 48.

13. Cheetham's career is sketched in Michael Durey, *Transatlantic Radicals and the Early American Republic* (Lawrence: University Press of Kansas, 1997), especially chapters 6 and 7.

14. See the summary in Isenberg, *Fallen Founder*, 243–56; and Nathan Schachner, *Aaron Burr: A Biography* (New York: A. S. Barnes, 1961), 219, 226–35.

15. James Cheetham to Thomas Jefferson, December 1801, in *Proceedings of the Massachusetts Historical Society* 1 (1907–8): 51.

16. Ibid., 56.

17. Isenberg, *Fallen Founder*, 243.

18. Cheetham, *View of the Political Conduct of Aaron Burr*, 14. Hereafter cited parenthetically in the text.

19. James Cheetham, *Nine Letters on the Subject of Aaron Burr's Political Defection* (New York: Denniston and Cheetham, 1802). Hereafter cited parenthetically in the text.

20. Joseph Ellis, *Founding Brothers: The Revolutionary Generation* (New York: Knopf, 2000).

21. Cheetham cites many such examples, the most famous being the 1802 Senate battle to repeal the Judiciary Act of 1801.

22. James Cheetham, *A Reply to Aristides* (New York: Cheetham, 1804), 110.

23. Gordon S. Wood, *Revolutionary Characters: What Made the Founders Different* (New York: Penguin, 2006), 230. Wood cites Milton Lomask's biography, which states, "'Things written remain,' he cautioned his clerks and his own adherence to the ancient caveat, especially in his political correspondence, would be the despair of future historians" (87). Milton Lomask, *Aaron Burr: The Years from Princeton to the Vice President, 1756–1805* (New York: Farrar, Straus and Giroux, 1979). Lomask's source, in turn, was an 1863 address to the Long Island Historical Society by Judge John Greenwood (reproduced in Charles Burr Todd's 1878 *General History of the Burr Family in America* [New York: E. Wells Sackett]), which asserted, "Col. Burr, in everything relating to business, and indeed in all his epistolary correspondence with men, had a special regard for the maxim that 'things written remain,' and was very careful as to what he wrote. But with regard to the other sex, such was his confidence in them, that he wrote to them with very little restraint" (124). Thus, a general maxim—presented with conflicting "evidence"—migrates to become a truism of Burrology and the actual words of Burr.

24. The toast is already satirized in the Maryland newspaper the *Republican, or Anti-Democrat* in March but begins to appear regularly in Cheetham's *American Citizen* after

late May 1802 and then figures prominently in *View of the Political Conduct of Aaron Burr*, published in July.

25. Wood, *Revolutionary Characters*, 225.

26. *American Citizen*, February 11, 1804.

27. Our numbers are based on searches of the Readex Newspaper Database and of several papers not included therein, such as Philadelphia's *Aurora*; we assume the text appeared in more papers than we have located.

28. There appears to have been only one translation of the report, which the *National Intelligencer* (August 5, 1801) attributes to the *Baltimore American*. We have been unable to locate the first version in the *Baltimore American*.

29. The earliest version we have found, with the title "Translated for the *National Intelligencer*. *The Constitution of the French Colony of St. Domingo*," is in the *New-York Commercial Advertiser*, August 17, 1801. We hereafter quote from this text.

30. Toussaint's name appears in Title 6, § 16; Title 8, §§ 28, 30 (twice), and 41; and Title 13, § 77. His signature concludes the text.

31. The texts we have just enumerated did not always appear together, though some combination generally did. The Constitution appeared in at least twenty-four papers, the promulgation texts in at least twenty-two, the convocation texts in at least five, and the character sketch in at least seventeen. The character sketch preceded the Constitution, appearing in some papers as early as June 11 (*American Intelligencer*), but became part of the constitutional sequence from August into December. The quotations in the text are from the *American Intelligencer* text.

32. See *Acts, Passed in the Island of Barbados, from 1643, to 1762, Inclusive*, ed. Richard Hall (London: R. Hall, 1764), 112–13.

33. See Eric Thomas Slauter, *The State as a Work of Art: The Cultural Origins of the Constitution* (Chicago: University of Chicago Press, 2009).

34. Think of Olaudah Equiano's or John Marrant's neglect of the American Revolution as a significant event, which was not a sign of Loyalism as much as a verdict on the independence movement of a slavery state. Two decades later, Boyrereau Brinch's *The Blind African Slave* offered a narrative of the Middle Passage and Caribbean slavery, giving way to a heroic account of British warfare, before collapsing into a farcical account of the American Revolution and slavery's long tentacles affecting life in rural Vermont. Jeffrey Brace, *The Blind African Slave, or, Memoirs of Boyrereau Brinch, Nicknamed Jeffrey Brace*, ed. Kari J. Winter (1810; repr., Madison: University of Wisconsin Press, 2004).

35. We recall here that Mason Weems's *Life of Washington* had been published in 1800. Paine enjoyed a brief flurry of coverage as he returned to the US from France aboard a US navy vessel, with Jefferson's permission.

36. This piece had originally appeared in the May 7, 1801, *Gazette of the United States* and was reactivated by the appearance of the Toussaint pieces.

37. *Aurora*, August 17, 1801.

38. The reference here is to Jefferson's 1801 inaugural address.

39. Thomas Paine, *Common Sense*, in *Paine: Collected Writings* (New York: Library of America, 1995), 16.

40. Anonymous, "Selections: A Sketch of the War of St. Domingo, from the Invasion of Leclerc to the Death of Toussaint," *Literary Magazine, and American Register* 2.14 (November 1804): 604–14, quotation from 613. The two additional quotations in the text are from the same page.

41. William Plumer, *William Plumer's Memorandum of Proceedings in the United States Senate, 1803–1807* (New York: Macmillan, 1923), 243–44.

42. Henry Adams to Henry Cabot Lodge, July 9, 1880, *The Letters of Henry Adams*, vol. 2, ed. J. C. Levenson (1982; repr., Cambridge: Belknap Press of Harvard University, 1988), 403.

43. Henry Adams to John Hay, October 8, 1882, in ibid., 475.

44. Henry Adams to John T. Morse, April 9, 1881, in ibid., 424.

45. See Eric Lott, *Love and Theft: Blackface Minstrelsy and the American Working Class* (New York: Oxford University Press, 1995), 22–25. We return to this problem in our conclusion.

46. Quoted in ibid., 24–25.

47. *American Citizen*, April 11, 1804.

48. "White privets fall, dark hyacinths stand." This is modified from Virgil's *Eclogues* II: "Alba ligustra cadunt, nigra varcinia *leguntur*" (White privets fall, dark hyacinths are gathered). In Virgil's poem, Alexis, the "fair" slave, is his "master's joy"; he rejects the sexual solicitation of Corydon, a shepherd working for the same master.

49. *Repertory* (Boston), September 21, 1804, 3.

50. Three installments appear in the *American Citizen*: August 31, September 9, and September 23, 1805.

51. *Kantikoy*: to dance as a form of religious worship; associated with Native Americans.

NOTES TO CHAPTER 5

1. *Reports of the Trials of Colonel Aaron Burr (Late Vice President of the United States,) for Treason, and for a Misdemeanor*, 2 vols. (Philadelphia: Hopkins and Earle, 1808), 2:337.

2. The oft-rehearsed catalogue includes Jonathan Dayton (Federalist senator from New Jersey), John Adair (senator from Kentucky), John Smith (senator from Ohio), Matthew Lyon (representative from Ohio), and Andrew Jackson (Tennessee supreme court justice).

3. We quote Nathan Bailey's *Universal Etymological English Dictionary*, which the OED lists as the most prominent source of the term.

4. See *Aurora*, May 22, 1804, which appears to reference Hamilton's letter, which circulated in the New York press in March and April. See, for example, the March 29 *Morning Chronicle*, "Extract of a Letter from Hamilton, Steuben County, Dated March 18."

5. *Aurora*, June 10, 1804.

6. "To the Republican Electors of the First Congressional District of Pennsylvania," *Aurora*, October 3, 1804.

7. Michel-Rolph Trouillot, *Silencing the Past: Power and the Production of History* (Boston: Beacon, 1995), 26.

8. Anonymous, "St. Domingo," *Literary Magazine, and American Register* 2.15 (1804): 655.

9. William Plumer, *William Plumer's Memorandum of Proceedings in the United States Senate, 1803–1807* (New York: Macmillan, 1923). Hereafter cited parenthetically in the text.

10. When the bill finally passed in February 1806, Burr, though long gone from the Senate, oddly once again draws Plumer's attention; Burr is dining with Jefferson on the twenty-second, he reports (Plumer, *William Plumer's Memorandum*, 436).

11. Walter Benjamin, "The Story-Teller," in *Selected Writings*, vol. 3, ed. Howard Eliand and Michael W. Jennings (Cambridge: Belknap Press of Harvard University, 2006), 154.

12. Christina Lupton, "Tristram Shandy, David Hume, and Epistemological Fiction," *Philosophy and Literature* 27.1 (2003): 110.

13. Joseph Ellis, *Founding Brothers: The Revolutionary Generation* (New York: Knopf, 2000), 43, 20.

14. Premiered on *Saturday Night Live*, series 31, episode 9, http://www.nbc.com/saturday-night-live/video/chronicles-of-narnia-lazy-sunday/2921/.

15. See here the first "Got Milk?" ad, in which such minutiae find their comic counterpart in the milk carton, almost empty when one's mouth is full of peanut butter: "Aaron Burr Milk Commercial," YouTube, uploaded June 30, 2008, by sycamorematt, http://www.youtube.com/watch?v=t1_soeWbaYI.

16. Hamilton's biographer Richard Brookhiser shows himself resistant to the Rube Goldberg tendency to obsess about details, writing, "Each particular of the duel—Hamilton's failure to explain himself; Burr's exasperation; the caliber and construction of the pistols; Hamilton's expressed intention of wasting his shot; Burr's evident intention of not wasting his—has been seized on by some historian, biographer, journalist, or partisan of one of the duelists, as unusual, and therefore requiring special explanation (which, if supplied, will explain the event, and the participants, usually in some revisionist fashion)." Brookhiser, *Alexander Hamilton, American* (New York: Free Press, 1999), 210. But Brookhiser cannot resist "imagin[ing] what [Hamilton] might have done had he lived out his natural life span. . . . The landmark cases of the next decades that used his arguments—*Fletcher v. Peck*, *McCullough v. Maryland*—might have been argued by him in person" (215).

17. Ellis, *Founding Brothers*, 46–47.

18. Joanne B. Freeman, *Affairs of Honor: National Politics in the New Republic* (New Haven: Yale University Press, 2001), 162.

19. Nancy Isenberg, *Fallen Founder: The Life of Aaron Burr* (New York: Viking, 2007), 292–97.

20. Aaron Burr to Theodosia, January 28, 1805, in *Memoirs of Aaron Burr*, 2 vols., ed. Matthew L. Davis (New York: Harper & Brothers, 1837), 2:355.

21. Ibid.

22. John Daly Burk, *The History of Virginia* (Petersburg, VA: Dickson and Pescud, 1805).

23. See, for example, the *Connecticut Herald*, May 1, 1804, 3.

24. *Balance, and Columbian Repository*, August 6, 1801.

25. Charles Brockden Brown, *An Address to the Government of the United States, on the Cession of Louisiana to the French, and on the Late Breach of Treaty by the Spaniards* (Philadelphia, 1803). Hereafter cited parenthetically in the text. The first advertisement of the pamphlet appears to be in the January 21, 1803, *Poulson's American Daily Advertiser*, among the leading Federalist papers.

26. Alan Axelrod, *Charles Brockden Brown: An American Tale* (Austin: University of Texas Press, 1983), 3.

27. *Gazette of the United States*, June 17, 1802.

28. *Aurora*, October 21, 1803.

29. *Aurora*, September 15, 1803.

30. Sylvestris (St. George Tucker), *Reflections, on the Cession of Louisiana to the United States* (Washington City, 1803), 25, 26.

31. *Aurora*, November 23, 1803.

32. Robert Livingston, "On This Question—Whether It Is Advantageous for France to Take Possession of Louisiana?," *Independent Chronicle*, July 4, 1803.

33. The first half on October 28, 1803, the second on October 31.

34. See also Connecticut Supreme Court Justice Roger Griswold's letter of March 1804, in *Documents Relating to New-England Federalism*, ed. Henry Adams (Boston: Little, Brown, 1877), 357.

35. William Plumer, *An Address to the Electors of New Hampshire* (Portsmouth, NH: William and Daniel Treadwell, 1804), 12.

36. See, for example, *New-York Commercial Advertiser*, February 23, 1804.

37. See William Jenks, *A Memoir of the Northern Kingdom* (Boston, 1808), 327–28; or see the modern annotation edited by Ed White, *Journal of the Early Republic* 30 (2010): 328.

38. Thomas Jefferson, *Fourth Annual Message to Congress*, November 8, 1804.

39. *The Constitution of the French Colony of St. Domingo*, in the *New York Commercial Advertizer*, August 17, 1801.

40. "St. Domingo Trade," *New York Morning Chronicle*, March 7, 1805, 2. See also Adams, *Documents*, 175. The bill passed both houses on March 2 and was sent for the president's signature the following day.

41. The United States did not recognize the independence of Haiti until 1862.

42. *Trial of Samuel Chase*, 5, 8.

43. Ibid., 23.

44. Ibid.

45. Uriah Tracy to James Gould, February 4, 1805, quoted in Isenberg, *Fallen Founder*, 276.

46. "Republican Simplicity," *New-York Herald*, March 30, 1805.

47. *United States Gazette*, January 12, 1805.

48. *New-Hampshire Sentinel*, December 22, 1804.

49. William Wirt's speech about Harman Blennerhassett and Burr during the trial became the most famous of these invocations; however, an earlier version was published in a long epic poem in the *Balance* in April and May 1806. Under the title "The Coalead" and the byline "Robert Rusticoat, Esquire," the three canto poem marshaled all the Miltonic machinery, with Burr as Satan gathering his forces after being thrown from Heaven—here, the governorship of New York. Only two of the promised cantos were published.

50. The reference is to John Fries. Randolph's transposition of murder for treason, the charge levied against Fries in 1800, is what generated such buzz. It goes without saying that the writer could not foresee the even greater irony that Burr was himself to stand accused of treason in the coming years.

51. "Extract of a Letter from Washington Dated February 9," *Balance* 4.9 (1805): 69.

52. Reprinted in the *Charleston City Gazette*, April 3, 1807.

53. *Democratic Press* (Philadelphia), April 1, 1807. In other words, for failing to carry out Jefferson's wish to depose Chase, Burr was now to suffer at the hands of the acquitted judge.

54. Slavoj Žižek, "Afterword: Lenin's Choice," in *Revolution at the Gates*, by Vladimir Ilyich Lenin (London: Verso, 2002), 278–79.

55. One thinks here of Douglas MacArthur's farewell address to Congress after his dismissal from active duty during the Korean War. MacArthur had threatened a filibuster of his own, criticizing President Truman for not going far enough against China. He was relieved for insubordination but then resurfaced as a fantasy object promising the fulfillment of the nation's "hope and dreams" in the 1952 presidential election.

56. Thomas Jefferson, "Presidential Message," in *American State Papers*, 9th Cong., 2nd sess., 1:468.

57. *Debates in the House of Representatives, on the Bill for Carrying into Effect the Louisiana Treaty* (Philadelphia, 1804), 78–79.

58. Albert J. Beveridge, *The Life of John Marshall*, vol. 3 (Boston: Houghton Mifflin, 1919), 304.

59. *American State Papers*, 9th Cong., 2nd sess., 1:469.

60. *Trenton Federalist*, March 16, 1807.

61. Edward Livingston, *A Faithful Picture of the Political Situation of New Orleans* (Boston, 1808).

62. Bernard Bailyn, *The Ideological Origins of the American Revolution* (Cambridge: Harvard University Press, 1967), 138.

63. Peter Charles Hoffer, *The Great New York Conspiracy of 1741: Slavery, Crime, and Colonial Law* (Lawrence: University Press of Kansas, 2003), 23, 18, 24, 22.

64. *Argus*, June 10, 1807.

65. We exclude here the details of the trials in Kentucky and the Mississippi Territory, as they belong to the conspiratorial narrative.

66. *Reports of the Trials of Colonel Aaron Burr*, 1:76 (quoting Wickham for the defense) and 1:62 (quoting Wirt for the prosecution).

67. See, for example, the March 31, 1807, story in the *New York Balance & Columbian Repository*.

68. From an April 3, 1807, *Charleston City Gazette* story, quoting the *Aurora*.

69. *Richmond Enquirer*, April 28, 1807.

70. From the April 6, 1807, *Democratic Press* (Philadelphia), quoting the *Richmond Enquirer*.

71. *Democratic Press* (Philadelphia), April 1, 1807.

72. *Spirit of the Press*, June 1, 1807.

73. *Miller's Weekly* (Pendleton, SC), April 3, 1807.

74. *New-York Spectator*, January 12, 1807.

75. *Reports of the Trials of Colonel Aaron Burr*, 2:446.

76. For example, the June 6, 1807, *United States Gazette* editorialized, "It is evident from the communications made to the Aurora by the editor now at Richmond, that he expects the government will be able to prove nothing against Burr. He is accordingly endeavouring to prepare the minds of his readers for the result, by the most gross insinuations and the most indecent accusations."

77. *Aurora*, September 23, 1807

78. *Aurora*, September 24, 1807.

79. *Miller's Weekly* (Pendleton, SC), October 22, 1807.

80. See Isenberg, *Fallen Founder*, 367–68.

81. "On the Defensive, No. I," *Aurora*, October 29, 1807.

82. *Reports of the Trials of Colonel Aaron Burr*, 2:96–97.

83. Ibid., 2:123–24.

84. Aaron Burr to Theodosia, April 26, 1807, in *Memoirs of Aaron Burr*, 2:405.

NOTES TO THE CONCLUSION

1. John Davis, *Walter Kennedy: An Interesting American Tale* (London: J. F. Hughes, 1808), 19.

2. Ibid., 19, 20.

3. Ibid., 20–21.

4. *Port Folio*, July 10, 1802, 216. In the original appearance, it is signed "Asmodeo," which was a common pen name for one Robert H. Rose, according to Milton Ellis. See Ellis, "Joseph Dennie and His Circle: A Study in American Literature from 1792 to 1812," *Bulletin of the University of Texas* 40 (July 1915): 166. Thelma Louise Kellogg notes that Davis was a sometime contributor to the *Port Folio* from 1805 but had had some regular contact with Joseph Dennie years before. See Kellogg, *The Life and Works of John Davis 1774–1853* (Orono: University of Maine Press, 1924), chapters 3 and 5.

5. See the document at "Slave Conspiracy in North Carolina Bertie County," The Slave Rebellion Web Site, n.d., http://slaverebellion.org/index.php?page=slave-conspiracy -in-north-carolina-bertie-county.

6. Kellogg, *Life and Works*, chapters 4 and 5. Kellogg notes that *Walter Kennedy* appeared in US bookshops, imported from the London publisher, in early 1805, after Davis had returned to the United States.

7. Davis, *Walter Kennedy*, 20.

8. John Davis, *Travels of Four Years and a Half in the United States* (London, 1803), 378–89.

9. Ibid., 380. On the Congo Minuet and its possible Haitian origins, see Médéric L. E. Moreau de Saint-Méry, *Danse: Article extrait d'un ouvrage* (Philadelphia: Moreau de Saint-Méry, 1796), 33; and the brief discussion in Lillian Moore, "Moreau de Saint-Méry and 'Danse,'" in *Dance Index* 5.10 (October 1946): 232–60, especially 236 and 258.

10. Robert C. Toll, *Blacking Up: The Minstrel Show in Nineteenth-Century America* (New York: Oxford University Press, 1974), especially chapter 2; and Hans Nathan, *Dan Emmett and the Rise of Early Negro Minstrelsy* (Norman: University of Oklahoma Press, 1962), especially chapters 3 and 4. Among the early examples discussed by Nathan is the 1824 blackface performance, by James Roberts, of "Massa Georgee Washington"—an evocation of the Washington-Toussaint conflation of the first decade of the nineteenth century (34–44).

11. Eric Lott, *Love and Theft: Blackface Minstrelsy and the American Working Class* (New York: Oxford University Press, 1993). Our tremendous debt to Lott should be apparent here.

12. Leonora Sansay, *Secret History; or, The Horrors of St. Domingo*, in *"Secret History; or, The Horrors of St. Domingo" and "Laura,"* ed. Michael J. Drexler, 2nd ed. (Peterborough, ON: Broadview, 2007). Hereafter cited parenthetically in the text.

13. Quoted in Nancy Isenberg, *Fallen Founder: The Life of Aaron Burr* (New York: Viking, 2007), 370.

14. Drexler floated this claim in an essay predating our joint project. See "Brigands and Nuns: The Vernacular Sociology of Collectivity after the Haitian Revolution," in *Messy Beginnings: Postcoloniality and Early American Studies*, ed. Malini Johar Schueller and Edward Watts, 175–202 (New Brunswick: Rutgers University Press, 2003).

15. Joan Dayan and Jeremy Popkin, for instance, had placed Hassal/Sansay in dialogue with other eyewitness accounts of the Revolution. See Dayan, *Haiti, History, and the Gods* (Berkeley: University of California Press, 1996); and Popkin, *Facing Racial Revolution: Eyewitness Accounts of the Haitian Insurrection* (Chicago: University of Chicago Press, 2008).

16. See Tamika Nadine Walker, "Romance and Revolution in Leonora Sansay's *Secret History*" (unpublished ms.); Sîan Silyn-Roberts, "Dispossession and Cosmopolitan Sociability in Leonora Sansay's *Secret History*" (unpublished ms.); Elizabeth Dillon, "The Secret History of the Early American Novel: Leonora Sansay and Revolution in Saint Domingue," *Novel* 40.1–2 (2006): 77–103; Gretchen Woertendyke, "Romance to Novel: A Secret History," *Narrative* 17.3 (October 2009): 255–23. See also Melissa Adams-Campbell, "Romantic Revolutions: Love and Violence in Leonora Sansay's *Secret History, or the Horrors of St. Domingo*," *Studies in American Fiction* 39.2 (Fall 2012): 125–46; and Tessie P. Liu, "The

Secret beyond White Patriarchal Power: Race, Gender, and Freedom in the Last Days of Colonial Saint-Domingue," *French Historical Studies* 33.3 (Summer 2010): 387–416.

17. Michelle Burnham, "Female Bodies and Capitalist Drive: Leonora Sansay's *Secret History* in Transoceanic Contexts," *Legacy* 28.2 (2011): 177–204.

18. Jennifer van Bergen, the critic who has focused most carefully on the biographical details of the Burr-Sansay relationship, has argued that the larger record of Burr's relationship with women demonstrates Platonic patronage more than sexual management. Like many Burr scholars, she claims that literary historians sloppily repeat unsubstantiated claims made in the nineteenth century. But she also tautologically defends her claims using Sansay's writings as archive. See van Bergen, "Reconstructing Leonora Sansay," *Another World Is Possible*, January 3, 2010, http://www.a-w-i-p.com/index.php/2010/01/03/reconstructing-leonora-sansay.

19. Doreen B. Massey, *For Space* (Thousand Oaks, CA: Sage, 2005), 117–18.

20. See C. L. R. James, *The Black Jacobins: Toussaint L'Ouverture and the San Domingo Revolution* (New York: Penguin, 1989), 334.

21. See, for example, Sean Goudie, *Creole America: The West Indies and the Formation of Literature and Culture in the New Republic* (Philadelphia: University of Pennsylvania Press, 2006), 200–216.

22. Burnham, "Female Bodies and Capitalist Drive," 188.

23. Leonora Sansay, *Laura*, in *"Secret History; or, The Horrors of St. Domingo" and "Laura,"* 222. Hereafter cited parenthetically in the text.

24. Black Philadelphians were inaccurately thought to be immune to the fever. Many were convinced to remain behind to care for the sick. They also were attacked for price gouging and grave robbing, charges that leaders of the community disputed in print. See Absalom Jones and Richard Allen, *A Narrative of the Proceedings of the Black People during the Late Awful Calamity in Philadelphia in the Year 1793* (Philadelphia: Woodward, 1794). Additionally, West Indians and refugees from Saint-Domingue, in particular, were associated with the spread of the yellow fever. See J. Worth Estes and Billy G. Smith, eds., *A Melancholy Scene of Devastation: The Public Response to the 1793 Philadelphia Yellow Fever Epidemic* (Canton, MA: Published for the College of Physicians of Philadelphia and the Library Company of Philadelphia by Science History Publications/USA, 1997).

Index

About the Authors

Michael J. Drexler is Associate Professor of English at Bucknell University in Lewisburg, Pennsylvania. Ed White is Pierce Butler Associate Professor of American literature at Tulane University in New Orleans. Their joint essays have appeared in *American Literary History*, *Early American Literature*, and Blackwell's *Companion to American Fiction, 1780–1865*. They have also coedited *Beyond Douglass: Essays in Early African-American Literature*. Drexler is the editor of Leonora Sansay's *"Secret History; or, The Horrors of St. Domingo" and "Laura"* and coeditor of *Haiti and the Early US*. White is the author of *The Backcountry and the City: Colonization and Conflict in Early America* and the editor of Hugh Henry Brackenridge's *Modern Chivalry*.